Master Plans and Encroachments

THE CITY IN THE TWENTY-FIRST CENTURY

Series editors: Eugenie L. Birch and Susan M. Wachter

A complete list of books in the series is available from the publisher.

MASTER PLANS AND ENCROACHMENTS

The Architecture of Informality in Islamabad

Faiza Moatasim

PENN

UNIVERSITY OF PENNSYLVANIA PRESS

PHILADELPHIA

Publication of this book was aided by the Graham
Foundation for Advanced Studies in the Fine Arts.

Published by
University of Pennsylvania Press
Philadelphia, Pennsylvania 19104–4112
www.upenn.edu/pennpress

Printed in the United States of America on acid-free paper

10 9 8 7 6 5 4 3 2 1

Hardcover ISBN: 978-1-5128-2520-6
eBook ISBN: 978-1-5128-2519-0

A catalogue record for this book is available
from the Library of Congress

To Ammi and Abbo

CONTENTS

LIST OF ILLUSTRATIONS

A NOTE ON TRANSLITERATION AND TRANSLATION

I have used many words and phrases in Urdu and Punjabi in this book. All translations from these languages are mine. I have used a simple form of transliteration without diacritics. Proper names and Urdu terms (like *kat-chi abadis*, *qabza*, *tehsil*, *begum*) are spelled the way they appear in official documents and newspapers. Urdu and Punjabi words are italicized the first time they appear in the book. Urdu and Punjabi words have been pluralized in the English manner by adding an *s*.

Introduction

Making Master Plans and Encroachments

My earliest impression of Islamabad was that it was clean, green, and different from other cities in Pakistan. I first visited the city with my family when I was in elementary school, and I remember that during our visit, we became confused and lost in the rationally organized city as we drove around searching for our destination among various neighborhoods that all looked the same. Islamabad was unlike other large cities we had visited. The streets were wide and uncongested, there was generous greenery everywhere, and the neighborhoods—called sectors—all looked identical and were named with English alphabet letters combined with numbers, which added to the city's novelty. Islamabad as a whole seemed highly "organized," even if we found that organization somewhat disorienting. The first time I noticed France Colony (a low-income informal settlement) was while shopping at the high-end F-7 *markaz* (center) market (also known as the Jinnah Super market). On the southern side of the expensive market, France Colony's modest dwellings were stacked next to each other in a low-lying area, in sharp contrast to the wide avenues and upper-income, single-family residences all around. The visual disparity between the living conditions of the privileged and underprivileged residents—whose homes were in close spatial proximity—was and still is too powerful for me to ignore. In hindsight, I realize that what made this city seem "different" to me was highlighted particularly in these situations of sociospatial disparity, when the pristine and modern template of the master plan seemed to be interrupted by organically occurring spaces of poverty. These early impressions of Islamabad shaped my research interests as I started thinking about the histories of these informal places, how they came to be, and how they were able to stay in place.

As a child, I of course didn't realize that France Colony was an encroachment on Islamabad's master plan. The city was conceived on paper in the late 1950s and early 1960s to be the new capital of Pakistan. It was designed by Greek architect-planner Constantinos A. Doxiadis according to the principles of high-modernist planning that dominated for much of the twentieth century. These principles proceeded from the conviction that scientific and technical rationality, professional expertise, and comprehensive planning could address all present and future urban needs around the world. Modernist master plans conceived in advance of construction called for a strict designation of various urban functions in clearly defined and distinct zones. But in all newly built, high-modernist capital cities of the post–World War II era, such as Islamabad, Brasilia (national capital of Brazil), and Chandigarh (state capital of India), unanticipated spaces, including low-income informal housing, emerged as soon as these state-of-the-art projects took shape.

Because unanticipated spaces were not part of the high-modernist planning ideology, they were categorized in early research on Chandigarh and Brasilia as "unplanned" or contradictory urban phenomena.[1] This academic characterization aligns well with how people generally understand informal spaces as unplanned and spontaneous. In his seminal study on Brasilia, James Holston employs the framework of "premises and paradoxes" to explain the creation of the so-called unplanned spaces as contradictory elements embedded in the new capital city's planning program. Holston conceives of Brasilia as a city "founded on a paradox" since its basic "premise" was "a negation of the existing conditions in Brazil."[2] While Holston's critique of a high-modernist city successfully exposes the hegemonic ideology of high-modernist planning and its tendency to reject unaccounted-for urban phenomena, my chief concern in this book is to show how the modalities of informal spaces in Islamabad are predicated precisely on its modernist master plan and regulations. *Master Plans and Encroachments* reveals that the negation of existing conditions in the master plan creates and sustains certain kinds of informality and that this interplay between formal and informal processes can occasionally result in a revision of the master plan itself. Islamabad's master plan is not simply a blueprint that guides future urban development or makes its violations apparent; it is used by both state and nonstate actors to develop informal spaces that accommodate unfulfilled needs of those living and working in the city. The master-planned city offers a clear template of formal urban design and development within which encroaching spaces and informal processes could be clearly articulated.

Master Plans and Encroachments presents a contemporary history of the comprehensively planned city of Islamabad from the perspective of spaces that were not a part of its initial master plan but that play an integral role in its everyday functioning and long-term development. Informal spaces like squatter settlements and vendors' stalls normatively exist at the margins of architectural discourse and practice because of how they are perceived as everyday and "ordinary" spaces in contrast to the "high" architecture designed by professional architects and planners. By looking at the development of informal spaces under the supposed "laboratory" conditions of a city planned "from scratch," we may learn more about how spatial nonconformity contributes to urban development in many other kinds of urban settings as well.

In municipal administration, encroachments and other categories of informal spaces are considered violations of the official plans and regulations. Yet cities often function and develop through spatial processes that are not entirely legal. By attending to the ongoing mediation between encroachments and official plans in a city, we can learn more about the way people build and rebuild, live, and work. *Master Plans and Encroachments* attends to this mediation by demonstrating how people build encroachments that are oriented toward official plans to accommodate unfulfilled functions in Islamabad. Encroachments are often seen as spatial irregularities that contradict official plans and thus need to be corrected. But processes of building and tolerating encroachments are integral to the way many cities around the world function and develop today. This book unsettles negative assumptions associated with the breaking of planning rules. It shows how the only way marginalized communities often gain access to space is by building informally and how encroaching spaces that may be labeled or perceived as illegal infringements are in fact built with official permission. Moreover, encroachments that break the law can also shape plans and regulations by introducing changes that they have already addressed in advance. Far from being marginal, dysfunctional phenomena, encroachments embody a strategic and flexible use of space and resources within rigid planning systems.

As part of the research that led to this book, I started investigating the development of *katchi abadis* (temporary, or squatter settlements) and *khokhas* (commercial-use kiosks) in Islamabad. Katchi abadis and khokhas were my first focus because of how they stood out as the quintessential spaces of informality; their irregular material forms appeared to encroach on public greenbelts, and they fulfilled low-income residential and commercial functions in the city. Sweepers, maids, drivers, and gardeners who care for the city and its wealthy residents reside in clusters of self-built dwellings arranged in organic patterns that contrast with the strict geometry of the rectilinear plots and streets that occupy most of the city. These informal dwellings sit next to naturally occurring ravines that have been purposely retained in the official master plan as natural landscape elements in the middle of very expensive neighborhoods. Similarly, small khokhas (kiosks and tea stalls) and makeshift cafés, which are built throughout roadside greenbelts, offer economical food options in an otherwise expensive city.

While I could have easily identified these as informal spaces based on their material characteristics and the socioeconomic status of most of the people who build and use them, I began to notice many other violations of the master plan and regulations that did not look informal but were highly illegal. At the time, many large houses and mansions in some of the most expensive parts of Islamabad were being drastically retrofitted to illegally accommodate high-end commercial uses; while keeping the external appearance of residences, these buildings were effectively converted into beauty salons, restaurants, art galleries, home-furnishing stores, clothing boutiques, guest houses, embassies, and corporate offices.[3] I began fieldwork around the same time that a high-profile Pakistani Supreme Court case in 2013 highlighted a trend initiated by several influential citizens, including the then recently deposed military dictator General Pervez Musharraf, of building lavish farmhouses in an area reserved for the farming of fruits and vegetables.[4] The proliferation of both low- and high-end unauthorized spaces in Islamabad presented an opportunity to compare the encroachment practices of elites and nonelites and to ask how these "ordinary" and elite informal spaces sustain themselves in a highly planned city.

I have felt ambivalent about using the term *informal* to describe spaces that I encountered everywhere in Islamabad—spaces that were mostly in violation of the master plan but were often officially authorized in some way. I have chosen to use the term mainly because many spaces, such as squatter settlements and vendors' stalls, examined in this book routinely get recognized as "informal" in both academic and popular discourses; by keeping the term, I can build on these existing discourses while analyzing new variations on and meanings of the informal in urban development. In this book, I conceive of the *informal* as an aesthetic and material modality that exists along a legal–illegal continuum, is closely monitored by city officials, and is based on material strategies that ensure its long-term survival. Conversely, I understand the *formal* to be those spaces and procedures that essentially conform to the official master plan and planning regulations that are created by official planners and architects, approved by executive orders or the government cabinet, and enforced by building officials and inspectors. Yet the formal system does not preclude unauthorized and technically illegal planning decisions carried out either directly or indirectly by government officials, architects, and planners. The boundaries between the formal and informal are at best blurry.

In *Master Plans and Encroachments*, I trace informality not only through planning documents and legal parlance but also in its various material forms and aesthetics. People do not randomly build informal spaces; they strategically use building materials and techniques to support their informal claims to space. A central concern of mine is to show that spaces categorized as "informal" are not divorced from official planning procedures but rather that elite and nonelite people alike encroach by using bureaucratic and architectural strategies that give an impression of conformity to the master plan and regulations. I focus on spaces that were not a part of the initial master plan not because I want to show the failure of planning but to show how planning actually works in complex ways. The intersecting histories of informal spaces in Islamabad reveal that those spaces are not only tolerated because they accommodate important unfulfilled functions; informal spaces can also impact long-term urban development by introducing major structural changes to the official master plan and regulations.

Architectural Forms and Aesthetics

This book argues that architectural forms and aesthetics are central to how residents and businesspeople build encroachments and how city officials tolerate them in Islamabad at both elite and ordinary levels. Scholars have emphasized political negotiations and bureaucratic procedures as the keys to understanding informal building and uses in cities. For example, direct negotiation between street vendors and state actors has been identified as an essential feature of how vendors gain access to urban space, often in contingent, illegal, and discreet ways.[5] Moreover, spaces of informal urbanism have been termed "insurgent," a "nuisance," and "messy" to signify their legally contentious status.[6] Based on the recognition that most informal activities are located along a continuum of legitimacy, with some activities simultaneously conforming to and violating regulations, scholars of informality assert that the legally complicated status of informal spaces often configures the political terrain on which spatial claims can be made.[7] The participation of the urban poor in the legalization process of informally developed spaces mobilizes them to demand their rights not only to space but to citizenship as well.[8] It is important to note that existing scholarship captures the range of political achievements of marginalized populations involved in building informal spatial practices by focusing primarily on sociopolitical negotiations and strategies. But it pays little attention to how vendors, hawkers, and squatters actually build their structures and physically occupy public space to sustain themselves. As a result, urban studies scholarship has not produced robust analyses of how the materiality of low-income informal spaces plays a role in their long-term sustenance.

In a study on low-income informal housing in South Africa, Paula Meth found a strong link between the material qualities of informal spaces, such as the "hyper-permeability" of informal houses made from impermanent building materials and structural elements, and the perpetuation of negative social behavior, such as crime and anxieties.[9] Without denying the social implications of living and working in hyperpermeable informal structures, *Master Plans and Encroachments* explores how the permeable material characteristics of ordinary informal spaces may support low-income populations' efforts to make claims to urban space. The empirical evidence I present here shows that the perceived and physical impermanence (that is, hyperpermeability) of informal structures can in certain cases ensure their long-term persistence.

Master Plans and Encroachments asserts that the ways in which encroaching spaces are built usually contribute to their long-term survival. Squatters and vendors mostly build with mud, branches, and other salvageable materials that appear temporary but are in fact quite durable. Low-income vendors and middle-class shop owners use architectural strategies of daily assembly and disassembly to situate their businesses on public spaces like streets, sidewalks, and corridors. Wealthy homeowners interested in converting their large houses into furniture showrooms make drastic architectural changes to the houses' interiors by removing partition walls, doors, and even en suite bathrooms, while making sure the buildings—with their compulsory setbacks, boundary walls, and front lawns—still look like houses on the outside. Businesspeople belonging to different socioeconomic groups do not make arbitrary design decisions to create spaces of informality; they use architectural design as a means of making and sustaining territorial claims.

I use the terms *ordinary informality* and *elite informality* to differentiate how the material characteristics of encroaching spaces contribute to their development. *Ordinary informality* refers to the processes and practices that facilitate informal claims to space based on materiality and modalities that are perceived to be temporary. Ordinary informal spaces are built using construction materials and techniques that allow quick assembly and disassembly and contribute toward an overall aesthetics of "ordinariness"—the quality of being impermanent, makeshift, and irregular. The materiality and aesthetics of ordinariness play an important role in the classification of certain informal spaces (like squatter settlements and vendors' stalls) as "ordinary" and explains why "ordinary" informal spaces get easily labeled in official and public discourses as unauthorized, illegal, and unplanned.

Ordinariness is not a socioeconomic condition, since many middle- and upper-income residents and businesspeople engage in ordinary spatial practices to make informal claims to space. Recent scholarship on urban informality and elite geographies recognizes how very wealthy people now participate in spatial irregularities previously associated with marginalized communities.[10] These studies highlight how elite actors in cities around the world build lavish yet illegal constructions. But elites do not only make "glamorous" architecture; they also create informal spaces that are temporary and ordinary.[11] Moreover, though middle-class residents and businesspeople use ordinary spatial practices to usurp public space for personal use, their role is missing from the existing analysis of informality from "above" and "below."[12] As a material category based on an aesthetic of temporariness, ordinary informality thus helps explain how the middle class, in addition to low- and high-income people, use temporary spatial strategies to claim public spaces.

For instance, in Islamabad it is common for middle-income shopkeepers to extend their indoor display areas by encroaching on adjacent public corridors, sidewalks, and roads. Middle- and upper-class homeowners similarly claim open green spaces in front of their houses to install security barriers and guard booths or to create private lawns and parking areas. Many foreign embassies and government offices located in large houses in Islamabad install movable concrete barriers and portable security guard cabins, used for safety and surveillance, to encroach on greenbelts, sidewalks, and streets next to their buildings. All these encroachments benefiting middle- and upper-income people are designed to be presumptively provisional, as add-ons and not permanent architectural components of the building. Used by people with and without wealth and influence, ordinariness as an aesthetic is constituted through design decisions that satisfy functional needs in a way that attracts

less unwanted official attention than what a more permanent spatial violation might receive.

In contrast to ordinary encroachments, elite informal constructions look
highly planned and show no signs of impermanence and incremental development. Designed by professionals and built to the highest architectural standards, elite informal constructions appear to adhere to building codes and
planning regulations. They involve massive monetary investments that help
communicate the high socioeconomic status of their inhabitants; this display
of wealth through architecture can function as a deterrent to city authorities
who would otherwise attempt to prosecute influential encroachers. Elite informality thus emerges as an important modality of informal urbanization
not only because it involves privileged actors but also because it is based on
using material forms and aesthetics to defer legal action. These attributes
challenge the idea that the informal is only the everyday and ordinary. Attending to elite informality also shows us that not all informal spatial practices can be seen as acts of resistance and self-empowerment by working-class
people; the bold and ambitious ways that the urban elite reimagine and re-
purpose master-planned spaces in Islamabad are proof of the entitlements
and privileges they enjoy in an unequal society.

In considering Indian cities, Shubhra Gururani and Asher Ghertner identify large private developers as elite informal actors who work in collusion
with state officials, such as city administrators and judges, to legitimize their
informally created spaces through favorable zoning exemptions and court decisions.[13] Existing urban studies research typically envisions the urban elite
as a homogeneous category with a shared set of interests and goals, positioned
against the urban poor to usurp valuable urban land using informal practices and processes. This approach accords with how classical sociology has
characterized the elite in a given society—as minority groups, either ruling
or nonruling elite, who are strategically and inevitably positioned to control
and dominate others and influence political outcomes.[14]

But this conception, which sees the interests among privileged state and
nonstate actors as neatly aligned and coordinated, obscures and even neglects
the reality of the often contentious processes of elite informal urbanism, in
which various privileged actors assert their positions of power through their
competing visions for the development of urban space. Recent elite studies
scholarship also supports the contested nature of elite composition and practices. This scholarship challenges the assumption that elites form an a priori,
cohesive, and conspiring social group; instead, it analyzes elite power as re-

lational and place-specific and acknowledges conflict, diversity, and differences among elites in terms of how they organize, maintain their social status,
and gain political legitimacy.[15] Because elites depend on urban centers for
their work, recreational, and housing needs, cities emerge as the main sites
of elite practices and spatialities.[16] But cities do more than simply fulfill the
necessary spatial needs of elite actors; an engagement with the urban built
environment is one of the ways in which elites maintain their identities, social status, and power. Attention to the competing forces within elite informal processes in urban areas reveals how elite power over space is neither
assumed nor uncontested; the wealthy and influential still must defend their
spatial violations through various mechanisms of power, including the use
of political connections, community organizing, fabricated paper documents,
architectural design, monetary resources, and legal proceedings. A study of
elite informality also shows the unexpected yet necessary alliances between
elite and nonelite actors and the work that must be done by the elites to maintain their power (over space).

While private developers and state actors are certainly the main produc-
ers of high-end informality, the role of elite citizens—implicitly understood
as the users of elite informal spaces—is mostly missing in existing scholarship on urban politics.[17] The assumption that elite homeowners are passive
consumers of elite informality is incongruous with the reality of the active
role that urban middle- and upper-class homeowners now play in shaping
urban development discourses and practices in cities of the global South.[18]
Sociologist Amita Baviskar links exclusive urban reforms that target any visible signs of poverty and underdevelopment to "bourgeois environmental-
ism," a set of practices through which affluent members of resident associations
and civic organizations vehemently (and sometimes violently) defend urban
public spaces from the alleged environmental degradation caused by the urban poor.[19] Existing studies show that the demands of "proper citizens" are
met when the judiciary and city administrators enforce existing planning
laws; such enforcement also entails ruling against the informal encroachment
of squatters and street vendors in urban public spaces. While resisting the
informal encroachments of underprivileged populations, upper-class homeowners retreat to exclusive spaces of living and leisure that are developed in
urban peripheries and suburbs mainly through informal mechanisms.[20] This
book shows that elite homeowners themselves participate in informal practices to build lavish mansions for their personal use or use their large houses
for illegal commercial functions, while they lament the destruction of their

cities and public spaces by low-income vendors and squatters. This contradiction in elite behavior demonstrates a form of "elite exceptionalism," which allows wealthy and influential people to justify their own illegal constructions while criticizing those built by less affluent populations. Elites justify their actions and bolster their criticisms of others with the argument that Islamabad's municipal officials are corrupt and ineffective in meeting their genuine spatial needs on the one hand and in enforcing the law on the other.

Master Plans and Encroachments highlights how elite homebuilders and businesspeople manipulate bureaucratic procedures using architectural strategies, some of which resemble the ordinary tactics poor people employ to meet their basic needs for shelter and livelihood. Ordinary informal structures, built using temporary construction materials and techniques, acknowledge their provisional status within a highly planned context. In contrast, elite informal constructions are built to last, are designed according to the highest architectural standards, and appear to be in line with official building codes and regulations. Both strategies are based on material forms and aesthetics that help informal spaces appear legitimate and unthreatening to the overall planning framework. I argue that this *compliance without intent*—that is, the practice of building spaces that only appear to comply to official rules but are intended to be used for unauthorized uses—is central to the viability of non-conforming spaces. The strategic use of architectural forms and bureaucratic devices that attend to formal regulations not only helps elite and nonelite people make informal claims to space; it can also have lasting impacts on the overall formal planning framework.

Urban Informality as an Orientation to the Law

In my interviews of both the privileged and unprivileged builders of informal spaces, our conversations often focused on how their building practices were deeply enmeshed with bureaucratic processes. I quickly learned that many of the owners of roadside khokhas that sell snacks, cold drinks, and cigarettes claimed to do business with *ijazat* (permission). They would point to their license numbers, which were either painted in white on their cabin's exterior or printed on a copy of the official license pasted on one of the interior walls. Residents of France Colony made similar claims to legitimacy by taking me to the place where a foundation stone inaugurating their neighborhood was laid in the 1980s by the chairman of the city's municipal authority, CDA (Capital Development Authority). Owners of elite informal businesses operating from large houses or lavish mansions built in protected areas also claimed that they developed their constructions with some form of "official" permission or, at the very least, with the tacit knowledge of city officials.

The entwined connections between formal procedures and informal spaces emerged as a recurring theme as I traced histories of other apparently illegal constructions in Islamabad. In most cases, informal spaces had been established with some form of official consent. Where official permission had not been granted, residents and businesspeople fabricated pseudo-legal documents to bring an impression of legitimacy to their unauthorized constructions. In other words, people were not simply ignoring the law when they built encroachments; builders of encroachments paid attention to the laws as they tried to find ways to build new spaces of their own.

The concept of urban informality, or more precisely the "informal sector," was popularized during the 1970s when experts began writing about unregulated, people-based economic activities, in contrast to the government-regulated and government-monitored "formal sector" economy.[21] The informal sector also became associated with illegal housing and land markets serving poor populations in cities of the so-called developing world. The initial conception of informal economy and housing was based on the recognition that street hawking and squatting offered important survival opportunities for the urban poor but required policy measures aimed at integrating the informal with the formal sector. Characterized by irregular and unmonitored economic processes, the informal sector was thus framed in opposition to a formal sector, based on fixed wages, labor rights, and regulated finances that constituted the dualistic economic structure found in urban areas of the so-called developing world.[22] The dichotomous formal-informal model of housing and economy, however, was subsequently criticized because it failed to capture the dynamic social and economic processes that often straddle the two sides of the binary.[23]

Because of the proliferation of informal spatial and economic processes in urban transformations in many parts of the world, scholars began to challenge the idea that the informal sector necessarily involves marginalized entities that exist distinctly from and await integration into the formal sector. Rather than treating urban informality as a "sector," Ananya Roy conceptualized urban informality as "a mode of urbanization" and "an organizing logic." Roy's work was influential in recognizing extralegality as "inhering in the state."[24] Using India as her example, Roy asserts that the "planning regime is itself an informalized entity, one that is a state of deregulation, ambiguity, and exception." As a central feature of this planning regime, informality comprises "forms of deregulation and unmapping" that allow state actors to flexibly manage valuable land resources.[25]

But encroachments, violations, and other forms of informality are often the result of a strategic and partial conformity to law. In Islamabad, elite builders selected land in a protected nature reserve next to a lake precisely because of its demarcation in the master plan as a protected scenic area. These elite homebuilders then initiated a legal process that resulted in major structural changes to Islamabad's master plan and zoning regulations. In this case, informal constructions were not the result of deregulation or unmapping but entailed strategic use of the master plan to introduce new functions within the formal planning framework. Islamabad's master plan is a living document that is referred to and amended over time to accommodate nonconforming spaces. The master plan adapts because it has already been modified by the encroaching spaces that orient themselves toward it, creating an ongoing interplay between plans and encroachments.

Therefore, in this book I present informality as an orientation to law rather than an absence of law. While *master plans* and *encroachments* are normatively seen in architectural and planning discourses as fundamentally different and separate categories, plans regulate and create conditions for their own encroachments. Islamabad's master plan was based on an imaginary empty site, when in reality hundreds of small, rural communities had been living in the area for generations. To accommodate displaced villagers, city officials built "model villages" in a protected nature reserve where residential construction was strictly prohibited. Moreover, Islamabad's city officials regulate both licensed and unlicensed street vendors and tea-stall owners. Unlicensed vendors are not allowed to use permanent building materials and construction techniques, while licensed vendors can do business on the condition that their constructions can be removed on short notice. This attention to the materiality of encroachments is not coincidental; it is based on CDA's policy of tolerating encroachments under temporary, revocable terms. The master plan regulates this strategy, which allows CDA to maintain an impression of adherence to the law as it develops bureaucratic procedures for tolerating encroachments on a temporary basis.

My arguments regarding the co-constitutive relationship between master plans and encroachments builds on recent research on entwined formal-informal relations. Gautam Bhan shows how Delhi's various master plans helped produce and regulate several categories of illegal housing through selective and discretionary planning policies.[26] Seeing violations as an outcome of planning practices rather than as deviations from plans, Jayaraj Sundaresan argues that the urban planning regime in Bangalore, India, is shaped by social networks of various actors working inside and outside the government and that these vernacular practices produce violations either by an "appropriation" of the ideal plans (through monetary and political payoffs) or by "incorporating" violations into plans (through legislative reforms and exemptions).[27] Francesco Chiodelli and Stefano Moroni use the term *nomotropism*, meaning "acting in the light of rules," to explain how informal spaces in the global South are routinely developed with respect to existing planning rules and regulations rather than by an indifference to existing laws.[28] In his study of unauthorized mosques in Islamabad, Matthew Hull notes how various religious groups consult official maps to identify sites reserved for mosques in each sector with the help of land surveyors. By "literally honor[ing] the plans in the breach," interested religious groups "squat according to plan" on spaces designated for the construction of a mosque in the official master plan, all in an attempt to legitimize their illegal construction in the long run.[29] *Master Plans and Encroachments* asserts that the way people choose certain construction materials and techniques to build informal spaces matters to the political and monetary negotiations and legal reforms that must take place to ensure their long-term survival.

In the case studies I present here, the state reacted to encroachments in unpredictable and complicated ways. City officials in charge of the removal of illegal constructions maintain neighborhood-based lists of encroaching spaces and functions, which range from elite houses being used for illegal commercial uses to unlicensed ordinary kiosks built in roadside greenbelts. While city officials use these records to issue fines, receive bribes, confiscate property, or remove illegal construction, I encountered repeated evidence of how they frequently developed new bureaucratic procedures to tolerate existing encroaching spaces or to enable the creation of new ones. Moreover, there is a great deal of variation in official attitudes toward informal spaces. I observed a particular discord between the courts and Islamabad's powerful city municipal corporate body, CDA, over whether an illegal construction should be removed or allowed to exist. The heterogeneous workings of the state help to explain why certain informal spaces are forcefully removed while others are tolerated, often for long periods.

The Politics of City Planning in Islamabad

This book shows how master planning in a comprehensively planned city is shaped by encroaching and informal spaces that represent the competing and colluding interests of city officials, the judiciary, and people who live and work in the city. But why does planning work in this way in places like Islamabad? The answer has to do with how informal processes have arisen as a response to changing local and global pressures. As I discuss in detail in Chapter 1, Islamabad's initial high-modernist master plan was a product of intersecting national and global development regimes and dominant urban planning discourses in the post–World War II era. When the decision to build Islamabad was made, Pakistan was under the control of a military dictator who wanted to consolidate his power by making a new capital city close to the army's headquarters. This ambitious new city-building project aligned with the interests of western powers (particularly, the United States) in developmentalism, which promised to expand their political control in postcolonial "developing nations" by providing them with technical and financial support for various developmental projects. Western modernist architects and planners saw in the design commissions of new capital cities in places like Pakistan and India extraordinary opportunities to test their city planning ideals. High-modernist planning principles emerged as a popular design orientation in the 1950s and 1960s because these principles supported the interests and ambitions of a diverse group of local and global authoritarian regimes and planning professionals.

Changes in global and national political and economic events of the 1980s and 1990s profoundly affected the primacy of the centralized and comprehensive city planning framework in Islamabad. Long-standing global armed conflicts like the Soviet-Afghan War of the 1970s and 1980s and the Global War on Terrorism since 2001 put unexpected yet serious pressures on existing urban infrastructure and resources in Pakistan.[30] Millions of Afghan refugees have arrived in Pakistan in different waves since the 1970s and settled in various urban areas, including Islamabad. Moreover, since the 2000s, large cities like Islamabad have also received local, usually rural, populations from the northern and tribal areas of Pakistan, who have been forcefully displaced because of ongoing military operations and drone strikes carried out against terrorist hideouts in their native towns and villages. Most of the displaced Afghans and Pakistanis prefer to live in non-refugee-camp urban settings, where they find themselves without government-supported centralized relief programs. In Islamabad and other major cities, Afghan refugees and internally displaced Pakistanis mostly rely on informal systems to earn their living as laborers and daily wage workers, to buy land or build ethnically homogenous informal neighborhoods, to set up commercial activities, and to access necessary services (like schools and health care).[31]

In addition to fielding the economic and housing challenges of low-income refugees and internally displaced people, large cities in Pakistan, including Islamabad, have expanded into their adjacent agricultural and rural peripheries to accommodate higher-end residential and commercial schemes. Several factors have contributed to this trend of urban sprawl that caters to the upwardly mobile classes in large metropolitan areas. Fearing asset freezes and heightened surveillance of their incomes and financial transactions in the aftermath of the September 11 attacks, Pakistanis living in western countries transferred large amounts of their money back home.[32] They invested most of these home remittances in real estate, as it is a highly secure form of investment in Pakistan. Because land prices have increased consistently despite political and economic instabilities in the country, most upper-income Pakistanis also invest in urban residential plots in newly developed schemes with no intention to ever build their houses there. This trend of treating land as a commodity and an investment, often called the financialization of real estate, has resulted in an overinvestment in Pakistan's urban land market; consequently, it has contributed to urban sprawl into the agricultural and rural peripheries of large cities.[33] Local and foreign capital from China and the Middle East has further fueled periurban real estate development in the form of exclusive shopping malls and "lifestyle" gated residential communities, which offer "world-class" living to affluent people.[34]

Since the late 1980s, middle- and upper-income groups have used informal mechanisms to open up a large, protected nature reserve in Islamabad for housing and investment purposes. Moreover, in the 1990s, the boundaries of Islamabad Capital Territory Region were extended to include a large area located near the southern edge of the neighboring city of Rawalpindi. This additional area was incorporated into Islamabad's territory to facilitate the development of upper-income residential gated communities by a military-backed housing development authority called Defense Housing Authority.

Because CDA's main source of revenue is the auction of land under its control, opportunities to develop more residential and commercial schemes—even in previously protected regions—also align well with its financial interests. In Islamabad, like other large cities in Pakistan, a "nexus" comprising civil and military bureaucracies, city development authorities, and private developers plays an important role in creating higher-end housing and recreation spaces in agricultural and rural peripheries.[35] This nexus often uses illegal and coercive means to forcibly acquire land from local villagers and legitimize irregularities related to the land and housing development process. In various zones of Islamabad, CDA and other private development companies are now building large, gated residential enclaves using a piecemeal development process in a pattern that resembles sprawling suburban subdivisions around the world, in contrast to Doxiadis's centralized master plan and modular scheme for individual neighborhoods.

Last but not least, local conditions like the presence of existing rural communities in the Islamabad site and reconciliation of the interests and conflicts involving elites and nonelites have played an important role in Islamabad's planning and development. Recent research on new high-tech cities in India and China confirms the centrality of local processes and informal negotiations in shaping urban development.[36] For instance, established in the 1980s as a Special Economic Zone, Shenzhen, China, is now Asia's leading financial, technological, and manufacturing capital. Because of Shenzhen's unprecedented economic success over the course of four decades, it serves as a model for urban and economic growth. But Juan Du argues that "Shenzhen is not a formalized and easily replicable top-down model, but a complex and shifting set of bottom-up and informal negotiations" and local innovations, which often contradict its centralized planning and policy regime.[37] Du shows how preexisting agrarian communities all over the rapidly modernizing city now exist as "urban villages," which are self-built communities that offer affordable alternatives to Shenzhen's formal, expensive real estate and commercial market. Shenzhen's innovation and success depend on the availability of this ecosystem of affordable housing and facilities to new migrants. While top-down planning may determine a general direction for a city's future development, local conditions and informal processes ultimately decide how and why a city gets built in a certain way. This limitation of modern master plans is rooted in the fact that they deliberately imagine a future based on the negation of existing conditions and a denial of unanticipated challenges.

In Islamabad, it is the fragmented and informal land development systems rather than centralized master planning that have addressed myriad global and local pressures, including the influx of displaced populations, the desire of upper classes to live in exclusive enclaves, local politics, and the financialization of residential plots. This book is an attempt to show how elite and ordinary encroachments are outcomes of a system that must reconcile the realities of global and local economic and political pressures as well as the asymmetries of extreme power and destitution. I am arguing for the importance of paying attention to how plans conceived on paper by a centralized authority are contingent on competing visions of multiple people for the same space. These competing processes can be neither predicted nor eliminated; they exist in deeply entwined relationships, but they maintain material and legal differences.

Mapping Contentious Spaces

I conducted fieldwork for this book over two research trips in 2012 and 2014, with yearly follow-up visits thereafter. But the idea for the book was shaped by my long-term association with Islamabad. I grew up in nearby cities, and the capital city was a popular destination for many of my family and school trips because of how unique Islamabad felt. As a school student, I knew that Islamabad's distinctiveness was attributed to its design; it was our "planned" capital city. I also knew that it was an expensive and elite city, a place for people with a lot of wealth and privilege. But my first encounter with France Colony made me realize that people with modest means also lived and worked in Islamabad, often in the middle of very wealthy neighborhoods. Years later, as an undergraduate architecture student, I learned the term *katchi abadi* (informal settlement), which is used to describe places like France Colony where poor people live in illegal, self-built dwellings. It wasn't until I started the research on France Colony presented in this book that I learned that the widely held association between informal spaces and illegality is highly inaccurate.

Because most of the spaces I examine in this book are legally contentious, tracing their histories was necessarily a complex, protracted endeavor. I developed a research approach that combined ethnography, spatial analysis of visual materials and site materiality, and archival research using legal files, government documents, and newspaper records. Even though I had to improvise my research strategy, much like the builders of the informal spaces that I was examining, I generally traced histories of various informal spaces from the perspectives of both the officials and the residents or businesspeople. I interviewed roadside khokha owners, residents of a katchi abadi, low- and high-ranking government officials, wealthy homeowners and business-people, store managers, architects, real estate agents, political activists, and nongovernmental organization workers. I frequently visited the offices of different departments at two key administrative bodies, the Capital Development Authority (CDA) and Islamabad Capital Territory Administration (ICTA), to get the perspectives of city officials and official policies on informal spaces and functions, including katchi abadis, new housing schemes in a once-protected nature reserve, roadside khokhas, and non-conforming commercial uses in large houses. Some officials were helpful in providing information during my first visit, but I came to expect that multiple visits to the same office would be needed before receiving a response to my queries. Residents of France Colony were always gracious in sharing their stories with me whenever I showed up in their neighborhood. But they exercised caution while describing their relationship to and dealings with the state. I gained access to my interlocutor for the elite informal neighborhood of Bani Gala, whom I call Mrs. Nabila Sheikh, through one of my close undergraduate college friends, who is related to her. The level of response from people in many ways correlated with how secure they felt in the informal spaces they occupied in the city. Roadside *khokha* owners and elite store managers were often more cautious about sharing how they set up their businesses; katchi abadi dwellers and elite residents of Bani Gala tended to be more open.

I corroborated the narratives of my interviewees with documents from official and institutional spaces like CDA, ICTA, and Wafaqi Mohtasib (Federal Ombudsman) offices, record rooms at the Press Information Department, and the High and Supreme Courts of Pakistan, CDA Library, Constantinos A. Doxiadis Archives (Athens), and National Archives of Pakistan (Islamabad). I found archives for my two case-study neighborhoods (France Colony and Bani Gala) in the form of active files at CDA's Katchi Abadi Cell and court files that I was able to access in the Lahore High Court's Rawalpindi Bench record room. Access to these records, which provide rich information on the histories of both France Colony and Bani Gala but are not all uniformly open to the public, was granted at the discretion of the staff at the time of my visits.

I traced histories of informal spaces not only through official documents and oral histories but also through their material forms and aesthetics. In addition to relying on my architectural training to analyze plans and buildings, I interviewed architects involved in either designing new homes or retrofitting existing houses for commercial nonresidential uses to better understand the role of architectural drawings and building forms in concealing the intended non-conforming uses. I documented the transformation of greenbelts, sidewalks, corridors, and service roads over the course of a day, and over months (and sometimes years), to accommodate commercial activities in public spaces. I looked closely at the infrastructure of temporary stalls and what steps were involved in their daily assembly and disassembly, including where the merchandise and display stands were stored at night and how they were transported back to the site each day. I also examined how changes in building materials and construction techniques of dwellings in katchi abadis and khokhas corresponded closely to their legal status. Following informality through spatial practices and architectural forms allowed me to understand how legal impediments may impact the way people make informal claims to space. In particular, it helped me appreciate that the material forms and strategies people use to build informal spaces are not arbitrary; those forms and strategies depend on the proficiency of builders in using design to help mitigate the impact of illegal constructions.

Organization of the Book

Master Plans and Encroachments begins by showing how the master plan of Islamabad is not simply an official planning device that makes violations obvious; it also creates conditions to make them possible. Chapter 1 traces the modernist lineage of Islamabad's master plan in order to provide context and genealogy for spaces where encroachments normally flourish. It highlights how the master plan was based on an imaginary *tabula rasa* that effaced the generations-long history of rural communities in the area. Despite the erasure of existing communities in the official master plan, the development of Islamabad as a "planned" city remains contingent on the complex acquisition process of local villages for various master-planned purposes. The master plan thus created the conditions for unanticipated spaces like the "model villages" to accommodate displaced rural communities in a protected nature reserve where all residential construction was strictly prohibited. This chapter sets up my argument about the master plan of Islamabad as a living planning document that is referred to and amended over time to accommodate important unfulfilled functions, an argument I explore further in the following chapters.

Chapter 2 highlights the role of the master plan and official procedures in the development of France Colony, a squatter settlement in the middle of an elite neighborhood in Islamabad. France Colony first developed in the 1970s, with official permission, to provide housing for low-level yet essential workers in the city, such as sweepers, drivers, maids, and clerks, many of whom are Christians in a predominantly Muslim city and are employed as municipal sanitary workers at the city's development authority. The chapter discusses how official authorities referred to the master plan to select a suitable site for this squatter settlement and developed new bureaucratic procedures to regularize this neighborhood. The residents of France Colony refer to the official procedures to sell their properties and to apply for electricity and gas connections. The chapter highlights the entwined relationship between the formal and the informal as an essential feature of the everyday functioning and long-term development of France Colony.

In Chapter 3, I consider ordinary commercial spaces like kiosks and tea stalls that are built on roadside greenbelts all over Islamabad. I argue that the long-term sustenance of such spaces depends on architectural forms and aesthetics, deliberately used by the builders, that help create an appearance of temporariness. In my analysis of the official strategies and everyday practices that allow encroachments to last for long periods, I propose the term *long-term temporariness*. A seeming oxymoron, *long-term temporariness* refers to official allowances for certain encroachments as long as they can be categorized as temporary. Builders of roadside kiosks and tea stalls deliberately use temporary building materials and construction techniques as a strategy of survival. This chapter shows how maintaining an impression of temporariness is an important bureaucratic and everyday strategy for sustaining ordinary informal spaces.

Chapter 4 examines the processes involved in the construction and legal defense of million-dollar lakefront mansions in Bani Gala—an illegal neighborhood built in a protected nature reserve. Elite homebuilders selected an exclusive scenic area based on its designation in the master plan as part of a large, protected nature reserve called the National Park. They mobilized their networks of personal resources and political connections with other elites, developed unlikely alliances with nonelites, and mimicked bureaucratic devices to legitimize their neighborhood through favorable court rulings. The revisions of the master plan and zoning regulations were based on the legitimization of encroachments like Bani Gala that had been oriented toward them.

Chapter 5 focuses on elite non-conforming spaces, an official term for regulation-violating construction by wealthy people on land that they legally own. Non-conforming spaces include large houses in residential areas used for illegal commercial purposes or lavish mansions built on what is ostensibly protected parkland. Elite non-conforming spaces in residential sectors sustain themselves by maintaining their external appearances as houses, even if their internal spatial arrangements have been drastically altered for commercial purposes. Elite non-conforming spaces do not simply function as violations of existing plans and laws; occasionally, they can displace the laws that had declared them illegal. A history of zoning laws in Islamabad shows how the legal defense of elite mansions in the protected National Park area initiated a process that significantly altered the master plan and zoning regulations of Islamabad. This chapter concludes with a discussion of the unmaking of certain elite and ordinary informalities in Islamabad after a series of High Court decisions passed in 2014 and 2015. I offer insights into the role of architectural forms and aesthetics in the recovery of certain encroachments after their demolition.

The Conclusion links the ways in which encroachments and violations are built with an eye toward official plans and regulations. I reflect on the role of contingency in contemporary city-making as a mode of planning based on the entwined relationship between plans and encroachments. As contingent modes of planning are available to both the privileged and the unprivileged, they help create spaces that are accessible but also exclusionary. The challenge is to harness contingencies and flexibilities in the planning process at the institutional level in ways that democratize the planning process without enabling elites to exploit the process to accumulate more wealth and power.

CHAPTER 1

Model Villages in a Modern City

slamabad's history as a modern city began around 1960, when the Pakistani government commissioned Greek architect-planner Constantinos Apostolos Doxiadis (1913–1975) to design a new national capital. People who live in or visit Islamabad recognize it as a "planned" city based on its unique design. Neighborhoods in Islamabad, called "sectors," are consistently sized, square-shaped communities that repeat on a rectilinear grid. The main roads running through the grid are all wide and straight, and the density of the grid is relieved by abundant and regularly recurring green spaces. People locate an address in the city by doing a mental calculation of its placement on the master-planned grid: sector F-7, for instance, lies west of sector F-6 and north of sector G-7.[1] All these distinct design features, including a grid plan, abundant open spaces, an efficient street network, and rational neighborhood layout and classification systems, contribute to Islamabad's identity as a highly planned modern city.

Doxiadis conceived Islamabad's master plan according to the dominant high-modernist planning principles of the mid-twentieth century. His design assumed an imaginary *tabula rasa*, an empty site free from the constraints of existing circumstances, as its starting point. Therefore, one of the prerequisites of Doxiadis's master plan was the annihilation of existing site conditions, including hundreds of small rural communities that had existed for generations in the site selected for Islamabad. This erasure was necessary to maintain the illusion that Islamabad would be a new city created from scratch. But this negation of hundreds of small, existing communities has remained contingent on the complex acquisition process of their villages. While many existing rural communities were displaced to implement Doxiadis's master plan, there have been several instances in which the master plan has had to accommodate new and existing villages that were not a part of it. The realities of displacing and relocating residents were far more complicated than the imaginary simplicity of a *tabula rasa*, and Doxiadis's attempted erasure of these existing settlements would pose serious challenges to the successful implementation of his master plan.

In this chapter, I address those serious challenges, which the master plan created itself. The master plan of Islamabad is not simply a planning device that makes violations obvious; historically, it has often formed the basis of its own violations. By assuming the invisibility and displacement of existing communities, the master plan created the very conditions that would undermine its holistic, totalizing goals: in order to successfully implement the master plan, Pakistani officials have had to allocate spaces not included in the original plan, such as the "model villages," to accommodate displaced villagers. I will first trace the modernist lineage of Islamabad's master plan by highlighting the design of identical neighborhood units and the provision of plentiful green spaces. This discussion provides necessary context for the spaces where encroachments and various forms of informality, examined in detail later in the book, normally thrive in the city. This chapter ends with an examination of both the displacement of existing villages and the development of new ones as a necessary feature of the "successful" implementation of the master plan.

A New Capital for a New Nation

New capital cities are highly political projects that represent the agendas of powerful actors, including political leaders, professional architects, and state officials.[2] About a decade after the formation of Pakistan, political leadership in the country carried out an ambitious and expensive capital city–building project for both symbolic and pragmatic reasons. Britain's exit from the Indian subcontinent in 1947 resulted in the creation of the two independent nation-states of India and Pakistan. Pakistan at the time comprised two wings—East and West Pakistan—that were geographically separated by over a thousand miles of land that belonged to India. The city of Karachi, in West Pakistan, was declared the national capital at the time of independence. Initially developed as a port city in the early eighteenth century, Karachi was chosen as the capital owing to its standing as a vibrant metropolis with an active commercial and political life.[3] But these attributes proved inadequate in allowing Karachi to function as a viable national capital city in the face of the political instabilities and refugee crisis during the 1950s.

One of the repercussions of the 1947 partition was the migration of millions of people across the India-Pakistan border who wished to settle on the other side. This mass movement of people, particularly to the large cities in India and Pakistan, placed tremendous stress on existing facilities and resources. In Pakistan, Karachi received a massive influx of refugees that more than doubled its existing population and placed immense pressure on its existing infrastructure.[4] Because of the extraordinary nature of the 1947 partition, displaced populations were temporarily allowed to build their homes in existing public buildings, parks, and other open lands in the city. Various proposals from foreign consultants to rehabilitate migrant populations and develop a new capital city in Karachi were sought in the 1950s, but most remained unrealized.[5] The deteriorating political situation in Pakistan in the 1950s, which included the assassination of sitting prime minister Liaquat Ali Khan in 1951 and a military coup in 1958, further sidetracked efforts to develop Karachi as the administrative capital of Pakistan.

The decision to plan a purpose-built capital city in a new location was eventually made by Pakistan's first military dictator, Field Marshal Muhammad Ayub Khan, who served as the head of state during the period of martial-law rule from 1958 to 1962 and was later elected president, serving until he was ousted in 1969. Shortly after taking power, Khan approved the plan to build a new capital city near Rawalpindi, the military headquarters of the Pakistan Army. Even though the Pakistan Navy was headquartered in Karachi, Khan did not enjoy the same support in Karachi that he would receive (as an ex–army chief) by being physically close to the army headquarters in Rawalpindi. While the military dictatorship established the conditions for building a new national capital in Pakistan's western wing instead of its more populous and economically stronger eastern wing,[6] external interests facilitated this massive city-building project. The post–World War II foreign assistance policies of wealthier western nations like the United States provided the financial and technical support needed to carry out ambitious developmental projects in Pakistan, including the construction of its brand-new national capital.[7]

Doxiadis first arrived in Pakistan as a member of the Harvard Advisory Group entrusted with drafting Pakistan's First Five Year Plan, which received financial support from the Ford Foundation.[8] Prior to the Islamabad commission, Doxiadis had successfully carried out several housing, educational, and urban development projects around Pakistan with funding from the U.S.

Agency for International Development program and the Ford Foundation.[9] One of Doxiadis's major commissions was the design of a refugee resettlement township in the suburban area of Korangi in Karachi, where 14,000 houses were built for people displaced by the 1947 partition of British India.[10] As a result, Doxiadis was already a familiar figure in Pakistan's local architecture and urban planning scene when he was hired by Pakistani officials in the late 1950s to design a new capital.[11]

Doxiadis was a self-proclaimed generalist who sought solutions to twentieth-century urban problems through an interdisciplinary scientific analysis of existing human settlements. He graduated as an architect-engineer from Athens Technical University in 1935 and acquired a doctorate from Charlottenburg Technical College in Berlin (now Technical University of Berlin) in 1936. In 1937, at age twenty-three and only a year after completing his formal education, Doxiadis was appointed chief town planning officer for the greater Athens area.[12] During World War II, Doxiadis was appointed head of the Department of Regional and Town Planning in Greece in addition to serving as a corporal in the Greek army. Following the liberation of Greece in 1945, Doxiadis traveled to England, France, and the United States to represent his country in various conferences and discussions about postwar reconstruction strategies. From 1945 to 1951, Doxiadis was actively involved in the reconstruction and restoration of postwar Greece, and he worked in various official capacities in the Ministry of Housing and Reconstruction and the Ministry of Coordination. In 1947, Doxiadis was introduced to the international forum of the United Nations when he represented Greece at the United Nations International Conference on Housing, Planning, and Reconstruction. This turned out to be a critical point in his career, landing him commissions both as a U.N. and private consultant in many countries in Asia and Africa, where the United Nations was actively involved in housing and development activities.[13]

After representing Greece in his official capacity, Doxiadis founded a private consultancy in 1951. Within twelve years, the firm had grown into a global enterprise providing architectural, planning, and engineering services, with offices in five continents and approximately forty projects in different parts of the world. During the 1950s, Doxiadis developed a new science of human settlements that he called ekistics, based on the systematic and interdisciplinary study of a range of past and present human settlements.[14] Doxiadis believed that a coordinated and interdisciplinary study of human settlements was essential for their success and necessary to fully understand and address the complex problems involved.[15] Doxiadis emphasized the need to "create a framework within which . . . disciplines can contribute to the totality and gradually merge with the others to form a rational whole."[16] Therefore, Doxiadis saw the need for an architect to expand his or her knowledge to include a number of fields and assume the role of master coordinator and generalist rather than that of specialist. Doxiadis founded the Athens Technological Organization in 1959, which served as a research and technical training institute to teach young professionals in ekistics, and its subsidiary, the Athens Center for Ekistics, in 1963, which focused on research and publications related to ekistics.

From 1959 to 1963, Doxiadis was commissioned as chief consultant for the new capital city of Pakistan.[17] The site selected for the city, called the Islamabad Capital Territory (ICT), comprised an area of approximately 290 square miles (750 square kilometers) located at the southern base of the Margalla Hills, roughly 12 miles (20 kilometers) north of Rawalpindi.[18] In the early 1990s, the government declared an additional area of about 60 square miles (158 square kilometers) south of Rawalpindi as part of the Islamabad capital region. Rawalpindi functioned as the interim capital of Pakistan during the initial years of Islamabad's construction and provided important support by fulfilling the basic needs of infrastructure, roads, airfields, and labor, and thus helped cut the initial costs of establishing these facilities anew in Islamabad.

The initial master plan of Islamabad envisioned that Rawalpindi would be developed alongside the new capital city (Figure 1.1).[19] Doxiadis's master plan enclosed the existing city of Rawalpindi within the grid of regularized neighborhoods that he developed for Islamabad. Since Rawalpindi had developed over several centuries, its historically evolved urban fabric lacked the organizational clarity that modernist architects sought, and it therefore presented many challenges for Doxiadis's master plan. At the same time, Doxiadis wanted to avoid having Islamabad become an annex to Rawalpindi through the "physical intermingling of the two cities."[20] Distance and separation had to be maintained in a way that the residents of Islamabad could make use of the services offered by the existing city while avoiding the "disadvantages" and dangers of mixing existing old and new urban patterns.[21] A type of *cordon sanitaire* comprising a generous greenbelt, a highway, and light industries was planned as a dividing zone between the existing city of Rawalpindi and the new city of Islamabad.[22]

The implementation of Doxiadis's master plan for Islamabad began in 1961, but the proposal to develop newer parts of Rawalpindi along with Islamabad was never implemented. From its grid plan to its distinctive con-

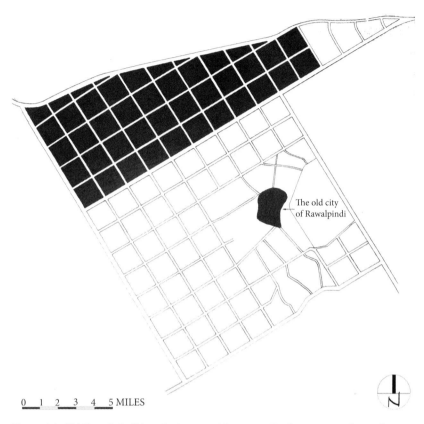

The old city of Rawalpindi

0   1   2   3   4   5 MILES

N

Figure 1.1. Old Rawalpindi in relation to grid pattern. Each square in the grid is 1.25 miles on each side. The black grid represents areas in Islamabad while the white grid area represents new areas in Rawalpindi. Source: Constantinos A. Doxiadis Archives, DOX-PA 168 (March 31, 1962), Periodical Report 76, p. 31 (Archive Files 36570). © Constantinos and Emma Doxiadis Foundation.

figuration of neighborhoods and expansive green spaces, Islamabad's "planned" built environment now stands in sharp contrast to the diverse urban patterns that exist in the historically evolved city of Rawalpindi.

Islamabad's Modernist Lineage

In Islamabad, Doxiadis got the opportunity to apply his planning approach of ekistics at the scale of an entirely new city.[23] Derived from the Greek word *oikos* (house or dwelling), ekistics proclaims that the livability of human settlements is based on a balanced relationship between five essential elements: nature, man, society, shells (buildings), and networks. To achieve an ideal balance among the five elements, ekistics specifies five planning principles: (1) *human happiness*; (2) *unity of purpose*, that is, unity in the economic, social, political, administrative, technical, and aesthetic spheres of a human settlement; (3) *hierarchy of functions*, which emphasizes the need to develop design based on different scales of human settlements to satisfy different human needs; (4) *four dimensions*, which includes three physical dimensions and a fourth dimension of time in order to accommodate changing functions and needs of human settlements; and (5) *many scales for many masters*, which emphasizes the need to design human settlements along different scales to ensure that machines serve human needs without becoming the master of human settlements. In addition to the five elements and five principles, ekistics is based on a fifteen-unit scale of social groupings in increasing population, with the anthropos (man) at the low end and the ecumenopolis (a universal city of fifty billion people that covers the entire earth) at the high end.[24]

By developing ekistics as a system of five elements, five principles, and fifteen units, Doxiadis's approach to urban design was like other modernist architects and planners who conceived of urban life in terms of distinct units that could be planned and manipulated in advance to achieve desired outcomes. Like other capitals built in the post–World War II era, including Brasilia in Brazil and Chandigarh in India, Islamabad was intended to be a symbol of progress and modernization centered on scientific rationality, professional expertise, and new technology. As members of the influential Congrès internationaux d'architecture moderne (CIAM), the architects and planners of Brasilia and Chandigarh developed their master plans according to CIAM's manifesto of urban planning called the Athens Charter.[25] Codified in 1933 by Le Corbusier, the Athens Charter conceptualized urbanism in terms of four functions—dwelling, work, leisure, and circulation—and called for a strict separation between functions to ensure efficiency.[26]

While the Athens Charter divided urban life into four basic functions, ekistics categorized human settlements into "a system of natural, social, and man-made elements."[27] Moreover, unlike CIAM's Athens Charter, as a manifesto of universal principles of modernist planning, ekistics privileged a study of local context and conditions in solving existing urban problems. Doxiadis insisted that planning should build on what is good in existing local conditions and import technology and experience only for areas in need of improvement.[28] As the discussion on existing villages later in this chapter will show, Doxiadis's ideological position on preserving the good in local contexts was often overshadowed by his professional partiality toward rational, standardized, and centralized planning.

Doxiadis was critical of utopian cities proposed by "experts" who sought solutions to harsh, existing realities by implementing unrealistic and unlivable schemes.[29] He explained that utopian ideas for future cities were infeasible because of the high costs associated with building fantastical cities like "great moving machines," "aerial clusters in space or inside pyramids in the desert or floating islands."[30] Additionally, such utopian cities were bad for human well-being, because life in a giant pyramid or in skyscrapers did not fulfill the basic social and psychological needs of anthropos. Doxiadis declared a utopian scheme a fiction in the "minds of . . . 'experts'" at best and a "a dys-utopia" at worst.[31] As an alternative to the experts' utopias, Doxiadis proposed the concept of *entopia*, or the desirable and feasible city. Doxiadis identified four anthropos-centric goals for entopia: happiness, safety, human development, and equal rights.[32] The approach to creating entopia was a realistic and optimistic one that did not turn away from the inevitable consequences of technological advancements and urbanization. Doxiadis declared that "to scream against the many highways is not enough and to stop them is wrong. What we need is to turn them from undesirable to desirable ones."[33] By using "knowledge, courage, and imagination" to predict the desirable and the inevitable, Doxiadis believed that all urban problems could be resolved to achieve a balance between technology and human comfort.[34]

One of the most distinguishing features of Islamabad's master plan, setting it apart from the roughly contemporaneous schemes for Brasilia or Chandigarh, is Doxiadis's emphasis on time and not space as "the real dimension of cities."[35] He conceived cities as dynamically growing organisms, which he called the *dynapolis* (dynamic city), that develop in one direction along a predetermined path. To enable Islamabad to thrive as a dynamic city of the future, in contrast to the static city of the past, Doxiadis's plan included provisions for the city to grow over time in a southwesterly direction.[36] In order to develop Islamabad as a dynapolis, Doxiadis planned a system of commercial and civic cores that would grow simultaneously with the city, thus diminishing the danger of the center being constricted by the overall growth of the city.

Doxiadis's master plan features a compartmentalization of various functions of the city in three clearly defined zones connected by an efficient circulation network. Man-made elements and existing natural elements like

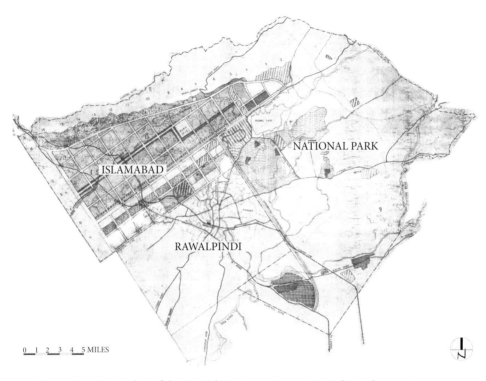

Figure 1.2. Master plan of the Capital Territory. Source: Capital Development Authority Planning Wing, Maps and Records Unit, Islamabad.

mountains and lakes delineate the boundaries and subdivisions of the metropolitan area. The city is bounded on the north and northwest by the Margalla Hills and on the southeast by the Soan River. A system of four highways generates three subdivisions in the metropolitan area. The three zones include Islamabad proper, Rawalpindi Town and Cantonments, and the National Park (Figure 1.2).[37] Islamabad proper was designed as a grid of identically arranged neighborhoods (called "sectors") that comprise communities of various scales and a hierarchical circulation network. The National Park area was imagined as a large open space of respite easily accessible to the citizens of the new city. While Doxiadis wanted to maintain separation between Islamabad and Rawalpindi, the inclusion of Rawalpindi Town and Cantonments in the metropolitan area of Islamabad shows how he also tried to regulate the development of the new areas in Rawalpindi along the same principles he used to plan Islamabad. But his proposal to develop Rawalpindi alongside Islamabad was never implemented because of a lack of political support for and the practical financial and administrative constraints associated with the simultaneous construction of not one but two cities.

Today, Islamabad continues to expand to the southwest, but this is not the only direction in which the city would eventually experience growth. Islamabad also has expanded in an area south of Rawalpindi; this region was incorporated into the capital territory at a later date (the 1990s) and is being developed by private and public entities into a number of gated enclaves that contradict the standardized grid pattern that Doxiadis planned originally. Even though Doxiadis conceived of Islamabad as a dynamically growing city, the basic structural element—the sector—was designed as a self-contained, fixed unit with little room for variation. Ironically, the sector is also the unit of geographical space in which the master plan has been undermined and transformed, as I show in the following chapters. But Doxiadis intended the sector as a highly rational spatial unit intended to regularize and control various aspects of social life.

The Sector

Each sector in Islamabad is a square-shaped parcel of land, 1.25 miles on a side, arranged in a grid generated by placing principal roads 2,200 yards apart. Doxiadis designed the sector as a self-contained community that could provide the basic needs of its resident population. The residential areas in Islamabad's sectors are equipped with large green spaces such as greenbelts, parks, and playgrounds; schools of different levels; and a central civic and commercial center called a *markaz* (Urdu for "center") located near the middle. Roads and streets of varying sizes were planned according to anticipated vehicular traffic. Doxiadis organized each sector based on a hierarchy of communities of various sizes, from a group of individuals to a community of 20,000 to 40,000 people.[38]

The predictability and clarity offered by the sector in Islamabad contrasts with the older neighborhoods, or *mohallahs*, in urban Pakistan, which owe much of their physical organization to their piecemeal development and gradually evolving social life. The disparities in street layout and functional zoning in mohallahs and sectors highlight their differences. Straight and wide streets intersect at right angles and provide direct and efficient access to various parts of the sector. In contrast, winding streets of varying widths lead to the deepest

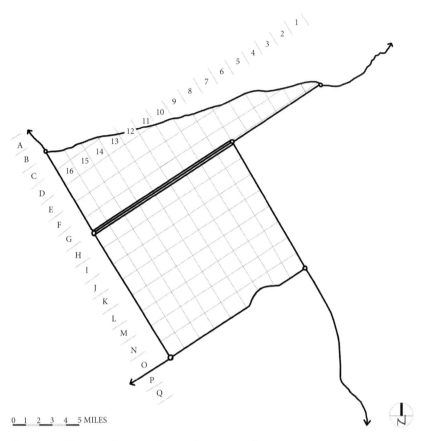

Figure 1.3. Naming of sectors. Drawn from Doxiadis Associates, DOX-PA 88, Periodical Report 32, p. 381 (Capital Development Authority Library, Islamabad).

part of the mohallah and often end in cul-de-sacs. Instead of being concentrated in a single central location, commercial and public buildings stand at important nodes and along market (*bazaar*) streets scattered all over the mohallah. Moreover, since mohallahs are high-density neighborhoods, they rarely have vast expanses of open spaces or parks the way the sectors do.

With the exception of highways and main roads, which bear the names of important persons and places in Pakistan, sectors are named according to their placement on the master-plan grid. The x-axis of the grid is numbered, while y-axis is assigned letters of the roman alphabet (Figure 1.3). The name of each sector hence consists of its coordinates on the x and y axes: a number and a letter. Moreover, each sector is further subdivided into four sub-sectors,

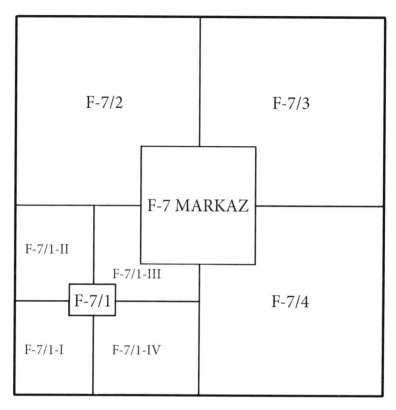

Figure 1.4. Naming of sector F-7 and subsector F-7/1 in Islamabad.

which are numbered 1 through 4 in a clockwise manner starting from the bottom-left corner. Thus, a sector with the coordinates of F along the y-axis and 7 along the x-axis is named F-7. Locations within sector F-7 can be further narrowed down according to sub-sector, referred to as, for example, F-7/1, F-7/2, F-7/3, or F-7/4 (Figure 1.4). Each sub-sector is further divided into four parts that are numbered using roman numerals I through IV (for instance, the sub-sectors in F-7/1 are F-7/1-I, F-7/1-II, F-7/1-III, and F-7/1-IV). Despite its incongruity in the Pakistani context, Doxiadis's rationalized system of naming sectors has been fully embraced by the residents and businesspeople of Islamabad.

The configuration of the sector in Islamabad developed out of the "neighborhood unit" concept, a planning ideal popularized by the practice and writings of American planner Clarence Perry during the early twentieth century.[39] Perry conceived of the neighborhood unit both "as a unit of a larger

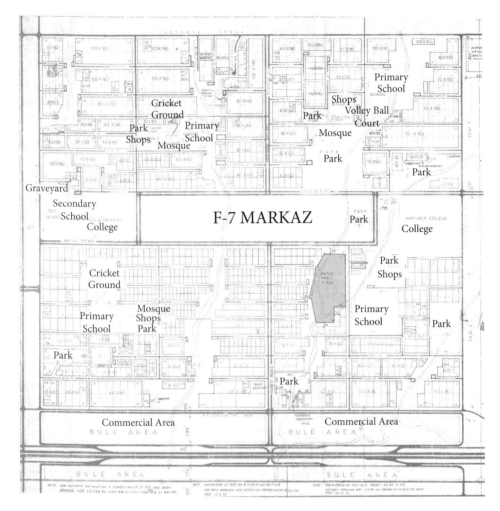

Figure 1.5. Master plan of sector F-7 with civic, educational, commercial, and recreational spaces. Drawn from layout plan of sector F-7, Capital Development Authority Planning Wing, Maps and Records Unit, Islamabad.

whole and as a distinct entity in itself."[40] It was designed as a self-contained ~mmunity organized around a school (along with other civic buildings and ~s) and as a walkable neighborhood in which pedestrians could reach dif-~menities within twenty minutes. Vehicular traffic was restricted in-~eighborhood unit, with arterial roads placed around the perimeter of the community and interior roads designed to slow traffic to ensure the safety of pedestrians moving around in the neighborhood.[41]

Doxiadis's sector follows Perry's neighborhood unit scheme quite closely, with only minor modifications (Figure 1.5). Doxiadis placed residential spaces on the periphery and commercial facilities in the center of the sector, as opposed to Perry's placement of shops on the periphery and institutional buildings in the middle of the residential neighborhood. Doxiadis similarly designed the sector as a walkable community with ample green spaces either in the form of parks and playgrounds or open spaces left vacant in the interstices of the grid, at the end of cul-de-sacs, and around streets and highways.

The concept of the neighborhood unit had already made an appearance in the South Asian region prior to construction of Islamabad. Sanjeev Vidyarthi traces the introduction of the neighborhood unit concept to the Indian subcontinent to the international practice of German architect-planner Otto Koenigsberger.[42] In his capacity as a planning consultant in colonial and postcolonial India, Koenigsberger used the neighborhood unit in his design for multiple new towns for industrial workers and refugees (for example, Bhubaneswar and Jamshedpur). In Pakistan as well, the neighborhood unit concept made an appearance in one of the unrealized proposals for the redevelopment of Karachi prepared in 1952 by the Swedish consultancy firm Merz Rendel Vatten (MRV). The MRV plan was based on a neighborhood unit of about one-by-two miles centered around public amenities and accommodating about forty thousand residents.[43] French architect and planner Michel Ecochard's refugee resettlement scheme in suburban Karachi, planned in 1953, was similarly organized around multiple neighborhood units.[44]

Residential communities inspired by the neighborhood unit concept formed an important design feature of high-modernist cities such as Brasilia and Chandigarh. In Brasilia, the neighborhood unit takes the form of four superblocks called superquadras, which are 240-by-240 meters (0.15-by-0.15 miles), each a residential module of identical, multistory apartment buildings clustered around open green spaces and nursery and elementary schools. Brazilian architect Lúcio Costa designed the neighborhood unit layout such that two superquadras share commercial, religious, sports, and recreational buildings. A longitudinal commercial center is located on one side of the superquadra, while a church, sports center, cinema, and a club form a cluster of communal spaces on the other side; this pattern is repeated throughout Brasilia's residential axis.

In Chandigarh, the neighborhood units, also called sectors, form an integral component of the master plan. Le Corbusier's master plan for the city was an adaptation of an initial scheme by two American designers, planner Albert Mayer and architect Matthew Nowicki.[45] Forgoing his earlier fascination with soaring towers in expansive park-like open spaces as visualized in his utopian schemes such as the Contemporary City (1922) and the Radiant City (1934), Le Corbusier accepted Mayer's proposal for neighborhood sectors made up of low-rise buildings in Chandigarh.[46] The sectors in Chandigarh have a smaller area than sectors in Islamabad, comprising rectangular modules of 800 meters (0.5 miles) by 1,200 meters (0.75 miles). As in Islamabad, these modules are organized in a grid to generate the overall master plan of Chandigarh. In Chandigarh, each sector is equipped with schools, shops, and civic and religious buildings, all within easy walking distance from the residential areas of the sector.

In the twentieth century, the neighborhood unit concept was a popular choice in different contexts because it gave physical form to the conviction that modern planning's organizational tenets could be used to model social behavior and forge social cohesion among people and their natural and built environments. In addition, the neighborhood unit made it possible for modern planners to manipulate the city by dividing it into smaller and more manageable "physical and social units."[47] This strategy was especially important in the administration of urban areas in postcolonial South Asia. Matthew Hull notes a fundamental shift in official attitudes toward urban communities and their management practices after the end of British colonial rule in India.[48] Whereas British colonial authorities preferred to administer and control cities by dealing with various existing communities (based on religion, ethnicity, caste, and so on), postcolonial administrators were more interested in producing new communities of citizens focused on place-based solidarity for the effective management of urban areas.[49] In addition to encouraging face-to-face human interactions as imagined by modern architects, the neighborhood unit fulfilled important aspirations for top-down control and management of urban spaces and populations.

While the neighborhood unit concept in its various iterations emerged as a popular planning strategy in state-led urban development projects around the world in the twentieth century, the implementation of these plans resulted in the creation of new kinds of spaces that had not been part of the master plan. In Islamabad, spaces and functions unanticipated in the master plan mostly developed to accommodate existing site conditions, unfulfilled needs of the underprivileged, and exclusionary practices of the elites. While unanticipated functions exist in both built and unbuilt spaces, some of the boldest and most pervasive encroachments in Islamabad have developed in expansive, open green areas—designated as the "lungs" of the city—that Doxiadis designed at the scales of the sector and the city as a whole.

Lungs of the City

Greenery and generous open spaces are an important feature of Islamabad's master plan, and these features distinguish it from other large cities in Pakistan. Doxiadis selectively incorporated certain natural site conditions to create parks, hiking trails, and nature reserves. For instance, the site for Islamabad is endowed with a series of natural ravines that cut across the site from north to south in many places. Doxiadis preserved these existing ravines as important landscape features in various sectors and placed walking trails, parks, gardens, playgrounds, and schools next to them.[50] Doxiadis referred to the ravines as the "lungs" of Islamabad, and he intended these spaces to provide relief and relaxation from the stresses of life in a modern city. But still, he made no attempt to preserve the natural undulating topography of Islamabad's site when imposing the rectilinear grid of his master plan, and he freely used cut-and-fill methods to level the site.

In describing green spaces as "lungs," Doxiadis invoked a metaphor used since the eighteenth century by planners, reformers, and thinkers, who considered open spaces necessary for the mental and moral well-being of people living in cities undergoing rapid urbanization.[51] In modern planning, the idea of allocating large, open green spaces as "lungs of the city" to improve its overall health was popularized by the American landscape architect Frederick Law Olmsted, who designed many large urban parks in major cities in the United States. Le Corbusier similarly used the term "lungs" to describe open spaces, which he declared necessary to accommodate high-density populations in his 1922 utopian proposal for "A Contemporary City of Three Million People."[52] Le Corbusier's master plan for Chandigarh similarly features interconnected bands of green spaces that run north to south and cut across all the sectors to provide breathing spaces for the city.

Islamabad's landscape features green spaces at various scales. In addition to dedicated spaces of leisure, such as parks, nature reserves, walking trails, and playgrounds, Doxiadis planned generous greenbelts adjacent to all roads.

Greenbelts separate residential lots from roads and sidewalks, punctuate the end of cul-de-sacs, and emerge in places where the geometric grid of streets meets natural site conditions such as ravines and slopes. In addition to open spaces interspersed throughout the planned sectors, Doxiadis reserved nearly one-third of the total site as a protected parkland called the National Park area. An important feature of this area is Rawal Lake, an artificial reservoir built next to Rawal Dam in the early 1960s to provide water to the residents of Rawalpindi and that now partially fulfills the water needs of Islamabad. Concern for pollution caused by excessive development in the catchment areas of Rawal Lake was one of the main reasons Doxiadis designated the surrounding region as the National Park area.[53]

As the rest of this book shows, the presence of large, open public areas throughout Islamabad presented opportune conditions for the development of new spaces that were not part of the master plan. While the plan provided a blueprint for the future growth of the city, it remained silent on the communities that already inhabited portions of the capital region, some for generations before Islamabad was ever conceived. While certain natural features like mountains, trees, and ravines were preserved, the plan to construct Islamabad "from scratch" meant that existing rural settlements had to be erased. The invisibility and displacement of small villages—a necessary precondition of the master plan—became one of the biggest challenges to its full implementation.

The Villages

The master plan of Islamabad is missing a sector. Like a missing piece of a puzzle, sector I-13 is left out of both the official blueprints and numbering system, which goes directly from I-12 to I-14. This is because the area earmarked for sector I-13 actually falls inside the Rawalpindi Cantonment area. Because the decision to develop Rawalpindi alongside Islamabad was eventually abandoned, areas that were in Rawalpindi Cantonment could not be included in the official master plan of Islamabad. Moreover, the site for Islamabad was selected without considering important existing conditions, such as the nontransferable nature of most cantonment lands. The absence of sector I-13 in Islamabad is one among many examples of its modernist grid being interrupted or warped by the presence of a preexisting fact. Despite its apparent rigidity, the modern grid flexibly accommodates existing conditions without compromising its overall geometric order.

The imagined emptiness of the site was particularly desirable for professional architects and planners who wished to test their planning ideals in laboratory-like conditions. Political leaders similarly saw in the creation of new cities an opportunity to circumvent unwanted existing socioeconomic and political issues. In the early 1950s, Indian prime minister Jawaharlal Nehru famously said of the new state capital of Chandigarh, "Let this be a new town, symbolic of the freedom of India, unfettered by the traditions of the past, an expression of the nation's faith in the future."[54] An official report on the location of the new capital of Pakistan compiled by a special commission chaired by army chief General Yahya Khan similarly justified the construction of new cities using medico-scientific metaphors: "We consume vitamins to rejuvenate our decayed tissues. We let fresh air and sunlight into our homes to accentuate vitality in living. . . . We build new cities and rehabilitate old ones to prevent decay eating into our national life."[55] The report eventually recommended an ideal site near the city of Rawalpindi for the development of a new capital in a "place where it cannot be overgrown into another crowded and sprawling city like Karachi."[56]

At the time of the development of Islamabad's master plan, there was a recorded population of over 54,000 people settled in 220 *mouzas* in the site chosen for the construction of the new capital.[57] A *mouza* is the smallest administrative unit of revenue estate in the records of the Revenue Department, having one or more villages or smaller rural settlements. While Doxiadis's plan preserved some existing topographical features of the capital site, including the lake, mountains, hills, and ravines, the master plan did not incorporate any of the existing rural communities. He even designed a vast barrier of open spaces and light industries between the new city of Islamabad and existing city of Rawalpindi in order to prevent mixing of new and old urban forms. According to the modernist logic under which Doxiadis worked, an erasure of all the existing settlements was a necessary precondition to develop Islamabad as a new modern city.

Doxiadis's approach toward existing local conditions reveals a contradiction in his design thinking. For all his international projects, Doxiadis emphasized "scientific" analysis of the context, which included site visits and collection of data on local climate, geology, culture, aesthetics, and building practices. But this knowledge of local conditions and cultural particularities—published in the form of numerous reports—was selectively applied in the final design proposals. In considering the 1950s restructuring of Baghdad as the modern capital of Iraq, Panayiota Pyla highlights that Doxiadis's use of local building elements (like overhangs, screens, and courtyards) appeared only as "relics of the past" within standardized plans that he designed as part of a "comprehensive order imposed from above."[58]

Doxiadis's approach to existing low-income communities in the cities that he helped modernize was simply to level the existing structures and displace the populations. In her study of informal mud and reed dwellings built by rural migrants in Baghdad, Huma Gupta shows how Doxiadis Associates declared existing migrant communities to be slums and justified their clearance and the resettlement of the residents in modern, standardized housing units.[59] For resettled rural migrants in Iraq, Doxiadis Associates designed sites-and-services schemes that offered fully developed and ready-to-build rectangular plots, a centralized civic center, education and recreation facilities, and streets of various widths. Rural migrants were required to build their houses following identical house plans that made "tokenistic references to local Iraqi building vocabularies."[60] In Doxiadis's design thinking, local spatial elements and conditions remained secondary to universalized modern planning principles of uniformity, standardization, and regularity.

To achieve the clean-slate condition that the Doxiadis master plan required, the official development authority in Islamabad, the Capital Development Authority (CDA), first had to acquire land from existing communities. In the 1960s, CDA started the process of acquiring small villages, which ranged in size from a handful to a few hundred dwellings each, according to the land acquisition policy outlined in the Capital Development Authority Ordinance of 1960. The ordinance gave CDA the power to acquire any land in the designated capital area as long the agency followed the prescribed acquisition process.

The official land acquisition process involves an order in writing—called an "award" (of compensation)—issued by the district commissioner of CDA. The "award" is CDA's official announcement of its compensation for a given parcel of land. The owners of the land to be acquired, called the "affectees" (of the displacement process), are compensated for both their land and existing buildings. The existing buildings are called built-up property (BuP), a designation that includes houses, shops, stores, cattle pens, and sheds. According to the current Land Acquisition and Rehabilitation Regulation (enacted in 2007), for every four *kanals* (0.5 acre) of acquired rural land, displaced landowners can receive smaller CDA-developed plots with utilities and physical and social infrastructure.[61] In the case of existing BuP, the government currently offers developed plots of 25-by-50 feet, in areas reserved for affected people as compensation for seized buildings. The minimum covered area requirement for a structure to qualify as a dwelling unit eligible for compensation under the current government policy was recently reduced from 1,000 square feet to 300 square feet.[62]

In practice, the acquisition and rehabilitation of land is a long process often mired in controversy and corruption. Government officials claim that many fake affectees have benefited from land acquisition and rehabilitation schemes over the years using a number of strategies. Local landowners and CDA staff believe that land scammers build fake houses, called dummy houses, overnight to qualify these structures for compensation as BuP. As quickly assembled structures made from a haphazard assortment of construction materials, often without any doors or windows, dummy houses are easily recognizable as structures solely meant to be counted as BuP and not appropriate for dwelling purposes. But this land scam involving dummy houses and fake affectees cannot be carried out without the participation of CDA's staff and officials. A local landowner explained the complicity of CDA staff in this process: "First a CDA official overestimates the value of the existing structures, and then another official called a checker verifies that the structure exists. Finally, the structure is demolished so there is no record of what was actually there."[63]

Another aspect of CDA's rehabilitation policy that often gets exploited is the provision of benefits to all existing households, even when multiple households share a single residential structure. CDA officials claim that this feature of the compensation policy for the capital territory has been exploited by villagers, who may assign a room in an existing dwelling to a relative living elsewhere in order to help them claim extra benefits. In some cases, a CDA revenue official claimed, residents of acquired villages strategically relocate to unacquired villages in order to exploit CDA's policy and receive compensation multiple times. A 2017 newspaper report describes the extent of fraud involved in the land acquisition process:

> As per Google image available a year back, only 137 houses existed on 237 kanals of land in area of Dhoke Azam and adjoining villages of Chak Shahzad. . . . However, some officials of CDA who are on deputation, for the sake of their interests and under some political pressure were also considering 700 fake claims of BuP in addition to 137 genuine cases. The CDA sources said the concerned officials of CDA were receiving bribe[s] from fake affected persons for allotment of 700 alternate plots, the total cost of which in the open market on allotment would be over Rs5 billion.[64]

The strategies developed by land speculators and impostor property owners have been prevalent enough to stall development work on new sectors. Mired in relocation benefit claims, CDA does not have the money to acquire the land needed to start the developmental process.

Even in the case of some villages it has already acquired, CDA faces a number of serious problems. Much of the land in the capital region was acquired in the 1960s and 1970s at then-prevailing market rates. As CDA carried out the process of developing new sectors, residents of acquired villages in places like the National Park were allowed to live there until the acquired land was needed for developmental purposes. In many cases, several decades passed before CDA needed the acquired land. When CDA demanded possession of it, residents refused to vacate on the grounds that while their elders had been compensated in the 1960s, they did not have any place to go. Others felt that their land had been acquired at a throwaway price in the 1960s and was worth a lot more now, which meant they should be given additional compensation.

In order to pacify these concerns and to clear land for developmental purposes without serious conflicts, CDA offered a second relocation package in the 1980s to the residents of villages already acquired in the 1960s. The package included a developed plot in one of CDA's "model villages." Conceived as a small community of residential plots, a model village is meant to provide land to displaced villagers and to generate revenue through the auctioning of additional plots. For instance, the existing village of Chak Shahzad, in the National Park area, was acquired in the 1960s as the intended site of various educational institutions. To gain possession from the residents of this village in the 1980s, CDA established a model village called Agro Village Chak Shahzad (also known as Shahzad Town) (Figure 1.6) in another location in the National Park. The layout of the model village includes rows of residential plots of mostly 30-by-70 feet along rectilinear streets, thus maximizing the number of plots that could be developed in the site. The model village is provided with basic infrastructure, including water, electricity, roads, and sewerage, along with assigned spaces for a school, mosque, park, and commercial shops. There are currently eight model communities in Islamabad: Rawal Town, Humak Model Town, Shahzad Town, Margalla Town, Nurpur Shahan, Farash Town (or Model Urban Shelter Project, discussed below), and Kuri and Tarlai Model Villages.[65] As Figure 1.7 shows, seven out of the eight model villages are located in the protected areas of the National Park and Margalla Hills National Park; they now serve as lower-middle-income neigh-

Figure 1.6. Aerial view of Agro Village Chak Shahzad, also known as Shahzad Town.

borhoods in the city. By declaring certain villages as "model," CDA was able to introduce new residential areas with rectilinear plots organized on a grid of straight streets in a protected region. In this way, city officials themselves established new spaces that did not exist on the master plan to accommodate residents of those settlements that needed to be cleared.

In 2001, CDA launched a sites-and-services housing project called the Model Urban Shelter Project (MUSP).[66] The purpose of this project is to resettle residents of eligible *katchi abadis* (squatter settlements) in Islamabad (discussed in Chapter 2) to Alipur Farash, a rural area in the protected National Park. MUSP, popularly known as Farash Town, is an extension of an earlier

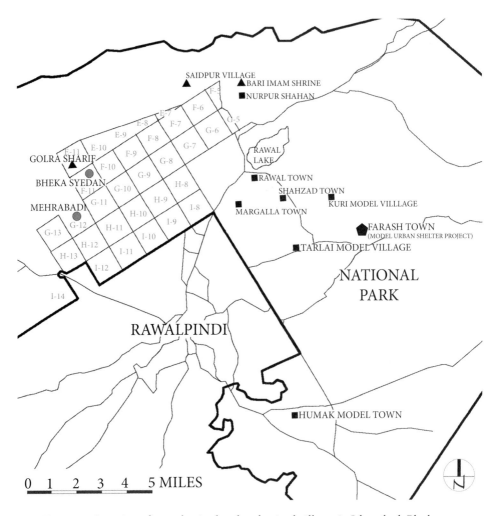

Figure 1.7. Location of unauthorized and authorized villages in Islamabad. Black squares mark the new model villages, and black triangles represent authorized spiritual and tourist villages. The black pentagon represents the Model Urban Shelter Project, a new sites-and-services project for resettled katchi abadi dwellers. Gray circles are the unauthorized villages.

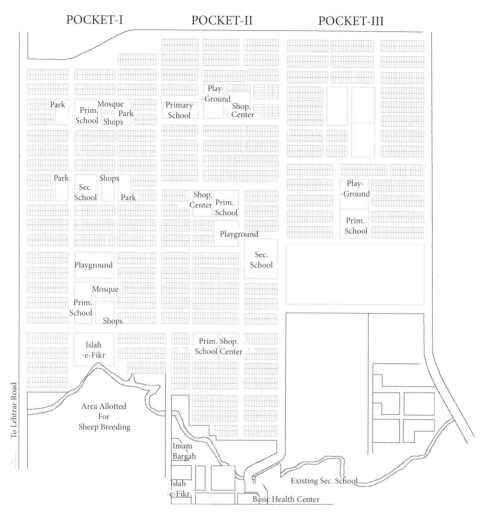

Figure 1.8. Master plan of the Model Urban Shelter Project, Islamabad. Redrawn from a Capital Development Authority map.

resettlement project, which was launched in the same area in the 1990s for people who were living in self-built dwellings on a site that was earmarked for a large park in sector F-9. MUSP's layout plan comprises approximately 4,000 small rectangular plots arranged on a grid of straight roads (about 30 to 70 feet wide) (Figure 1.8).[67] Schools, parks, mosques, and shopping centers are dispersed throughout the site of about 160 acres.

Figure 1.9. Aerial view of Saidpur village near sector F-6.

At the time of its creation, CDA offered residents of eligible squatter settlements plots of 20-by-40 feet on a temporary basis, with an understanding
that they would be allowed to live there (without legal title) free of cost for
the next 15 years. But the allottees were expected to make an initial payment of about 20,000 Pakistani rupees, a substantial amount for people with
limited incomes. The project was at a site anywhere from 9 to 12 miles away
from where the katchi abadi dwellers lived and worked. It lacked basic
amenities like water supply, sewerage, and garbage disposal and public
transportation facilities to urban areas of the city. MUSP ultimately failed
to attract the residents of existing katchi abadis located in the central, well-
serviced areas of Islamabad and fell prey to property speculation as many

allottees sold their plot allotments (using informal means) to lower-middle-income people.[68]

Besides planning new model communities to accommodate displaced af-fectees or katchi abadi dwellers, CDA has authorized certain villages based on their spiritual and touristic significance. For instance, the sixteenth-century village of Saidpur, located at the base of the Margalla Hills next to a beautiful ravine, was upgraded to a tourist village in 2006 (Figure 1.9). The Disneyfied upgrading of the village's historic core consisted of painting the existing sixteenth-century Hindu temple and a twentieth-century Sikh gurd-wara in bright colors, converting an existing building into an art gallery, and creating new restaurants and cafés.[69] Golra Sharif provides another example of special permission given to an existing village of spiritual significance. Located in the middle of sector E-11, the Golra Sharif village is the site of a mosque and shrine complex of a nineteenth-century revered Sufi saint, Peer Meher Ali Shah. Sector E-11 provides a contrasting urban pattern that in-cludes new residential areas with regular plots and rectilinear streets around the labyrinthine form of the village.

In addition to the officially recognized model, tourist, and spiritual vil-lages, certain unacquired rural communities still exist in the city. Residents of these villages accuse CDA officials of violating the terms of their acquisi-tion contracts, corruption, and delayed payments. Bheka Syedan, a small vil-lage located across the street from the elite and exclusive shopping *markaz* of sector F-11, provides an example of a site where negotiations between CDA and local villagers have stalled for nearly forty years (Figures 1.10 and 1.11). CDA announced three awards in the 1980s to acquire land in sector F-11 from the residents of Bheka Syedan, and in 1990 reached an agreement granting them cash compensation or developed plots in the same or a nearby sector.[70] In early 2003, CDA decided to unilaterally change the terms of the agreement by offering replacement plots in an undeveloped sector located at a distance from the original village. Many residents of Bheka Syedan refused to accept this new offer, but CDA allegedly went ahead in constructing luxury hous-ing in F-11 on land that was acquired from Bheka Syedan residents without compensation.[71] Today, a cluster of small houses belonging to the uncompen-sated villagers, who have taken CDA to court and are literally holding their ground until they are offered a more acceptable option, sits in the middle of a fully developed, otherwise elite sector.

While Bheka Syedan exists as a minor disruption to the planned order of sector F-11, the village of Mehrabadi challenges the discipline of the modernist

Figure 1.10. Aerial view of Bheka Syedan village in the middle of sector F-11.

grid on a much larger scale. According to the official master plan, the space occupied by Mehrabadi should have been sector G-12. Plans to acquire the village of Mehrabadi were announced in the 1980s, but the original terms CDA offered were unacceptable to the local community.[72] This situation was further complicated by the fact that many land speculators quickly started building structures in this village so that they might benefit from CDA's relocation and acquisition policy. As organically evolved settlements, existing villages disguise the new extensions made by private land speculators often in collusion with CDA officials. Despite several attempts by CDA to forcefully acquire land in Mehrabadi, the area still remains under the control of locals. Taking up the geometric space of an entire sector and bounded on three

Figure 1.11. Bheka Syedan village (left) and luxury apartments (right) in sector F-11. Photograph by author.

sides by fully developed sectors, this village continues to thrive as a low-income residential area built in an organic form; its auto-repair workshops, building-material shops, restaurants, and other businesses offer affordable services to the residents of Islamabad. The erasure of existing human communities—a necessary precondition of the master plan—has paradoxically aided the development of both unacquired and model villages in Islamabad. These old and new villages appear as stark interruptions of the master plan, which resumes immediately beyond the boundaries of the villages.

Conclusion

Informal spaces in comprehensively planned cities have been mostly conceptualized as contradictions to the ideal "plan." Existing critiques of high-modernist cities like Brasilia and Chandigarh explain the emergence of informal housing as "spontaneous" or "unplanned" and as paradoxical urban phenomena.[73] While these critiques successfully expose the hegemonic ideology of high modernism and its tendency to reject unaccounted-for urban phenomena, they do not consider how informal spaces work in direct relation to the master plan and planning regulations. This chapter showed that the master plan makes its violations both apparent and possible. By leaving nothing to chance and accounting for all essential functions in a presumably empty site, modern architects like Doxiadis claimed that their master plans could combat the issues of congestion, pollution, and laissez-faire development that were prevalent in existing cities. But top-down planning works in complex, uneven ways. Markus Daechsel sees Islamabad as an instance of "ideological displacement" or "misplaced ekistics" because of how Doxiadis's ideas and approach to address the "problems" or "crisis" of urbanization did not quite exist in the remote region of Islamabad.[74] And the "problems" and conditions that did exist in the site selected for Islamabad received no consideration in Doxiadis's use of ekistics as a planning ideology. This ideological displacement did not represent a failure of top-down planning but contributed to its fragmentation, which provided avenues for both the city officials and citizens to participate in the development of unanticipated urban phenomena.[75]

A clean-slate site was a necessary precondition for achieving the goals of efficient and idealized urban living promised by high-modernist planning. In Islamabad, the *tabula rasa* assumed in the master plan had to be achieved by displacing existing rural communities. While the master plan necessitated an erasure of existing villages, in practice, Islamabad could only be developed with the accommodation of small village communities or even the creation of new "model villages." CDA officials built new communities that did not exist in the master plan in areas that were designated as a nature reserve. In this way, city officials themselves inaugurated the practice of using numerous, open public spaces, a characteristic feature of high-modernist planning, as sites of encroachment in Islamabad.

Islamabad's high-modernist master plan is a living document that has been added to and modified in order to accommodate its encroachments. The master plan accommodates informal spaces either as temporary provisions or as permanent additions. Adherence to official rules and regulations has a very different purchase in societies in which "law itself is a means of manipulation, complication, stratagem, and violence" to help both the privileged and underprivileged further their illegal claims to space.[76] This emerges as an important feature of the history of encroachments and violations in Islamabad, where elite and nonelite citizens and state actors alike have been and continue to be involved in devising new ways of making informal claims to space while paying close attention to the master plan and formal planning procedures. The rest of the book will focus on how the city officials, residents, and businesspeople of Islamabad try to reconcile their personal and political agendas with Doxiadis's high-modernist blueprints.

CHAPTER 2

Ordinary Informality

Across Bhitai Road, at the southern edge of the elite markaz of sector F-7, sits a cluster of small dwellings. Built in an outwardly irregular form, these dwellings contrast starkly with the freestanding mansions that sit on deep, rectangular plots all around. Inhabited primarily by city sanitation workers, these dwellings are noticeably smaller and more tightly packed. A white-painted brick wall surrounds the dwellings, yet many social activities spill over on the adjacent streets and sidewalks: children playing and teenagers hanging out with friends, men socializing or doing business, and women and men going to or returning from work as sweepers in the homes and offices of the wealthy or for the city. This is France Colony—an ordinary informal community built in the middle of a master-planned sector. France Colony got its name from a landmark within sector F-7, the Embassy of France, which was located nearby when France Colony was first settled.[1] The name caught on when people started referring to the new low-income neighborhood as the colony near the Embassy of France, hence, France Colony.[2]

A white plaque sits on a wall extending awkwardly from the side of a brick house in France Colony. It bears the following inscription: "The foundation stone of *Basti-e-Karkunan* [worker's settlement] was laid by Chairman CDA, Brig. (r) Jan Nadir Khan, on 30 April 1985" (Figure 2.1). France Colony is one of the six katchi abadis (squatter settlements, or literally flimsy/raw settlements) that were established with official consent in the 1970s.[3] Foundation stones are celebratory objects that commemorate the beginning of a construction project or site. They are usually "inaugurated" by an important person and placed in a prominent location. Today, France Colony's foundation stone stands almost hidden in a narrow side alley. A resident took me to its location

Figure 2.1. Foundation stone in France Colony. Photograph by author.

during an interview as proof of a forgotten promise of rehabilitation and proprietary rights that the city's municipal and development authority, CDA, once made to the residents of this neighborhood. While initially placed on a freestanding brick wall, the foundation stone is now a structural part of a modest brick dwelling. At the time of my visit, a pile of recycled bricks was stored next to it, while a blue plastic water pipe and an electricity cable dangled precariously in front of the wall, providing essential utilities to the adjacent dwelling. Despite its present state of neglect, the foundation stone is not forgotten, nor does it face the threat of annihilation. Longtime residents of France Colony bring it up in conversations about the legitimacy of their neighborhood and understand the importance of preserving this inscription, literally set in stone, as proof of CDA's complicity in setting up this neighborhood.

Why did a highly ranked municipal official in Islamabad lay the foundation stone of a so-called katchi abadi? One of the myths of squatter settlements is that they are unplanned and built illegally, without official permission. This chapter presents the history of France Colony, revealing that the reality of this kind of informal settlement differs significantly from its myth. Self-built housing outside of the master plan first emerged in Islamabad's undeveloped sectors with official consent. One of the oldest low-income informal settlements in Islamabad, France Colony was first authorized in the late 1970s to accommodate low-level CDA employees, mostly sanitation workers. Using France Colony as a case study, this chapter elaborates how city officials create and manage informal settlements by referring to the master plan and developing new bureaucratic procedures that help legitimize encroachments. An investigation of the modalities of the transaction of land and property within France Colony shows how the residents themselves mimic bureaucratic procedures to create the impression of legitimacy for their otherwise informal claims to space. This chapter thus explains informality as a relation and orientation to the law by examining the development and functioning of France Colony as an ordinary informal space in the middle of one of Islamabad's master-planned sectors.

Authorized Transgressions

Low-income informal settlements first developed as labor camps in Islamabad in the early 1960s to provide places of residence to laborers and other workers who had migrated from other parts of Pakistan to participate in the massive city-building project. While many smaller settlements existed near different construction sites, there were two large labor camps: one next to the existing rural settlement of Bari Imam and the other in a vacant site reserved for subsector G-8/3.[4] Not all those who settled in these labor colonies were laborers, as landless farmers (primarily from rural Punjab and the North-West Frontier Province) also moved into these camps in search of work and residence in the new capital city. Toward the end of the 1970s, residents of the G-8/3 labor colony received eviction notices from CDA.[5] The agency needed the site to build a large hospital complex as specified by the master plan. After making several failed attempts to clear the site and when talks between the residents and CDA broke down over the issue of the date of voluntary relocation, CDA launched an aggressive anti-encroachment "operation" in August 1979 to forcefully demolish the labor camp.[6] A clash during the operation between the laborers and CDA staff resulted in serious casualties on both sides.[7]

CDA staff returned to the labor colony a few days later, this time accompanied by a large contingent of armed police to carry out a military-style operation in the presence of then CDA chairman Syed Ali Nawaz Gardezi. CDA was ultimately successful in demolishing many of the huts in the labor camp and getting the remaining residents to agree to leave the site "voluntarily" within one month.[8] At the time of the operation, Chairman Gardezi announced to the residents of the labor colony that CDA would devise a relocation plan for the genuine "affectees" of the eviction process, because he believed that not everyone who lived in the labor colony belonged to the labor community.[9] He claimed that living among the genuine laborers in the labor colony were property speculators who had built huts that were either rented out or left vacant in the hope of benefiting from a government rehabilitation scheme down the road.[10] It was in light of these promises that some evicted residents were officially allowed to build clusters of small dwellings, using their own resources, in and around the yet-to-be-developed sectors of Islamabad.[11]

CDA officials at the time gave "temporary" permission to settle "eligible" affectees within various sites reserved for sectors F and G. Those evicted from the G-8/3 labor colony included both Muslim and Christian residents. Religious identity became an important factor in this resettlement process as CDA negotiated separately with the union leaders and members of both religious communities and offered them different relocation options. The Christian residents and their leaders were more successful in realizing their demand to stay close to the nascent city's central areas; the majority of the six relocation settlements within the city limits were allocated to the Christian affectees. Conversely, most of the Muslim residents of the labor colony were relocated to the peripheral areas of Islamabad.

These early low-income informal settlements in Islamabad present a rare example of preferential treatment given to a small Christian community, in contrast with the long history of violence and marginalization against religious minorities in Pakistan.[12] Pakistan is a Muslim-majority state with only 3.5 percent of the population identifying as non-Muslim, according to the most recent census carried out in 2017.[13] Hindus compose the next largest group at 1.7 percent, while Christians, who mostly reside in the province of

Punjab, constitute 1.3 percent of the total population. The majority of low-income Christians in Pakistan were previously poor, low-caste Hindus (Dalits) engaged in jobs that were considered polluting and menial.[14] Most of them converted to Christianity during the British colonial period to escape their inferior position in the Hindu caste system.[15] Conversion to another religion, however, has done very little for the social and economic uplift of these marginalized members of the society; as Christians, they still suffer from violence and discrimination. Most low-income Christians find their employment options limited to undesirable work as sweepers, garbage collectors, and sewer cleaners. They are underpaid and work without any protective equipment, and they are treated with scorn because of the supposedly unsanitary nature of their work. Keeping in line with the discrimination, danger, and humiliation they face at work, low-income Christians in Pakistan (and other countries in South Asia) mostly have no choice but to live in religiously homogenous, and therefore segregated, village communities and informal urban settlements.[16]

Islamabad's first Christian-majority abadis were established to resettle the labor colony Christian evictees in centrally located yet undeveloped areas, which now fall right in the middle of the city's most expensive sectors. One of the reasons why Christians received preferential treatment to reside within city limits after their eviction from the labor colony was in part because Muslim residents had played an active role in resisting CDA's eviction process (most of the police arrests made during the demolition operation were of Muslim leaders).[17] News reports from the late 1970s mention the name of Muslim leader Buland Bakht, who actively participated in the resistance against CDA's plans to demolish the labor colony. Depending on which news report one reads, Bakht is either hailed as the president of the Labor Colony Union or denounced as a ringleader. The main reason why CDA may have favored a religious minority group in the relocation and rehabilitation process is that the overwhelming majority of the city's municipal sanitation staff were Christians. A longtime resident of France Colony recalled that a large group of CDA's Christian sanitation workers marched to the President's House (which was in Rawalpindi at the time) to demand housing closer to their place of employment. They explained that they were Christian municipal workers without *milkiyyat* (property ownership) and therefore they needed the government's assistance: "Milkiyyat nahi thi, sadi koi jagah nahi. Naukari karte hain, rahaish kahan se layein" (We didn't have property ownership; we had no place. We perform service and need to know where we can get a place to live).

Because of their employment by CDA, Christian workers were also well represented in the CDA Union, which negotiated aggressively with higher officials to meet their demands. In contrast, most of the displaced Muslims were daily wage laborers whose work would be less in demand once major construction projects in Islamabad were complete. The residents of France Colony may have been Christian, but it was the importance of their labor—as sanitation workers—that determined their ability to secure a settlement in an affluent sector of Islamabad.

The selective resettlement and rehabilitation of the labor camp evictees, based on their utility in municipal functions, was in keeping with CDA's official policies. A 1980s policy states that resettlement priority is to be given to those associated with "any function of development, civic or municipal maintenance."[18] The policy report prioritizes accommodation to people who fall under the category of a "follower" (a term for sweepers borrowed from military jargon) defined as "an adult (male or female) citizen of Pakistan holding a national identity card engaged in the occupation of sanitary worker, khakrobe (sweeper) or a profession related to civic or municipal functions, permanently residing and essentially required in Islamabad."[19] In contrast, the policy calls for the eviction of squatters who are not functionally useful to the city, such as "unskilled labour and all other encroachers," and recommends they be "removed permanently in an organized and planned manner."[20]

City officials allowed essential municipal workers to build their dwellings in open green spaces in Islamabad, but they ignored Doxiadis's recommendations for building housing for the laborers and workers necessary for the city's maintenance. While the planners of Brasilia and Chandigarh have been accused of not accommodating low-income populations in their grand master plans, Doxiadis and his team were mindful of the housing needs of people needed to build and care for the city. A report prepared by the Islamabad office of Doxiadis Associates in June 1962 entitled "Plots and Houses for Labour Force" shows that Doxiadis was aware of the labor housing problems in Brasilia and Chandigarh and wanted to avoid the development of self-built housing for laborers and workers.[21] The report cautioned, "We should be guided by the experience gained in the recent completion of two similar projects of Chandigarh and Brazil where this problem [labor housing] was not foreseen and no provision was made for the same. In both these projects labourers built their own houses in an unauthorized and uncontrolled way."[22]

The report details housing provisions for both the existing and incoming laborers near construction sites in Islamabad and not in adjacent cities or villages to avoid long commutes and inadequate housing. Depending on workers' short- or long-term engagement in Islamabad, the report also proposed accommodation for the labor force in the form of temporary labor camps and permanent plots and houses. The report recommended that CDA facilitate private enterprises and contractors involved in the construction of Islamabad to build cheap, if not free, houses for the labor force. Furthermore, records show that in October 1962, Doxiadis Associates also sent architectural working drawings of houses specially designed for the labor force to CDA. The house plans were for both single workers and workers with families on plots that varied from 20-by-45 feet to 20-by-50 feet in dimension, while temporary labor colonies were planned in two sectors of I-9 and I-10.

In the report on labor housing, Doxiadis Associates also attempted to broaden the definition of citizens in Islamabad to include all those involved in the construction of the new city, from the chief engineer in charge to the skilled and unskilled laborers, and proposed suitable permanent housing or plots for each category of citizen. Providing decent housing for the permanent laborer-citizens of Islamabad was declared essential for the peaceful coexistence of different socioeconomic groups. The authors of the report explained that the disparity in living conditions between the laborers in tents and temporary shacks and the higher standards of government houses may lead to "a lot of grumbling and complaints on the part of the government servants due to sanitary and hygienic reasons" found in labor colonies and "feelings of jealousy and hostility amongst the workmen, who, after all, are and will be going to build Islamabad."[23] Doxiadis thus conceived of the labor force as constituting the future citizens of the new capital city and not as a temporary population expected to leave at the end of the initial construction phase.

But Doxiadis's proposal for low-income housing for laborers and other workers of Islamabad was never implemented. CDA did build a few modest quarters for low-level staff in sites that its officials considered appropriate for informal housing, that is, low-lying open spaces near existing *nalas* (ravines) in sectors F-6 and G-7. Other low-income government workers built their own dwellings in vacant areas around these quarters to form larger squatter settlements, now known as *sau*-quarters (100-quarters), *chhiyasaṭh*-quarters (66-quarters), and *artalis*-quarters (48-quarters) based on the number of CDA-built quarters in each location.[24] In addition, CDA authorized municipal workers to build housing on their own on a "temporary" basis. CDA ignored Doxiadis Associates' proposed plan to build housing for essential municipal workers and laborers. Instead, city officials chose to inaugurate the process of squatting in Islamabad.

Finding Places to Encroach

CDA officials selected interstitial open spaces according to the master plan to resettle the labor colony evictees. Islamabad is built on an undulating site that slopes naturally from north to south. To maintain the straight lines of Islamabad's grid as conceived on paper, level differences have been minimized using cut-and-fill techniques. The sloping terrain remains, however, and is most pronounced in areas next to the nalas that occur naturally all over Islamabad. Narrow and low-lying strips of land next to nalas—officially designated the "green lungs" of the city—were selected as the sites for settling low-income government workers. Site selection for these early authorized "katchi" abadis, as a senior CDA planner explained to me, was based on the premise that allowing "temporary" settlements in areas next to nalas "would not disturb" the overall layout of the master plan. This insight foregrounds a split between the official obligation to preserve the master plan and the need to accommodate essential functions like housing for lower-level employees. CDA officials identified sites suitable for violating the master plan in interstitial spaces between regular plots and natural ravines, places where the master plan would not be "disturbed." Based on this criterion set by CDA officials, land-grabbers, with the help of under-the-table negotiations with city officials, have built squatter settlements in low-lying areas next to ravines in other parts of the city.

France Colony is sited next to a markaz market called Jinnah Super in the elite sector of F-7.[25] A nala fed by two tributaries flows toward one edge of this low-income community. Once a natural ravine, this nala is now an open drain that receives trash and sewage from the dwellings in France Colony. During rainy season, it overflows and causes devastation to property and life in this neighborhood. Distance from the nala determines one's social and legal status. Older residents with official recognition live on higher ground in regular-shaped plots along relatively straight lanes farther away from the nala. Late arrivals have built their homes in available spaces, dangerously close to the open drain. In one of my visits, I met the mother of a young man who had recently died from an accidental fall into the nala at night. While the nala creates interstitial, leftover spaces in a grid-planned city where informal settlements are officially tolerated, it contributes to a dangerous and socially and environmentally degrading living situation.

Doxiadis envisioned sector F-7 as a middle- and upper-income neighborhood. Consequently, he designed large residential plots, ranging in size from 4,200 square feet to 25,200 square feet. The development of France Colony (shaded gray in Figure 2.2) as a densely packed, organic settlement within the planned geometric grid has not only disturbed the socioeconomic uniformity sought by Doxiadis but also created sharp contrasts in form, density, and scale. In contrast to the generous rectangular plots of the sector, plots in France Colony come in all shapes and sizes and fall within the range of 675 to 1,125 square feet. Due to the small sizes of the plots, houses in France Colony are built edge to edge, while houses in the master-planned areas have mandatory setbacks on all four sides.

CDA officials assumed that allowing communities to build housing in open areas next to nalas would not upset the designed spaces. But they did not foresee the social conflict that would result from very privileged and unprivileged people living together in the same neighborhood. While elite homeowners in Islamabad hire people to clean their homes and make tea for them in their offices, they do not want their low-level staff and servants to be their neighbors. It is expected that low-level city workers, like sweepers, gardeners, and domestic help, work in the city but reside outside of it, spending hours commuting each day to their places of work.

The presence of CDA-authorized, low-income informal communities in Islamabad is thus a source of resentment among elite homeowners who decry rising crime and immorality and decreasing property values in their neighborhoods. This interclass conflict is further exacerbated by the low-income community's predominantly Christian composition. Elite Muslim residents attach to the cultural and religious differences of France Colony's low-income Christian residents an assumption of moral failings and undesirable vices, like alcohol consumption, crime, and prostitution. For instance, in Pakistan, sale and consumption of alcohol is banned for all Muslim nationals, but non-Muslims can purchase alcohol from authorized vendors after obtaining government-issued licenses. Some Christian men with official permits in France Colony sell alcohol to Muslims who do not possess the same legal privileges to buy or sell alcohol. Some city residents consider this side business a source of moral corruption. Similarly, the morality of Christian women is often questioned by middle- and upper-class Muslims. Because of the nature of their work in the public realm, women sweepers move more

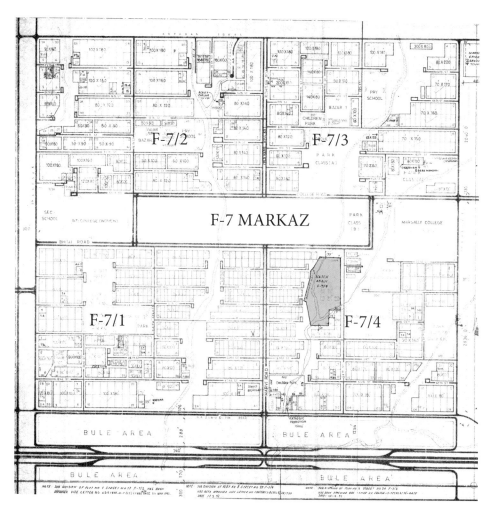

Figure 2.2. Layout plan of sector F-7. France Colony is shown in gray in subsector F-7/4. Source: Layout plan of sector F-7, Capital Development Authority Planning Wing, Maps and Records Unit, Islamabad.

freely and openly both inside and outside the walls of France Colony in comparison to the women of low-income Muslim communities who are unemployed and observe *pardah* (literally, screen), which refers to the physical and visual segregation between men and women.[26] Christian residents of France Colony experience stigmatization on multiple levels as they try to live and work in an ostensibly elite city.

Sociocultural biases based on religious differences and supplemented by economic disparity between elite and marginalized communities residing in proximity have provoked several instances of conflict over space. Mr. Ahmed, who lives in a house on Street 48, shared with me the plight of homeowners, in particular how their safety and security in both private and public areas is threatened by the residents of France Colony. Mr. Ahmed listed numerous instances of how nothing is safe even inside his boundary wall: "My nephew's bicycle, parked outside our house, was stolen from inside our [walled] premises. We would hang our clothes outside for drying, but they would be gone in the morning. We would find empty alcohol bottles in our lawn. Manhole covers have been stolen from inside our premises. Our streetlights have been vandalized. Initially we had a four-foot boundary wall, but we had to raise it after the police told us to do so to avoid these incidents of theft." Outside their boundary wall, the situation is even worse: "Another problem in the area is prostitution. There are girls who walk all around the abadi looking for work. Men in cars come to pick up girls from this area. Now these girls looking for work have started dressing up like doctors (wearing white lab coats). . . . Taxis used to be parked here constantly, but now those have been asked to move. Prostitutes used to be delivered using these taxis as well as to aid thieves to get away. As a result, our women and children can't even walk on the streets because they get harassed by those interested in picking up prostitutes."

Mr. Ahmed once went inside France Colony to look for a boy who had allegedly snatched his daughter's wallet. Horrified by the "disturbing and highly congested" scene inside the settlement, Mr. Ahmed realized, "If someone took someone there and killed that person, no one would know." He considers France Colony *alaqa-i-ghair* (Urdu for "foreign land," which refers to the semiautonomous tribal areas of Pakistan where criminals are believed to take refuge to escape prosecution) as it is impossible to retrieve anything that goes inside the confines of the abadi.

While speaking about his feelings of victimization—a sentiment shared by many middle-class residents in cities around the world because they see the state as protecting the interests of illegal squatters and vendors in their neighborhoods—Mr. Ahmed declared, "We feel like we are living in a jail, a sub-jail, in our own houses. Our women and children feel like they are under house arrest." Mr. Ahmed also claimed that many families living in the immediate vicinity of France Colony had to move from this area because of its deteriorating environment. He finds relief in the fact that at least his house, which is the first house on his street, is located farthest away from France Colony, but the houses right next to France Colony are more adversely affected. One of his neighbors who had a house adjacent to France Colony had to relocate because he did not feel it was the right kind of place to raise a family. He also agonized over the decrease in land prices and rental values of the houses next to France Colony because of their proximity to a neighborhood of thieves, drug dealers, and prostitutes.[27]

CDA's earliest response to elite property owners' concerns was to physically contain the outward expansion of informal settlements in the city. In the late 1980s, a six-foot brick wall was built around all "squatter" settlements that had been officially selected for onsite upgrading. Because of their low-lying sites, walled squatter settlements in most cases remain hidden from their adjacent master-planned areas. But sharp elevation differences betray the obscuring effect of the walls, visually connecting disparate sociospatial conditions from certain vantage points. France Colony, for instance, is totally visible from the main road next to the expensive stores in Jinnah Super despite being enclosed in a wall (Figure 2.3). The construction of the wall reveals CDA's attempt to physically control the outward growth of an encroachment that the agency itself helped create.

Members of different residents' associations see the walling of France Colony as a superficial solution to the problem of squatting in their neighborhood and a sign of CDA's complicity in creating a violation.[28] In a written complaint from 1998, association members living in streets 48 and 49 of F-7/4 noted that at the time of construction of the boundary wall around France Colony, CDA staff had deliberately and unnecessarily extended their wall all the way up to the boundary walls of the corner houses in their streets in order to give more space to the France Colony residents.

To appease the agitated homeowners, CDA made a controversial decision to close all side entrances into France Colony in 2004. The residents of France Colony rejected this decision because a single entry point in an organically organized settlement would make their movement through the colony arduous; it would take them about fifteen to twenty minutes to get from one side to the other.[29] France Colony residents held protests that invoked their rights on humanitarian and moral grounds and argued that "they had as much of a right as rich people to go in and out of their homes and walk in the streets."[30] Because of the immense political pressure on CDA from its sanitation staff, who lived in France Colony, city officials eventually abandoned their plan, much to the dismay of wealthy homeowners nearby.

FRANCE COLONY

MARKAZ

Figure 2.3. View of France Colony from one of the main roads in sector F-7 next to the markaz. Photograph by author.

CDA had initially authorized France Colony and other settlements on a temporary basis to fulfill an urgent need. But in 1999, political pressure from the federal government about the burgeoning housing crisis and growth of squatter settlements in the capital city prompted CDA to develop the following official katchi abadi policy based on residency and location criteria: "The katchi abadis (squatter settlements) existing in sensitive areas or in right of way of roads or encroaching planned plots should be demolished whereas other katchi abadis may be upgraded at their existing locations. Only the houses surveyed upto [sic] 1995 should be regularized."[31] According to this policy, CDA "recognized" eleven katchi abadis in the city. Recognition is an important first step in the delivery of services and allotment of land titles in informal settlements through processes that are referred to as "regularization" or "rehabilitation."

Out of these eleven recognized settlements, CDA decided to rehabilitate six settlements in their existing locations, while the remaining five settlements were to be relocated to alternate sites.[32] It is worth noting here that five out of six settlements slated for on-site rehabilitation are the same settlements that G-8 evictees were allowed to build. The settlements selected for relocation are in areas no more "sensitive" than those selected for on-site rehabilitation. Interestingly, settlements selected for on-site rehabilitation are in highly desirable locations in some of Islamabad's most elite sectors, while settlements selected for relocation are located toward the edge of the city in areas dominated by industries and wholesale markets. All except one of the eleven settlements are along the banks of natural ravines. The obvious difference between the two categories of recognized squatter settlements is the association of their residents with CDA. The neighborhoods approved for on-site rehabilitation primarily house CDA and other government employees, while residents of the settlements to be relocated are self-employed as daily-wage workers and laborers.

To implement its policy, CDA received financial support from the United Nations Development Programme from 1999 to 2001 to develop a centralized household database for the eleven recognized squatter settlements. The household classification system—based on surveying and mapping—is one of the main ways that CDA and other authorities recognize squatter settlements in Islamabad. CDA developed a numeric system for recognized settlements based on the temporal and material characteristics of built property. This process entails an "invention" of new bureaucratic systems necessary for legalizing encroachments like France Colony. Enlistment in official records—a complex process that involves mediation between official staff and the local community over who gets counted—helps differentiate between those "eligible" or "ineligible" for the rehabilitation process.[33] But in France Colony and other squatter settlements in Islamabad, the regularization process was never completed. Access to services and other benefits to listed and unlisted households continues, however, using a range of bureaucratic procedures and everyday practices.

Katcha and Pakka Numbers

The entrance walls of several houses in France Colony bear address numbers starting with the letter C (Figures 2.4 and 2.5). These are called C-numbers, or *pakka* (permanent, solid), numbers based on a household classification survey that CDA carried out in the late 1990s. Residents who could prove they had been living in a settlement before 1995 were given a CDA-number or a C-number. Renters and people who did not meet the residency requirement remained unnumbered. CDA allotted 339 C-numbers in France Colony, while a total of 86 housing units remained unnumbered since they were believed to have been built after 1995.[34] A community activist and longtime resident of France Colony, Anthony James, explained that a C-number is "a form of a Non-Objection Certificate (NOC)," issued by CDA, giving legal housing rights to its allottee.[35] Residents of France Colony believe that CDA staff will not disturb holders of C-numbers until a proper resettlement plan, in keeping with government and CDA policies, is prepared in either the existing or an alternate location. But more immediately, a C-number on a housing unit gives its residents the right to apply for legal door-to-door electricity and gas connections.

C-numbers in France Colony and other settlements were allotted based on identifiable *chardewari* (literally a four-walled enclosure). Chardewari is an old civic concept in South Asia. The household (instead of the individual) was the main unit of urban census (*khanah shumari*) during the sixteenth-century Mughal era.[36] Chardewari is also closely linked to the protected domestic space under the logic of pardah. In the case of Islamabad's squatter settlements, chardewari takes on a different definition to delineate space based on occupancy and enclosure, irrespective of the actual number of households and concerns for privacy.

CDA defines chardewari as a single-walled domestic space within an existing squatter settlement, regardless of the number of people or families occupy-

Figure 2.4. C-number plate. Photograph by author.

Figure 2.5. C-number marking. Photograph by author.

ing the walled space. It is not uncommon in France Colony for multiple families to live within a single chardewari. Yet, according to CDA policy, each C-number allottee is eligible for ownership of a single plot in the future. This policy of one chardewari per plot was challenged in the Wafaqi Mohtasib (Federal Ombudsman) on a number of occasions but could not be revoked due to CDA's reasoning that it was beyond its means and resources to allot different C-numbers, and hence plots, to multiple families living within a chardewari.[37] In the late 1990s, CDA started the process of giving land allotments to the residents of one of the recognized settlements (in G-8/1). In 1996, a resident of this settlement who shared the same chardewari with other members of his family complained to the Wafaqi Mohtasib about CDA's decision to allot only one plot per chardewari. The Wafaqi Mohtasib decided that while it may not be possible for CDA to allot multiple plots according to the number of families per chardewari, it must give joint title to all the heads of families residing in a single enclosure.[38] This policy of joint allotment applies to all multifamily units (siblings or acquaintances living together). But in those cases where fathers live with the families of their adult children, the father is considered the head of the family and allottee of the C-number, and hence the plot will be allotted in his name only.[39] These rules for multifamily units create a complicated situation for the legal inheritance or subdivision of the allotted plot.

In 2002, CDA carried out another survey of France Colony and introduced a new classification system based on "serial" numbers. Serial numbers are printed on the application forms that CDA issued to eligible households during its second survey. Residents refer to serial numbers as *katcha* (temporary) numbers because CDA has not yet processed the application forms. About 82 serial numbers were issued to the residents of France Colony. At the time of CDA's first survey, about 86 houses had not been assigned numbers because they were believed to have been built after 1995. The increase in number from 339 to 421 in the second survey appears to be a concession CDA officials made to their own policy by including the households that were missed in the first survey. Like a C-number, a serial number refers to the allottees' inclusion, albeit incomplete, in an official categorization system.

Allotment of C- and serial numbers marks the first step in the regularization process. The final step in this process is the allocation of ownership rights of a single plot of land (either in an existing or a new location). However, except for some residents in only one settlement (G-8/1) in Islamabad, most recognized katchi abadi dwellers have yet to pass the final stage of regularization. At the time of my fieldwork in 2012–13, there were 6,500 people living in 642 housing units in France Colony. Of those units, 421 had either a C- or serial number and the remaining 200 houses were unlisted. While the process of regularization remains incomplete, recipients of C-numbers and the less exalted serial numbers are generally considered safe from forced evictions and enjoy benefits like private electricity and gas connections. Residents of unlisted houses are ineligible to apply for door-to-door services. But city officials and the electricity supply company have authorized an alternative electricity distribution system to provide electricity to people without the official numbers.

Islamabad Electric Supply Company (IESCO), a government-approved corporate entity, is the sole supplier, distributor, and seller of electricity in the city. In the early 2000s, residents of France Colony were given electricity for a flat monthly fee via a *thekedari* (literally contractor-based) system, which preceded the door-to-door connections. IESCO installed two big commercial meters for France Colony because of political pressure and financial support by local elected politicians. Meant as a "temporary" arrangement before door-to-door connections could be given to the eligible residents of France Colony, the contractor-based electricity supply system was a bureaucratic innovation. According to IESCO rules, electricity connections could only be issued in the name of an individual. To meet this requirement, a twenty-one-member residents' committee in France Colony nominated one resident in whose name the electricity meters were issued for the entire colony. This person was responsible for laying out networks of connections to others in France Colony, collecting monthly fees, and paying a collective bill for the entire neighborhood. In this instance, IESCO and CDA officials concocted a new system of issuing an electricity connection in the name of an individual according to a rule that is effectively emptied of its intended meaning. The officials thus figured out a way to maintain an illusion of conformity to the law without changing it.

By the late 2000s, residents with C- and serial numbers received independent door-to-door connections for gas and electricity. The process of creating individual electricity and gas connections involved a CDA-issued NOC accompanied by a list of residents with official numbers to the concerned electricity or gas supply company. The less desirable contractor-supplied electricity is now mostly used by unlisted residents who are not eligible for door-to-door connections.[40] While the management of this semilegal system of electricity distribution among multiple households is difficult, it is prone to exploitation by the contractor as well. The contractor-supplied electricity is believed to be uneconomical as it is based on a flat rate pre-decided for all the people irrespective of individual consumption.

Based on the abandonment of individual electricity meters in one of Islamabad's squatter settlements, where inaccurate and inflated billing forced
some residents to go back to the contractor-based system, Ijlal Naqvi observes
that "formal rights seem to be worth very little" in such situations.[41] While my
research similarly confirms that formal rights are neither the only nor even
the most desirable way for residents to get access to services, I see little distinction between formal rights and informal systems that replace them in places
like France Colony. C- and serial numbers are elements of an incomplete and
stalled "formal" regularization system, yet they are central to the understanding and distribution of rights and privileges in informal settlements. Moreover, formal rights (either in the form of services or property titles) are often
based on official concessions to accommodate complex and messy conditions.

We can see in the household classification system that formal rules consider local conditions, such as the multifamily configuration of a chardewari
or, in the case of the contractor-based electricity system, pseudo-legal arrangements concocted by IESCO and CDA to provide services to squatter settlements by using laws differently from their intention. In this way, residents of
informal settlements are not the only ones who "take liberty with rules" to
benefit from government schemes; city officials themselves invent bureaucratic
systems as concessions to existing restrictive laws.[42] Formal laws and informal
practices are not isolated from each other but work very much in conjunction
to ensure the management and functioning of places like France Colony.

The interplay between formal and informal systems is similarly evident
in the way space is claimed and traded within France Colony. As the next
section shows, spatial claims and property transactions in France Colony are
not divorced from official systems; they depend on both socially and officially
established rules and procedures.

Property Transactions

One day, Baji Perveen mentioned how her previous next-door neighbor, Zara,
sold her house to another woman, Faheema, who also lives in France Colony.[43]
Baji Perveen explained that she was unhappy with this secretive property
transaction because had she known that Zara was looking for a buyer, she
would have certainly made an offer. Baji Perveen is originally from the city
of Faisalabad in Punjab, where her family worked at a *bhatta* (brick kiln).
She came to France Colony as a renter in the mid-1990s. Before moving to

France Colony, Baji Perveen lived with her husband and children in an accommodation provided by her husband's employer. Her husband, a skilled *mistari* (construction worker), lost his job after sustaining head injuries while working on a construction site. Without a place to live, they came to France Colony with hopes to stay with their relatives, but the relatives refused to put them up. Baji Perveen remembers that it was strangers who gave her family shelter while they got back on their feet. As soon as they were able to afford it, Baji Perveen and her family moved into a rental house in France Colony. After renting for two years, they purchased an empty plot using a land transaction process and built their current home incrementally over time. While her husband is unable to work now, she works as a domestic "maid," and three of their adult sons' salaries supplement their total family income.

Baji Perveen currently lives with fourteen family members, and having the additional space in Zara's adjacent unit would have improved their living situation. While Zara and Faheema's property deal soured the relationship between next-door neighbors, I include this example here to highlight how routine property transactions occur in a place like France Colony, where residents do not possess legal property rights. France Colony was initially settled to accommodate evicted workers, but today it is home to many low-income renters and homeowners who arrived later from other towns and who rented or purchased existing houses or built new ones in vacant areas. Although none of the residents of France Colony have legal title to their houses or to the land on which they are built, this fact does not discourage them from selling, buying, and renting units.

How do people buy and sell land that does not legally belong to them? An investigation of the modalities of land and property transactions within France Colony shows how claims to land are made on tenancy status. Just as CDA officials fabricated new procedures to allow services in France Colony, residents in "illegal" property transactions selectively attended to bureaucratic procedures for the sale and purchase of property to create the effect of legitimacy and conformity to law.

To understand how domestic space is organized and transacted in France Colony, consider the term *makan* (literally house), which is related to the concept of chardewari. The term *makan* is used to refer to the space (mostly rental) occupied by a single (tenant) individual or family. The way this usage differs from the concept of a house in general is that a single chardewari can have more than one makan. For instance, within the confines of a housing unit, it is possible for the owner to live in one makan and rent the second one. Another example is that of two or more brothers and their families liv-ing in separate makans within a single chardewari. Each makan primarily consists of a multipurpose room plus a space, either open or enclosed, desig-nated as the kitchen for a family. The makan may have an independent bath-room, although it is more common to find bathrooms being shared by different families living in separate makans in the case of a multifamily chardewari. Two makans can be stacked on top of each other, with each family occupying different levels. CDA restricts constructions in katchi aba-dis to single-story structures, but this rule is widely violated. Most housing units have at least two floors; indeed, some even have three (Figure 2.6). The rooftop in nearly every unit constitutes an open or partially covered usable personal or rental space. While occupying different levels of the same dwell-ing makes it easier to maintain privacy among different households, spatial boundaries of individual makans of multiple families living on the same level are socially negotiated and clearly maintained.

But these multifamily arrangements in different makans within a single chardewari cause contentious situations, especially in the allocation of C-numbers. In a 2003 case filed with the Wafaqi Mohtasib, the separation and subdivision of spaces according to families within the confines of a charde-wari ended up being an important factor in the court's final decision.[44] In this case, complainant X, a resident of the recognized informal settlement of Muslim Colony, went to the Wafaqi Mohtasib to make corrections to the spelling of his name in CDA's official record. During the proceedings, an-other individual, Z, made claims to the chardewari allotted to complainant X. When CDA's field staff went to Muslim Colony for verification of Z's claim, they found that resident Y, along with his family, was living in said charde-wari. While the field staff rejected Z's claim, they reported that there were in fact two families living in the chardewari that bore a single C-number issued in the name of complainant X. Based on previous legal rulings, the Wafaqi Mohtasib decided to give joint allotment of the chardewari to both X and Y.

Complainant X objected to the co-ownership on the grounds that only his family resided in his chardewari. In a written statement, resident Y claimed that a partition wall had existed between the spaces used by the two families until 1993. This partition wall was taken down by X in 1993, while resident Y was briefly out of town. According to CDA's record, no partition wall existed in the chardewari at the time of its survey in 2001. Despite the missing physical division that apparently once separated the spaces used by the two families, CDA's field staff found out that there were four rooms with two kitchens in the existing chardewari. The Wafaqi Mohtasib considered the layout of the space within the chardewari to ascertain the truthfulness of complainant X's claim to single occupancy and ownership. The presence of two kitchens proved that there were indeed two makans and was used as evidence to support resident Y's claim that he and his family were the co-occupants of the chardewari.

The concept of makan helps to explain the way independence and boundaries are maintained within densely inhabited spaces and reveals how the rental property market works within informal settlements. Makan space in France Colony allows multiple households to live in the same chardewari as well as carve out rental properties to supplement their incomes. A family may decide to generate extra income by renting a makan within their chardewari. Some financially stable homeowners with more than one chardewari live in one unit and rent the additional unit in its entirety, often to multiple tenants. Depending on the size of the rental unit, multiple families in the same chardewari have independent cooking areas but typically share a bathroom. While no two housing units in France Colony have precisely the same layout, the following examples illustrate some of the general principles of the organization of rental space in France Colony.

Rental Makans

There are three main types of rental accommodation in France Colony: rental units within the same chardewari, a dedicated chardewari consisting entirely of rental makans, and a single stand-alone rental makan. The first two types of dwellings have a similar organization and function: different households (mostly a husband, a wife, and their children) live in separate makans within the confines of a single chardewari. Each makan may be rented to a different family, and all the tenant families share the common spaces like the bathroom and courtyard (if available) but maintain separate cooking areas.

Figure 2.7 shows the layout of a multifamily chardewari that includes a rental space in France Colony. Four brothers and their families live in this chardewari along with a tenant. The rooms on the first floor belong to the brothers and their families, while the unit on the second level is rented. The rental unit has an independent bathroom, an open terrace, and independent entry access via a bamboo ladder. The brothers' families mostly cook separately, either in the second-floor kitchen or the first-floor cooking space, but share the main bathroom on the first-floor level. The bathroom on the second

Figure 2.6. Multistoried dwellings in France Colony. Photograph by author.

floor is padlocked from the outside when not in use. This bathroom was paid for by one of the brothers and is used exclusively by his family. While this is an example of a rental space carved out of a chardewari shared by multiple households belonging to the same family, there are dedicated single and multifamily rental properties in France Colony.

Stand-alone Rental Makan

When I met them during my research, Shaheena and Tariq were living with their two young sons in a one-room stand-alone rental unit. Located next to

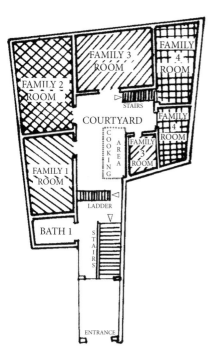 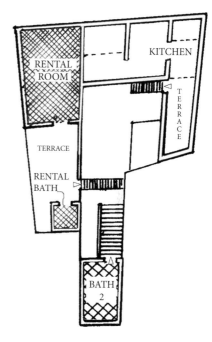

FIRST FLOOR PLAN   SECOND FLOOR PLAN

Figure 2.7. Diagrams of a multifamily unit in France Colony. Rooms used by a particular family are hatched in the same style. The shared bathroom and kitchen areas are left unhatched.

the nala, their rental makan comprised a 10-by-10-foot room with a door but no window on the first floor. A bathroom, accessible from an external staircase, was located on the second floor. They cooked and slept inside the main room (Figure 2.8). The owners of the rental lived across the street in an independent two-story unit (Figure 2.9). Shaheena and Tariq had moved to Islamabad from the city of Gujrat in Punjab after one of their relatives convinced them that he would help Tariq find a good job in the capital city. After arriving in Islamabad, they found that the relative was all bluster and could not help Tariq secure a good job. Before relocating to France Colony, Shaheena and Tariq shared a room with their relative in another katchi abadi in Islamabad but found it uncomfortable to live in a room with another couple and their

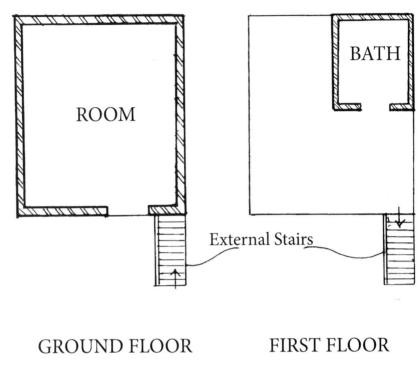

GROUND FLOOR   FIRST FLOOR

Figure 2.8. Diagram of a rental unit in France Colony.

children. Tariq was eventually able to find work in a corporate office tower in Blue Area, the main business and commercial hub of Islamabad. Tariq's job was a twenty-minute walk from his France Colony accommodation. Their children were not in school at the time of our meeting, but the couple planned to get them in school soon. With rental costs taking nearly half his salary, Tariq was unhappy with his family's situation and wanted to return to Gujrat. Shaheena tried to maintain a positive outlook and encouraged Tariq to stay on for a little longer.

Rental housing in France Colony offers newly arriving families in Islamabad an affordable lodging option. When financial situations improve over time, families may invest in a new or existing home in this informal neighborhood. How do people build new dwellings or purchase property on land that does not legally belong to them? In an existing informal settlement like France Colony, people control vacant and built-up spaces using a land occupation process called *qabza* (literally possession).

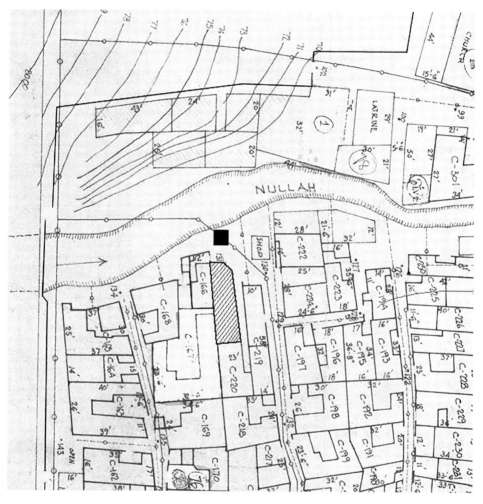

Figure 2.9. Tariq and Shaheena's rental property shown in black, with the landlord's house in hatch.

Taking Qabza

Qabza, or land-grabbing, is a common land acquisition process in Pakistan that involves the forced takeover of land by someone who does not legally own it yet claims rights over it based on its physical possession. Because this process of land-grabbing is carried out by the France Colony residents themselves, it differs from the way external land mafias, also called "qabza groups," work as developers of elite gated communities and low-income kat-chi abadis in places like Pakistan. In France Colony, most people who built houses there in recent years acquired land from long-term residents who had taken qabza of empty land. I often heard residents who had recently arrived in France Colony say, "I bought qabza of this plot in [Year] for [Amount] ru-pees" from [a longtime resident]. France Colony is now fully developed, with almost no vacant spaces left to be sold for building new houses. But I found small parcels of land occupied under the qabza system near one of the side entrances (Figure 2.10). At first glance, these spaces seem peculiar due to the metal fencing all around, but they illustrate one of the ways of taking physical possession of land. The size of these spaces is too small for residential purposes but can be sold or rented out as shop space or for other commer-cial purposes.

Saima and her family's housing situation illustrates an instance of how a single family gained qabza of multiple parcels of land over time using their longtime association with France Colony and personal connections with CDA staff. Saima is a thirty-nine-year-old single mother who works as a domestic servant for a wealthy family in Rawalpindi. She lives with her five children in a two-story, unnumbered makan in a peripheral location of France Colony across the nala (Figure 2.11). She grew up in France Col-ony in her parents' house. Saima's family is originally from Narowal, a small town in Punjab, where they farmed their land. They moved to Islam-abad's labor colony after one of Saima's older brothers found work as a sweeper at a government school. Saima's father is a sweeper by profession who worked for CDA and was one of the labor colony evictees who settled in France Colony with CDA's permission. Saima's father remembers that CDA gave him and others permission to make their houses on roughly 3 *marlas* (1 marla is approximately 272 square feet, or 30 square yards). Saima's parents' house was allotted a C-number in the first CDA survey (Figure 2.12).

Saima moved to the neighboring city of Rawalpindi after getting married. During the mid-1990s, she left her abusive husband and returned to France Colony with her children to live closer to her family. When Saima decided to move back to France Colony, her family started to look for an alternate site in the neighborhood where she could live independently with her children. They built a home on the empty space across the nala where Saima moved with her children (Figure 2.13).

Figure 2.10. View of a lane in France Colony with caged qabza spaces on both sides. Photograph by author.

Figure 2.11. Dwellings without a number on the other side of the nala. Photograph by author.

Saima has four brothers who live in France Colony. As the family grew with the marriages of elder sons, Saima's family decided to make a third home to accommodate their growing housing needs. The family once again took possession of a plot next to Saima's makan across the nala from where her parents moved, leaving their old home to their four sons and their families (Figure 2.14). Saima often referred to one of her brothers, also employed with CDA, as someone who gets things done based on his CDA connections. Her brother claimed that vacant space was easily obtainable across the nala when Saima's family were looking for additional land to build their second and third houses. When I probed further, Saima confessed that there were other claimants to this open and unclaimed land. In the end, it was Saima's brothers who prevailed and staked a claim to the land.

Qabza allows longtime and well-connected residents of France Colony to take up available public land for their personal use or to generate income. Residents make claims based on the length of their residency and the power they wield in the neighborhood. These alternative forms of property ownership are recognized by people interested in renting or buying property here, and qabza fuels the real-estate market for low-income people. While the sale of vacant plots and built-up units by people who do not own them is technically illegal, people interested in living in a low-income community in a central location regularly buy properties in France Colony using pseudo-legal processes.

Sale and Purchase

Consider the question once more: How do people buy and sell land and properties without legal titles? Transaction of property and land in France Colony is based on mimicking official procedures for real estate transactions. This performative imitation of official procedures helps lend an impression of legitimacy to otherwise informal claims to space. The case of Faheema, a successful Muslim female entrepreneur who has lived in France Colony for over fifteen years, illuminates the modalities of property transactions in France Colony. When she was twelve years old, Faheema started working as domestic help in the house of a Foreign Service officer and traveled with his family to Saudi Arabia and Afghanistan when he was appointed the ambassador there. She eventually quit her job when she demanded proper pay

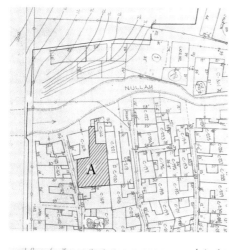

Figure 2.12. Saima's parents' house (A). It has a C-number.

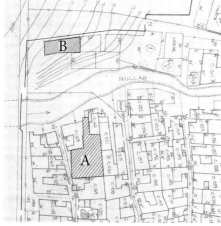

Figure 2.13. Saima's house (B) across the nala. It has not been assigned a C-number.

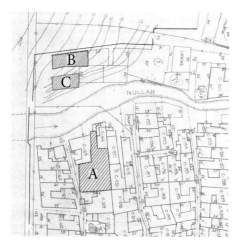

Figure 2.14. Saima's parents' new house (C) across the nala. It does not have a C-number.

for her work after the ambassador got posted to Vienna and he refused. Faheema returned to her hometown of Deira Ismail Khan in the North-West Frontier Province to live with her family, but because of economic hardships at home, she returned to Islamabad, along with her younger brother, in search of work.

Faheema found a job as an *aya* (low-level female helper) at a school in Islamabad while attending a tailoring course at a vocational training center. She used this tailoring expertise to set up a shop and hired tailors to do the work while she supervised the business. By age thirty, she had cultivated a successful tailoring business in two leased shops in Jinnah Super market. But Faheema lost both shops when, after getting married, she had to leave the business in the hands of her husband to raise her children.

In the late 1990s, Faheema bought the rights to build (qabza) on a 2.5-marla (about 680 square feet, or 75 square yards) plot from another resident in France Colony for 25,000 rupees and built a makan for her family across the nala near the western edge of France Colony. Her first business investment in France Colony was in the form of a water well dug near her makan. In France Colony water is supplied by private wells, each shared by 8 to 10 houses (Figure 2.15). CDA also provides water to this neighborhood, but people primarily rely on shared tube wells because CDA does not provide enough water. This water-sharing is an important feature of life in France Colony; rubber pipes snake through the streets of France Colony throughout the day, and women and young girls can be seen dragging these pipes from one house to another (Figure 2.16).

With a natural knack for business, Faheema saw in this an opportunity to earn extra income, and she decided to bore a well near her house. At the time, she looked for investors to help offset the high cost of about 75,000 to 100,000 rupees (about $1,600 to $2,200 in the late 1990s), but nobody was willing to take the risk since there was no guarantee they would find water in the selected location. So she went ahead alone in this venture; luckily, her risk paid off, and she found water of good quality. Faheema now sells water to about twenty houses and was able to get full return on her initial investment after a few years.

With the money saved from her water supply business and other smaller businesses, including work as a broker for household items sold on installments, Faheema bought a second house in France Colony where she relocated with her family, and she then began to rent her first house. In her old house,

Faheema rented three makans for 5,000 to 6,000 rupees per unit to male sales-men who worked in the nearby F-7 markaz. The chardewari where she cur-rently lived had three rooms and two bathrooms. To help with the payment of her house, Faheema rented two rooms and one bathroom. Her family used the other bathroom and the third room for her children. On the second floor, she made a semi-covered structure that functioned as a multipurpose cook-ing, living, and sleeping area for her and her husband. One of her two rental units was being used as a part-time workshop by a tailor who paid her a hefty 8,000 rupees (the rate of a makan at the time was around 5,000) per month for using the space a few hours each day. Faheema told me that she chose her tenants carefully and only rented out to employed men who spend most hours of the day at work and who are either single or have families living in other cities or villages.

Faheema bought her second home from Zara, who was introduced earlier in this chapter. Zara was a community activist during her days as a resident of France Colony. Zara migrated from Karachi to Islamabad in 1998 and bought a place in France Colony. In 2002, her house was listed in the CDA serial-number classification system. Around 2011, Zara decided to sell the house because she felt that the living environment in the neighborhood had deteriorated with the rise in alcohol sales and prostitution: "Halaat kharab ho gaye thay, mahol nahi acha" (Circumstances had deteriorated; the [social] climate is not good). She also needed to satisfy a more immediate concern of generating money to marry off her daughter.

Generally speaking, the sale of built houses in France Colony involves the drafting of an agreement between both parties on stamp paper. This type of document, which includes a preprinted stamp, was initially used as a tax col-lection tool in the British colonial period. It's now commonly used in South Asia to legitimize leases, to transfer deeds for property, or to write up con-tracts. Since the property owner does not own the land, the cost of the prop-erty is determined based on the cost of the building material and a reasonable margin of profit for the sellers. Terms of the transaction are drafted on the stamp paper, including the amount of payment and a waiver by the owner of all rights to the property. In her transaction with Faheema, Zara transferred the serial number to Faheema on a stamp paper and handed her the document bearing the serial number issued by CDA.[45] Even though this property transaction bears no legal value, it gives the outward appearance and the feel of legality.

Figure 2.15. Shared tube-well. Photograph by author.

Interestingly, this is exactly the way "plot files" are exchanged between middle- and upper-income people in urban Pakistan. Plots in new housing developments are mostly balloted, and the ballot winners are free to sell their plot files to interested individuals or entities. A plot file includes an affidavit on a stamp paper (issued by the property developer) in which the seller surrenders the plot file back to the developer, and this process allows the transfer of the plot to a new buyer.[46] A plot file is often left "open" to facilitate tax evasion and property speculation. An "open file" means that only the seller's name is mentioned, while the buyer's name is deliberately left out of the transaction document. It allows the buyer undocumented possession of the plot. Whoever holds the "possession" of the file becomes the owner of the plot, and

Figure 2.16. Sharing water. Photograph by author.

the new owner may sell the open file again using the same process.[47] The actual physical custody of the open plot file is an essential feature of this transaction process.

While the development and ownership of real estate in Islamabad is shaped by market forces and property rights, ownership and development of land within the walls of France Colony is largely based on socially accepted rules like land rights established by precedence in physical possession and property transactions that mimic official procedures. Moreover, social relationships are integral to how space is claimed and exchanged in informal settlements. Nearly all the France Colony residents I interviewed moved to Islamabad in search of better employment opportunities, but social ties also shaped their decision to move to this city. Originally from smaller towns in Punjab, low-income Christians arriving in Islamabad mostly received shelter and other assistance from family members or friends living in one of Islamabad's katchi abadis or in affordable areas of the twin city of Rawalpindi. As soon as possible, new arrivals would rent a makan in informal settlements like France Colony. Those renters who transitioned to homeownership purchased land or property, again using their social connections in the community. The denial of such social relations led to the disappointment that Baji Perveen felt toward her neighbor Zara.

As residents rely on socially recognized rules for land development and ownership, the influence and control of the state in France Colony may appear to be minimal. But in this community-based real estate development process, neighbors' buy-in is very important. Even adding a room can be costly because it might invite a complaint to city officials and a visit from CDA's anti-encroachment staff. CDA's file on France Colony includes several written complaints by its residents against one another. For instance, in 2000, a resident with a C-number requested that CDA officials remedy a fraudulent change in the ownership of his property; his next-door neighbor had apparently gotten the official records altered to become the owner of the complainant's house. In a 2010 matter, several residents of France Colony and a government representative for minorities requested CDA officials to clear "encroachments" on one of the main pathways in France Colony. They complained that a group of individuals had illegally set up a *kabaar khana* (scrap yard), a tea stall, shops, and an animal pen near one of France Colony entrances, which obstructed passageways and caused a nuisance for residents coming in and out of the settlement.[48] In 2013, a resident accused his neighbor of "ghair qanooni tameer" (illegal construction) after the neighbor had built a room over a lane behind the complainant's house.

These complaints show that in situations of conflict over "encroachments" inside France Colony, residents seek CDA officials' help; the conflicts therefore can turn into opportunities for CDA's field staff to receive bribes from the violating party. A few years ago, Baji Perveen added a room upstairs to accommodate the growing needs of her large family. But a *chaudhry* (explained next) complained to CDA's anti-encroachment staff, and CDA agents came to her house and took 3,000 rupees (about $30 at the time) as a bribe. Even if communal networks and socially established rules largely shape the development and transaction of land in France Colony, the state selectively intervenes in constructions inside the walls.

The figure of the chaudhry sheds further light on the social and class dynamics at work in bureaucratic procedures and interventions within encroachments, including official classification systems, pseudo-legal transactions, and mediation over encroached space. In Pakistan, chaudhry is a title of honor traditionally associated with land ownership, especially in rural Punjab. In contemporary usage, chaudhry is an honorific used either before or after a name. In France Colony, the title still bears its connotations of honor and power; it identifies residents seen as carrying political clout within France Colony. Chaudhrys are some of the earliest settlers of this neighborhood, as Zara explained: "Pahle baithy hue thay, woh apne aap ko chaudhry kahte hain" (Those who had been sitting/squatting from before, they call themselves chaudhry). She also referred to them as *upar walay* (those on top), that is, those located on the higher (and the more desirable) side of the nala. Her definitions suggest how this title is sometimes self-proclaimed ("they call themselves chaudhry") and how the superior political position of chaudhrys is based on their spatial and temporal association with France Colony.

As residents with comparatively more wealth than their neighbors, chaudhrys are often suspected of owning shops and houses not only in France Colony but elsewhere in the city.[49] While chaudhrys are important people with the power to get work done in France Colony, most people feel some contempt toward these self-proclaimed leaders of the neighborhood. Chaudhrys are the representatives of the neighborhood and are normally the first people approached when national or international nongovernmental organizations want to launch a welfare or development project in France Colony. Residents eye these chaudhrys with suspicion, as they are believed to be self-promoting and corrupt; many have been accused of pocketing significant sums of money given to them by nongovernmental organizations for community uplift projects. As people with connections to CDA officials, chaudhrys have been known to throw their weight around, especially among residents without official recognition. Some residents (like Baji Perveen) claimed that the chaudhrys complained to CDA staff about new additions to their dwellings or threatened people from building on open areas across the nala.

Chaudhrys see themselves as deserving the title of honor based on the services they have given to the neighborhood and its residents. During a conversation I had with Anthony James, a community organizer–cum–chaudhry, he spoke of "when [he] became a chaudhry," referring to the fact that it is an honor earned over time.[50] As one of the people involved in community organization since the early 1990s and whose father is one of the first generation of chaudhrys, Anthony explained his commitment to the cause of social welfare:

> Social work is something I have inherited from my father, a part of my family heritage. But it's not like *jagir dari* (feudalism). I don't have a birthright to it. Anyone can be in my position; it's only a matter of volunteering time and working for the benefit of the people. Most people ask why they should go after other people's problems? What is in it for them? When I go visit an official (CDA), not only do I have to take time off from work but I also have to spend money, for *chai/samosa* (tea/snack) for the officer. Once a trainer [of a workshop for community organizers] called people like me *sar-phiray* (mad). We are volunteers and do this without any salary.

The authority of chaudhrys is reinforced by the structure of what may be considered an extension of the concept of "street-level bureaucracy," which alludes to the encounters that take place between ordinary citizens and the state via street bureaucrats.[51] Police, schoolteachers, and social workers are all examples of street bureaucrats who act as mediators of policies constructed elsewhere and who are in a position to exercise political power in very localized settings. While chaudhrys do not have the same level of legitimacy enjoyed by street bureaucrats, they possess political influence because of their position in the community and their recognition by CDA and local and international nonprofit organizations. Anthony James showed me the stamp that he uses to create different types of pseudo-official documents for the residents of the colony, including proof-of-residence letters needed by France Colony parents who wish to send their children to the nearby government school.[52] In the F-7/4 girls' middle school, for instance, Anthony's proof-of-residence letter holds value because the principal of the school personally knows Anthony. Similarly, he also issues *rah dari*—a kind of authenticating document used for animals that includes a full description—a requirement meant to curb the theft of animals and for the legal movement of the animal within and outside the city. Like the use of a stamp paper for drawing up legal transactions or the concoction of a contractor-based electricity supply system, the chaudhry mimics official roles and procedures that shape the everyday functioning of an informal settlement.

Conclusion

One of the biggest misconceptions about informal spaces is that they are unauthorized and hence illegal. Histories of ordinary informal spaces like squatter settlements and vendors' stalls (discussed in the next chapter) reveal the central role of official policy in the creation of these encroachments. These violations are authorized and tolerated because they provide a material and political space to fulfill necessary functions that the official master plan cannot accommodate as effectively. Encroachments in Islamabad developed in relation to its master plan and regulations; officials referred to the master plan to select a suitable site for informal settlements and developed new bureaucratic procedures to regularize their dwellings. Moreover, the municipal government's contradictory and conflicting official positions on encroachments like France Colony necessitated various bureaucratic and material responses, from the installation of walls to the provision of electricity and gas services.

An examination of the everyday functioning of France Colony reveals an entwined relationship between this neighborhood and officially developed spaces and procedures. Residents neutralize external threats to their neighborhood through political protests and negotiations with CDA. Within the walls, they use long-term occupancy to claim land that does not legally belong to them. While residents make claims to space based on socially accepted norms, they legitimize their land and property transactions by mimicking bureaucratic procedures. Both the residents and government officials are involved in developing low-income housing in Islamabad through concurrently formal and informal processes, which helps create an impression of legitimacy of informal spaces and allows them to exist often for long periods of time. The next chapter explores the long-term sustenance of informal spaces from the perspective of their materiality and aesthetics.

CHAPTER 3

Long-Term Temporariness

For over eighteen years, Tariq has been selling ready-made garments and clothing accessories from a parking area in one of Islamabad's busiest markaz markets.[1] Every morning, Tariq brings out collapsible tables, stands, and merchandise from a nearby rented storage space and assembles a display area under a canopy made from tarp, ropes, and poles. He repeats this process in reverse every night when he disassembles the stall and stows the tables, stands, and merchandise in a nearby storeroom. Vending and hawking are labor-intensive processes that involve rituals of daily assembly and disassembly. To access streets, sidewalks, and other public spaces as places of livelihood, vendors like Tariq must build their stalls and stands to last during work hours. One early morning, as Tariq was busy setting up his display by hooking shirts on plastic hangers to stretched ropes, I asked if he had ever considered building a more permanent structure.[2] Tariq immediately brushed aside this suggestion by saying "that would be absolutely illegal."[3] Tariq's association of the word "illegal" with permanent construction and not with his business obstructing a service road and parking area, which he framed as "*zarurat*" (necessity), suggests a strategic and partial conformity to law through architecture and building practices. An analysis of ordinary encroachments, including vendors' and hawkers' stalls and stands, reveals that their builders select construction materials and techniques that help maintain conformity to law by appearing to be temporary. These architectural strategies are integral to the way vendors and hawkers claim public spaces every day, often for long periods.

The strategy of temporarily allowing the occupation of public spaces is often mirrored in official policies concerning informal spaces. I repeatedly noticed the use of the word *temporary* in official documents and laws that allow violations and encroachments in Islamabad. Consider the following example of a certificate issued to the evictees of the G-8/3 labor colony in the late 1970s by the director of enforcement, the officer in charge of keeping the city free of encroachment: "Mr. X sweeper s/o [son of] Y presently resident of labor camp G-8/3, Islamabad, you are given a land on temporary basis by CDA in Sector G-8/1 (at Qadir Colony). You are requested to shift from labor camp to allocated location while doing arrangements for your residence by your own [sic]."[4] Chapter 2 described the circumstances and aftermath of CDA's forced eviction of the G-8/3 labor colony in the late 1970s. As people were evicted from their dwellings, the director of enforcement issued "temporary" permission (in the form of the abovementioned certificate) to male evictees who were considered eligible for resettlement. While the language in the document does not suggest this, all the certificate holders with whom I spoke believe the certificate promised them temporary residence in their current designated locations next to nalas, without any threat of eviction, until an acceptable relocation plan is developed. The official relocation of evicted labor colony dwellers to open green spaces was intended as a provisional housing solution for essential municipal workers until a more permanent plan could be developed. An important aspect of this so-called temporary permission is its endurance over time. These "temporarily" resettled neighborhoods in officially "allocated" sites are now over forty years old and sit right in the middle of Islamabad's most expensive sectors.

This chapter explores how "temporary" building practices and bureaucratic procedures help sustain ordinary encroachments for long periods. I use the term *long-term temporariness* to explain this paradox. Temporariness is a condition of provisional existence. An apparent oxymoron, *long-term temporariness* refers to special allowances that permit certain activities at odds with the official master plan to take place for long periods provided they are categorized as temporary. Labeling something "temporary" creates the effect of tolerance, of making concessions for activities that otherwise would not be allowed on a permanent basis. When CDA officials designate an encroachment as temporary, they engage in a creative bureaucratic strategy based on the assumption that temporary violations will be resolved permanently at a later stage. But that stage may or may never be reached. Vendors, hawkers, and shop owners similarly make claims to public spaces using temporary building practices, forms, and aesthetics to appear less "illegal," as Tariq explains above. The notion of long-term temporariness is apparent in both the spatial practices and bureaucratic procedures that sustain ordinary encroachments, often for long periods.

My concept of long-term temporariness builds on Oren Yiftachel's concept of *permanent temporariness*, which refers to state policies and procedures that sustain legally ambiguous gray spaces, activities, and populations that are "concurrently tolerated and condemned, perpetually waiting 'to be corrected.'"[5] But in my experience, long-term temporariness is not only a strategy that officials use to control the spatial practices of destitute populations; it is also a way for people to make informal claims to public space on a routine basis. While I recognize the draconian power that the state may possess by maintaining control through uncertainty, here I emphasize how informal spaces can also be tolerated for long periods by deliberately maintaining an impression of temporariness, at both official and unofficial levels. In the case of ordinary encroachments, the strategy of long-term temporariness functions as a means of negotiation, however uneven, between vendors and city officials. And while this strategy may condemn ordinary informal spaces to the state of being "perpetually waiting 'to be corrected,'" it can also allow those spaces a long-term durability.[6]

This enduring aspect of temporary informal spaces is often used by the middle-class and elite actors who build ordinary structures to claim open spaces next to their homes to create private lawns and parking areas. In this chapter, I show how middle-class shopkeepers create additional retail space in adjacent public spaces in commercial markets by using ordinary spatial practices that they must repeat on a daily basis. Ordinary encroachments—based on the notion of long-term temporariness—not only provide essential relief to underprivileged populations; they often allow middle- and upper-income people to use public spaces for private activities.

This chapter begins with an analysis of official procedures that regulate ordinary encroachments through the issuance of monthly licenses to hawkers and vendors based on the condition that their constructions are temporary and can be removed on short notice. These official concessions for certain kinds of encroachments are written into the municipal bylaws, resulting in an inconsistency between Islamabad's master plan and the city's planning regulations. Next, the chapter analyzes how hawkers, vendors, and shopkeepers claim public space by maintaining routines of daily assembly and disassembly. They use salvageable building materials and impermanent construction techniques that contribute to an aesthetic of temporariness to help sustain ordinary encroachments as impermanent infractions.

I argue that architectural forms and aesthetics are integral to this process of *compliance without intent* and are essential to the long-term viability of non-conforming spaces.

Licensed Encroachments

During my fieldwork in Islamabad, I rarely sat down to eat at a restaurant or café. I found them to be both expensive and slow in service. My typical (though not healthy) diet during work hours included bags of chips and cold drinks bought from some of the conveniently located and affordable roadside khokhas and tea stalls. None of these kiosks and tea stalls are built according to the Doxiadis master plan, but they can be found nearly everywhere in greenbelts along roads. In addition to small shops that sell food items, makeshift pop-up stalls that sell household and personal items are routinely set up along busy roads and at intersections. As people drive through the city, these open-air display areas attract (and perhaps distract) them to pull over to buy fresh fruits, fish, area rugs and carpets, inflatable wading pools and toys, and fake designer sunglasses. These outdoor shops mostly sell a single item that sometimes corresponds to seasonal changes and consumer needs: sunglasses and inflatable pools during the summer, flags around Independence Day, and, more recently, face masks during the pandemic. Outdoor commercial spaces increase the closer you get to the master-planned shopping areas, where vendors and hawkers line roads, sidewalks, and verandas of commercial buildings to sell their merchandise and services.

How do businesspeople in Islamabad occupy and sell from public spaces that are not zoned for commercial activities? I answer this question by tracing a history of street vending in Islamabad and municipal policies that "temporarily" allow encroachments in the city. I show how builders of both authorized and unauthorized encroachments use architectural forms, materials, and techniques perceived to be temporary to claim public space on a routine basis, often for long periods.

Street vending first emerged in Islamabad in the 1960s, when construction work on the city had just started. The only places to shop at that time were in the existing villages of Bari Imam and Saidpur. To meet the everyday needs of laborers and other workers, CDA encouraged businesspeople to set up food facilities in the city. The general secretary of the Khokha Association, a coalition of khokha owners formed in the early 1970s, claimed that "CDA was more than welcoming" at that time to anyone willing to set up food and refreshment shops in Islamabad. But doing business during the early years of Islamabad's construction was not easy. He explained that early khokha owners had to "carry goods from the neighboring city of Rawalpindi on their heads" and bring drinking water from distant natural springs so that the *baniyan-i-Islamabad* (literally founders of Islamabad, a reference to construction laborers) could get food, water, and other necessities with relative ease.[7] Meant as a temporary provision for temporary needs, these small-scale shops continued to do business even after the completion of the master-planned markets.

CDA tried various ad hoc and partially implemented policies to relocate khokha owners from open public areas to small CDA-built shops in markaz markets. For instance, in 1975–76 it was decided that khokha operators would be allotted space in a class-III shopping center, which comprised small shops on the ground floor and apartments on the floor above. But only a few khokha owners benefited from these allotments. Around the mid-1980s, CDA staff carried out a survey of all existing khokha owners in Islamabad as part of a more comprehensive policy. CDA abandoned its earlier plan to accommodate khokha owners in one of the designated shopping centers and decided that those on the survey list would first be given "temporary" licenses and eventually allotted permanent kiosks or tea stalls in their existing or alternate locations.[8] But the transition from temporary licenses to permanent allotments remains incomplete even in 2023; many khokha owners on CDA's list have been doing business for decades on provisional licenses without receiving allotments.

The system of temporary licenses and permanent allotments for street commerce in Islamabad has become a controversial issue in the early 2010s. Newspaper reports and anecdotal evidence indicate that many well-connected and wealthy people have entered the khokha business and received licenses and allotments to open kiosks in prime locations in Islamabad by using political influence and bribes. For a nominal monthly license fee, khokha owners can obtain access to prime locations, including parks and greenbelts in central sectors; this saves them from the high rental prices they would pay for commercial spaces in one of Islamabad's formal markets.[9]

In 2012 the Islamabad High Court placed a ban on issuing new khokha licenses after a case was filed against a particular kiosk operating in a public park in sector F-7, one of the city's most elite neighborhoods.[10] This case brought to light fraudulent mechanisms used to issue licenses to people doing business in the city and the controversial involvement of well-to-do business-men in the khokha enterprise, as the owner of this kiosk in F-7 was a rich businessman and the brother of the interior minister of Pakistan at that time. The scandalous involvement of elite actors in the khokha business, conven-tionally associated with providing much-needed economic relief to destitute populations, illustrates how ordinary encroachments are better categorized by their material forms and aesthetics than by the socioeconomic status of their builders. Commenting on how elite businessmen are now involved in stereotypically nonelite encroachments, a senior Enforcement Directorate of-ficial said, "VIP log VIPon walay kam nahin kartay" (VIP people do not par-take in VIP-like work/actions).[11]

But most of the street vendors and hawkers in Islamabad are financially underprivileged and rely on their stalls and stands to make ends meet. CDA's Anti-encroachment Wing confiscates goods and demolishes kiosks and other structures like food stalls, counters, cabins, and sheds encroaching on side-walks and parking areas during its routine anti-encroachment "operations." I discussed the difficulty of enforcing government regulations on hawker stands and vendor stalls with an officer from the Directorate of Municipal Administration (DMA), a CDA department concerned with the regulation of all commercial activities in Islamabad.[12] The officer noted that the confis-cation of items from illegal hawkers is a particularly unpleasant task because of "how bad it feels to take away the source of income from poor people." He added, "ham log bhi insan hain" (we are human as well), referring to the dif-ficulty of administering official protocols that are sometimes devoid of hu-manity. He spoke about the dilemma faced by DMA staff "when a poor person wearing old shoes walks in [their office] to retrieve his [confiscated] stuff." He mentioned personally knowing a "chips-wala" (a person selling chips) who earned a living from selling hot French fries in a veranda of a commercial building. The officer knew that the chips-wala and his family would not be able to survive if the DMA staff confiscated the vendor's portable deep-fryer.

It would be an oversimplification to view such instances of nonenforce-ment of municipal regulations as "corruption" or "incompetence" by the DMA staff. It would also be inaccurate to see humanitarianism as the sole or even primary reason for why they forsake anti-encroachment regulations. City officials in places like Islamabad must reconcile bureaucratic planning systems with pressing global challenges such as urban poverty and lack of re-sources. This reconciliation may result in what Jonathan S. Anjaria calls "daily, if unofficial, negotiations" based on monetary transactions and extralegal arrangements between street hawkers and officials.[13] In addition to under-the-table arrangements and monetary negotiations, architectural forms and aesthetics of ordinary encroachments play an important role in the daily reconciliation between builders of informal spaces and city officials. Moreover, an attention to building forms and spatial practices is integral to the bureaucratic procedures and laws that tolerate the long-term subsistence of hawkers' stands and vendors' stalls.

Forms and Aesthetics

According to the *Islamabad Capital Territory Municipal Bye-Laws of 1968–69*, "encroachment"—defined as erecting "an immovable structure, hut or khokha or overhanging structure" on government land or obstructing "pedestrian traffic in circulation verandahs of all the markets of Islamabad"—is illegal "under any circumstances."[14] Special concessions, however, are written into these bylaws for encroachments that have been issued monthly "licenses": "roofless movable stalls" no more than 16 square feet and the condition that "the license shall be revocable by a 12 hours notice."[15] It is obvious from these terms and conditions that formal bylaws make allowances for "licensed encroachments" to exist in the planned city of Islamabad, according to the implicit logic of temporariness—that small-scale encroachments in the official master plan can be tolerated if they can be easily removed when need be. Moreover, issued licenses must be renewed on a monthly basis and can be revoked on short notice, revealing another guiding principle of temporariness: the right to revoke the temporary. Just as temporariness creates the conditions for extraordinary provisions, city officials can withdraw those same provisions precisely because of their temporary nature. We can also see how the material characteristics of "licensed encroachments" contribute to the logic of temporariness, as the stalls for which these licenses can be issued are characterized in the bylaws as "roofless" and "movable" structures that can be easily removed.[16]

Anyone carrying out business in Islamabad is required by law to obtain licenses from the DMA. In a master-planned city containing clearly designated commercial spaces, hawking is one of the thirteen licensable trades according to the municipal bylaws. The bylaw defines *hawking* as "exposing or carrying goods for sale, either in the hand, or any part of the body, or in a cart, wheelbarrow or any other wheeled conveyance, and shall include setting up a stall or otherwise selling or exposing for sale on a street."[17] It allows "hawkers and squatters dealing in goods, eatables, perishable or imperishable, selling wares of any kind or description at a specified place or on cycles, taxis or by any other means . . . within the municipal limits of Islamabad" as long as they have been issued a monthly pass for a fee.[18]

DMA issues "temporary" licenses to mobile hawking carts in small blue books that are kept with mobile hawkers and to stationery vendors in the form of a three-page document. The license documents include the terms and conditions for vending and hawking written in English. Given the low literacy level of most hawkers, the language choice indicates that these documents serve as a bureaucratic formality rather than an actual means of communicating municipal rules to the license holders. Issuing licenses to hawkers and vendors is a common practice in older cities in Pakistan and elsewhere. It is based on the state's desire to monitor and control every aspect of trading by imposing a formal structure on indigenous modes of economy. But in a place like Islamabad, there is no room in the modernist master plan for roadside kiosks or tea stalls; the licensing of encroachments like street hawking and vending functions in reverse to legitimize and introduce informal elements of the economy into a master-planned city. The inconsistency between Islamabad's master plan and the de facto regulations thus serves as an important aspect of the development of informality in Islamabad.

Regulation of ordinary encroachments like vendors' stalls does not end with the issuance of a paper license; city officials specify the exact location of each licensed khokha on the master plan. CDA maintains large maps of individual sectors, drafted by hand on translucent tracing paper. These maps represent the general layout of a given Doxiadis sector, each containing four residential communities around a commercial center. If you look closely at these maps, you can find additions or changes to the original master plan: new markings or old lines that have been scratched off the tracing paper using a blade (Figures 3.1 and 3.2). Most of these changes and additions accommodate new needs and functions, such as large plots subdivided into two plots to accommodate multiple owners and "temporary" approved stand-alone structures like toilets, sheds, and reception areas in greenbelts. Figure 3.1 shows the location and size of licensed kiosks marked as small boxes in greenbelts next to major roads or in other commercially strategic locations in the G-9 sector. Geometric markings are accompanied by freehand notes around the main drawing, which specify the location, date, and file number of the approved changes (Figure 3.2). The strict symmetry of the original drawing

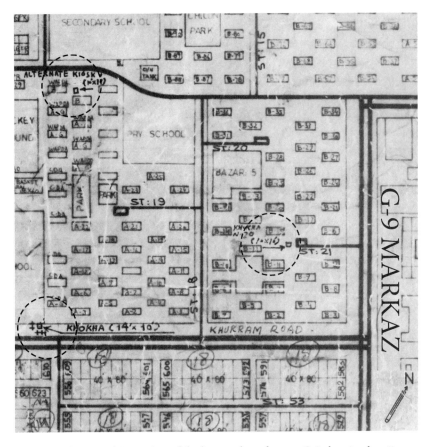

Figure 3.1: A zoomed-in section of the layout plan of sector G-9 showing location sites of licensed khokhas/kiosks. Dashed circles around khokha locations are added for emphasis. Source: Layout plan of sector G-9, Capital Development Authority, Maps and Records Unit, Planning and Design Wing, Islamabad.

is visually interrupted by the notes and markings that reveal changes made over time. The messiness of city-making is literally etched on the surface of the master plan document.

In addition to issuing licenses in the form of paper documents and specifying the location of licensed khokhas on the master plan, CDA regulates the "design" of licensed khokhas. This exercise of control over architectural design is an official strategy to standardize authorized encroachments and to differentiate them from unauthorized encroachments. As a senior mem-

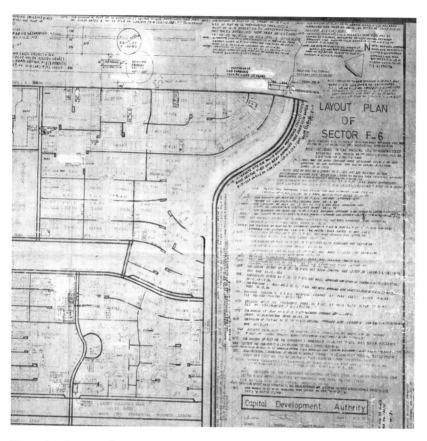

Figure 3.2: A zoomed-in section of the layout plan of sector F-6 showing
handwritten notes on changes to the master plan. Erasures by hand have resulted
in certain areas of the map being lighter in color. Source: Layout plan of sector F-6,
Capital Development Authority, Maps and Records Unit, Planning and Design
Wing, Islamabad.

ber of the Khokha Association explained, "Permission stepwise *hoti hai. Jab*
regular *kartay hain, tu* design *milta hai*" (Permission is stepwise. When they
make [your khokha] regular, then [you] receive the design). He further elaborated that CDA's enforcement staff does not allow unlicensed khokha owners
to build according to the CDA "design." Building with this "design" is a privilege only given to licensed kiosk owners, a distinction diligently enforced
by CDA staff. Even if the city tolerates violations of the master plan, it makes
sure to regulate the violations' architectural design.

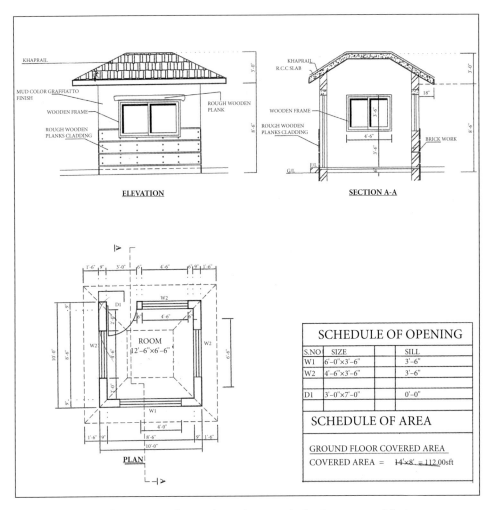

Figure 3.3. Earlier version of Capital Development Authority–approved design of a licensed tea stall/kiosk with a concrete roof. Source: Capital Development Authority, Architecture Directorate, Planning and Design Wing, Islamabad.

CDA's Architecture Directorate issues an authorized kiosk design to vendors when their license application is approved. The approved design is issued in the form of a computer-drafted architectural drawing that includes a plan, elevation, and section, which specify all design and construction details including the overall building form, construction materials and techniques, and size of doors and windows.[19] After receiving the paper drawing,

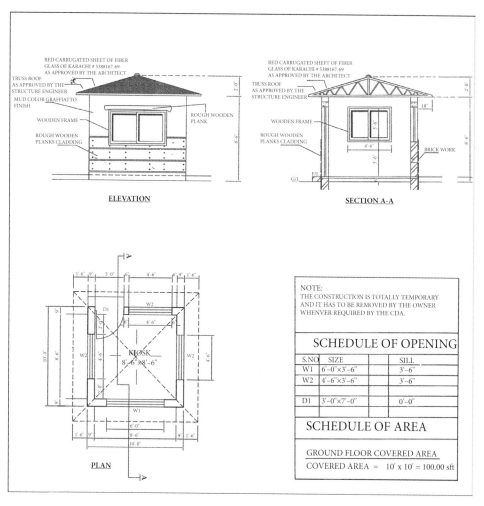

Figure 3.4. Capital Development Authority–approved design of a licensed tea stall/
kiosk with a steel truss roof. Source: Capital Development Authority, Architecture
Directorate, Planning and Design Wing.

the licensed vendor uses his own money, labor, and resources to build his kiosk according to the prescribed design. Figures 3.3 and 3.4 show an old and
new iteration of the officially approved design for licensed kiosks. The kiosk
in both versions is a simple structure made with brick masonry walls on a
concrete slab foundation. The roof in the earlier version (Figure 3.3) is made
from reinforced concrete and covered with terracotta tiles, while a later design

(Figure 3.4) incorporates a steel truss structure with corrugated fiberglass roofing. An official in the Architecture Directorate explained to me that this change in the roofing material and technology was based on the administrative desire to make these structures easy to dismantle and relocate to another site if needed. A concrete roof cannot be moved without destroying the building material completely, while steel-truss roofing can be disassembled and reassembled. A note in the legend of the architectural drawing issued to the kiosk licensees in the later version underscores this point: "The construction is totally temporary and it has to be removed by the owner whenever required by the CDA."

While tea-stall and kiosk owners may withstand tremendous financial damage as a result of the removal process, the restrictions on building materials and construction techniques in official discourse and licensing terms are in keeping with the logic of temporariness and its reliance on ease of revocation. Even though brick and steel are not impermanent materials, they can be reused and reassembled for simple structures without losing their structural integrity, especially in comparison to the properties of glass and poured concrete, which shatter or break during the demolition process. *Temporariness* and *permanence* in this way do not describe the actual strength of the building materials but whether the materials have salvageable and reusable properties. Additionally, by stipulating that constructions for hawking and vending be removable, CDA officials themselves participate in maintaining the impression of temporariness of an illegal yet necessary function.

According to an official survey reported in 2013, there were 1,339 kiosks operating in Islamabad, out of which only 539 were licensed under existing municipal bylaws.[20] This means that the majority of kiosks in Islamabad are unlicensed. Additionally, many of the licensed vendors rarely confine their businesses to their officially allocated space. Since *dhabas* (cafés) and tea stalls are located on roadside greenbelts, their owners commonly use outdoor areas for cooking and seating and end up taking much more space than allotted by CDA. Even in the case of kiosks offering only prepackaged snacks, adjacent outdoor areas may be used as ancillary vending space for displaying stands of bagged chips or refrigerators carrying bottled drinks. These unauthorized spillover spaces next to licensed businesses can be either open to the sky or semicovered.

This lapse in the legality of unlicensed and licensed encroachments is apparent in their material forms. For instance, unauthorized extensions of licensed tea stalls are made from semipermanent building materials and techniques (Figure 3.5). Similarly, unlicensed tea stalls in Islamabad use mud, branches, and mortarless stone or concrete blocks for walls and flooring. Their proprietors build roofs out of roughly assembled branches, tarp, plastic, and steel sheets supported by tree trunks (Figure 3.6). By avoiding the use of building materials and techniques considered to be permanent, unlicensed stall and kiosk owners deliberately adopt an aesthetic of temporariness as a tactic of survival. The aesthetics of temporariness complement the presumed physical properties of building materials and construction techniques for ordinary informal businesses: mud and wood are not weak building materials but are selected by builders of unlicensed encroachments who recognize the importance of participating in the rhetoric of temporariness in making claims to public space. Because of the longevity of building materials and techniques that are presumed to be temporary but are in fact quite durable, the logic of temporariness does not indicate structural vulnerability but rather a performance and aesthetic of provisional existence.

Given the temporary-revocable terms of the licenses, the legal status of licensed encroachments is always tenuous, and their builders must work under a constant and implicit threat of losing their licenses and becoming illegal almost instantaneously. CDA's anti-encroachment drives against licensed encroachments illustrate the insecurity and vulnerability of working under this system. In 2013, CDA demolished several licensed kiosks in a greenbelt in front of a large hospital in sector G-8/3 (which is coincidentally the same hospital that was built on the site of the labor colony evicted in the 1970s). A few months later, CDA demolished a larger structure built by a philanthropic organization for providing free food to the needy, especially the poor families and attendants of hospital patients.

The administration of the free-food distribution facility claimed they had received permission from CDA in 2009 for a 60-by-60-foot area at the rate of 6,000 rupees per month for their set-up.[21] The kiosk owners similarly claimed they had been selling low-cost food and other items of daily use to the staff and visitors of the hospital after receiving licenses from CDA and that CDA had canceled their licenses without any prior notification. The owner of one of the demolished kiosks complained that "if the CDA has the authority to withdraw permission of tuck shops or give alternative place to us, then why they did not issue prior notices to us?"[22] He added that the kiosk owners would have moved voluntarily if CDA had given them previous warning. Another owner of a demolished kiosk used the metaphor of

Figure 3.5. A licensed kiosk in Islamabad built using brick masonry walls and steel roofing. The shed on the side is an illegal extension, using semipermanent materials and construction techniques. Photograph by author.

attacking an enemy's post to describe the military-style anti-encroachment operation carried out by a large, two-hundred-person team of CDA staff and policemen. In the view of one kiosk owner, vendors who had been paying their license fees regularly were following the law; it was CDA that had acted illegally.[23]

The reason behind all these intense demolition activities was that CDA had auctioned two plots for commercial buildings in the greenbelt occupied by licensed structures.[24] When CDA found a more lucrative use for the space, it withdrew its permission to kiosk owners, turning their licensed businesses

Figure 3.6. An unauthorized roadside *dhaba* (café) that looks *katcha* (temporary) using materials considered less permanent, such as mud, wood, and thatch. Photograph by author.

into illegal encroachments almost overnight; "temporary" allowances for khokhas, which had been in effect for years, were rendered illegal almost instantaneously to make way for more profitable functions.

Modalities of Temporariness

The notion of maintaining an impression of temporariness is more than a bureaucratic innovation that allows the construction of ordinary encroachments;

it is a deliberate attempt on the part of entrepreneurs to make their stands and stalls in public spaces appear provisional and hence more tolerable. We can observe this correlation between materiality and sustenance of the stands and stalls in commercial areas built according to the master plan. Businesspeople occupy parking spaces, sidewalks, and building verandas in master-planned markets according to *modalities of temporariness*. I use this term to refer to the material forms and practices of ordinary encroachments based on daily rituals of assembly and disassembly and socially recognized rules about rights to adjacent public space. Islamabad has clearly demarcated and seemingly abundant commercial spaces dispersed throughout the city. There is a markaz market in each sector and a central business district, called the Blue Area, for the entire city. But various forms of informal trading and businesses thrive, often in and around the officially designated commercial areas.

The coexistence of formal and informal commercial activities in master-planned shops, on sidewalks, and in parking areas and building corridors is most apparent in the G-9 markaz market. Sector G-9 is a predominantly middle-class neighborhood with smaller residential plots for lower-middle-income groups and mid-rise apartments for lower-level government employees (Figure 3.7). Located in the geometrical center of the sector is the G-9 markaz, where various civic and commercial amenities such as a post office, bookshops, restaurants, and clothing stores are housed in mid-rise buildings mostly two to three stories high. G-9 markaz is popularly known as Karachi Company because it was once the location of a construction company from Karachi involved in the early construction of Islamabad. Karachi Company is the busiest commercial markaz in Islamabad, known for its affordable prices for everyday necessities in contrast to most commercial areas in the city. The affordability and popularity of Karachi Company can be attributed to the range of informal commerce that takes place in greenbelts and circulation spaces in and around the planned markaz market. The prevalence of encroachments in Karachi Company is often lamented as a failure of municipal administration in Islamabad.[25] Commenting on the extent of encroachments in this market, a CDA official once declared, "G-9 markaz has become Raja bazaar now."[26] Raja bazaar is one of the busiest and most outwardly chaotic old commercial areas in Rawalpindi, a far cry from the superficial orderliness of Islamabad's master-planned markets. Various forms of hawking and vending thrive in Karachi Company both in spite of and because of master-planned commercial areas.

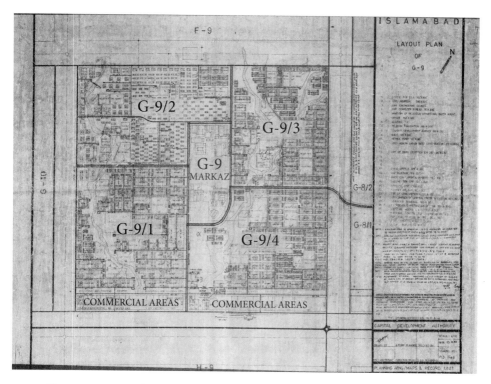

Figure 3.7. Layout plan of sector G-9 with Karachi Company (G-9 Markaz) in the middle. Source: Layout plan of sector G-9, Capital Development Authority, Maps and Records Unit, Planning and Design Wing, Islamabad.

A visit to one of the stores, banks, or offices in Karachi Company typically involves walking past a variety of temporary stalls on sidewalks, service roads, and parking areas (Figure 3.8). Depending on the nature of the enterprise, vendors and hawkers sell their services and products from displays positioned on their bodies, on hand-drawn carts and bicycles, or in simple tent-like structures. Mobile hawking is based on the principle of portability, so the nature of the equipment used for selling depends on the means of conducting business. Those without any mechanical modes of transportation use simple lightweight structures or small display cases that can be carried on their bodies and transported with ease. Others sell their goods on the move, using bicycles, pushcarts, or pickup vans (Figures 3.9 and 3.10). These types of hawkers typically remain on the go, avoiding the need for any ancillary structures for their businesses.

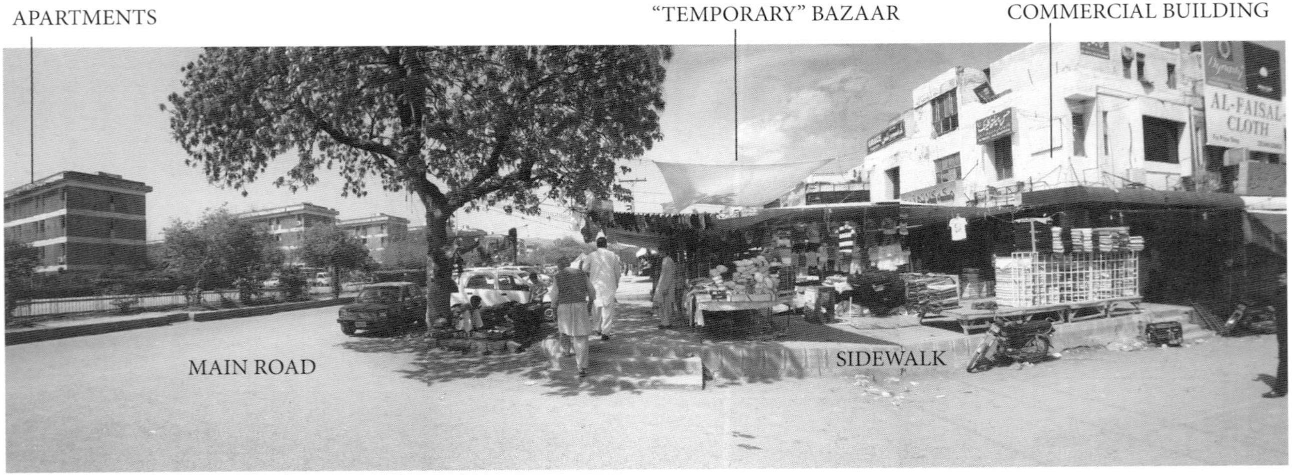
APARTMENTS
"TEMPORARY" BAZAAR
COMMERCIAL BUILDING
AL-FAISAL CLOTH
MAIN ROAD
SIDEWALK

Figure 3.8. Hawking in public areas of Karachi Company (G-9 Markaz). Photograph by author.

Figure 3.9. Mobile hawkers selling toasted corn nuts and popcorn and hand-woven baskets. Photograph by author.

Stationery hawkers and vendors, in contrast, use a range of more advanced spatial arrangements primarily based on the principle of daily assembly and disassembly. Amjad and Naveed are two vendors who assemble their stalls daily, next to each other on a busy sidewalk in Karachi Company (Figure 3.11). Both vendors migrated to Islamabad from smaller cities in Punjab in search of better employment opportunities. Amjad sells an impressive range of kitchen and household items mostly made from plastic, such as buckets, cups, laundry baskets, and food containers. Amjad's is the largest stall in the area, and his display space comprises part of the sidewalk and a raised platform assembled in the adjacent open area every day. Right next to Amjad's stall,

sunglasses displayed on a stand made from styrofoam sheets covered with brown packing tape

a bamboo stick supports the display case

plastic stool for the vendor

bricks tied to ropes to keep the tarp from shifting

Figure 3.10. Portable display case for sunglasses placed on a sidewalk in Karachi Company. Photograph by author.

Naveed sells personal grooming items and clothing accessories like socks, underwear, vests, combs, buttons, and scissors, which are displayed on a waterproof sheet placed directly on the sidewalk. Next to Naveed, a man on a plastic chair sits under a colorful beach umbrella and lets passersby check their body weight on his "weighing machine" (scale) for a few rupees. Nearby, a vendor sells fresh seasonal fruits in baskets placed on wooden crates. On the other side of the sidewalk, a vendor sells soda water from a small stall and a hawker sells pieces of sugar cane from his parked pushcart.

I noticed that none of the vendors and hawkers in this corner fully obstructed the sidewalk; there appeared to be an invisible straight line that func-

Figure 3.11. Street vendors on a sidewalk in Karachi Company. Photograph by author.

tions almost like a "building line." A building line is a legally designated line beyond which a building cannot extend; it is meant to create uniformity among buildings and to avoid obstruction of public rights of way. Vendors observe an agreed-on setback for their stalls for similar reasons: they recognize the importance of appearing organized and of avoiding being accused of sidewalk obstruction. Even the temporary shading system that they erect daily over their stalls is supported by vertical poles anchored on either side of the sidewalk. While Amjad recognizes the significance of keeping sidewalks clear for pedestrians, he also feels that the vendors have a right to use this public space to earn a living: "I am a citizen of this country and not some foreigner. It is in the government's interest that people like me are earning a living."[27] Vendors like Amjad (and Tariq, discussed earlier) do not simply claim public space on moral grounds; their temporary occupation of public space uses material forms and strategies that support their political claims.

Amjad and other vendors in Karachi Company disassemble their stalls every night at closing. This process can take a while in the case of large stalls, as the merchandise has to be carefully packed in boxes and bags and tables and other equipment completely dismantled and transported to storage. Interestingly, the sale of items continues as vendors perform the nightly disassembling process. Amjad rents a nearby storage space in the markaz market to store his equipment and merchandise. He explained that vendors in his corner try not to leave any signs of their business activity; they remove their stalls and merchandise completely and mostly take down the temporary shading system. Amjad thinks that this helps "keep CDA staff away when they do their morning rounds. But then again, they can come any time, so there's always a risk" of getting their merchandise and display equipment confiscated.

Despite the temporariness and uncertainty of selling on sidewalks and in parking areas, there exists a level of regularity in the way vendors set up their stalls every day. Most vendors occupy a rectilinear-shaped space on the sidewalk, greenbelt, and parking area. Each stall has a clear boundary defined by its display area and shading system. Even though vendors dismantle their stalls at the end of the day, they usually do not risk losing their spots the next morning. Both Amjad and Naveed confirmed that their particular location on the sidewalk is "permanent," an arrangement that is consistently respected by all doing business in their corner. Amjad has been doing business in this area for more than eighteen years, and Naveed for over two years. Despite their temporary configuration, vendors' stalls achieve a kind of permanence in the repetition of their daily assembly and disassembly.

Shopkeepers similarly encroach on adjacent public spaces to increase their retail space. Public space in front of an existing shop is often claimed by its shopkeeper, a practice that is mutually observed by all doing business in the area. This conforms to the general practice of shopkeepers in urban Pakistan claiming public space (including corridors, footpaths, and even parking spots) in front of their stores. The prevalence of this practice can be illustrated in the everyday usurpation of public spaces by well-to-do businesspeople who work in Blue Area. Doxiadis planned Blue Area as the commercial and business hub of Islamabad. In Blue Area, commercial buildings are situated on both sides of an expansive boulevard called Jinnah Avenue (Figure 3.12). High-rise office buildings are located on the north side of Jinnah Avenue, while mid-rise shopping markets sit on the south side. Blue Area offers expensive retail space to corporate offices and elite businesses like clothing

CORPORATE TOWERS

COMMERCIAL BUILDINGS

JINNAH AVE

SIDEWALK

GREEN BELT

Figure 3.12. A view of Blue Area, with commercial buildings on either side of Jinnah Avenue. Photograph by author.

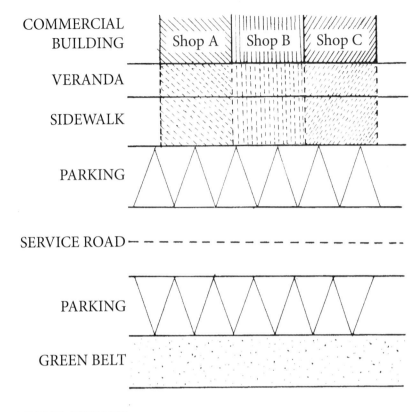

COMMERCIAL
BUILDING   Shop A | Shop B | Shop C

VERANDA

SIDEWALK

PARKING

SERVICE ROAD – – – – – – – – – – – – – – – – – – –

PARKING

GREEN BELT

JINNAH AVENUE

Figure 3.13. Diagram showing an aerial view of public spaces in Blue Area.

stores, restaurants, and showrooms. Even a small store in one of the commercial markets rents for several hundred thousand rupees.

Middle- and upper-class shopkeepers in commercial markets like Blue Area use ordinary informal spatial strategies to claim public spaces for personal use. Blue Area's mid-rise commercial buildings typically comprise a linear arrangement of stores and offices facing covered verandas. The verandas open onto wide footpaths, parking areas, and service roads (Figure 3.13). It is not unusual to find parts of the corridor, footpaths, or parking spots right in front of shops blocked by their owners with planters or concrete blocks (Figure 3.14). Shopkeepers believe this unhindered visual and spatial access to their stores helps improve business. Even more striking is the large number of shopkeepers who undergo the daily ritual of moving their merchandise—often expensive electronics like televisions, washing machines, or air conditioners—out to the public spaces in the morning and returning them back inside at closing time (Figure 3.15). This strategy effectively allows some of them to nearly double their display space. But claims to adjacent public space are limited to the area in front of the shops in commercial markets; they do not extend into the spaces on each side, which are to be claimed by the adjacent shop owners. When a shop owner's usurped public space exceeds personal needs, he may rent it out to vendors. Vendors' stalls in master-planned markets often enjoy the patronage of middle-class shopkeepers because of their renting arrangements over the use of public space.

Not surprisingly, Karachi Company provides informative examples of the entwined relationship between vendors' stalls and brick-and-mortar stores. On the southwestern side of Karachi Company, several stores in a three-story building sell unstitched fabric and ready-made clothes. As the sketch in Figure 3.16 shows, the footpaths, service road, and parking area next to these stores are occupied by another kind of market made up of temporary stalls and stands that sell affordable ready-made clothes, underwear, shoes, and clothing accessories. Sunshades for the outdoor stalls are made from sheets of tarp or similar material stretched horizontally or at an angle using a web of nylon ropes that attaches to pegs drilled into the walls of the commercial building (Figure 3.17). Metal poles or bamboo posts are propped to provide additional vertical support, while other structural reinforcements include using the weight of bricks tied to ropes or tarp pegs driven into the ground to keep the tarp structures from shifting. Vendors display their merchandise either on the ground, on collapsible wood or metal tables and platforms, or hung from ropes. They disassemble their display areas, store their merchandise, and retreat from public spaces daily at closing time (Figure 3.18).

I learned about mutually beneficial arrangements between vendors and shopkeepers from Waseem, a vendor who sells shoes from a parking area in front of a store. Waseem pays the storekeeper rent for use of the space and for providing electricity for lighting to help facilitate his business after sunset. Waseem said that he didn't mind paying the shopkeeper, "as times were tough and the shopkeepers are only looking for ways to earn income."[28] Vendors like Waseem also rent space in the markaz market to store their merchandise at night. The daily modalities of businesspeople operating from planned shops or vendors' stalls blur the distinction between formal

Figure 3.14. Planters enable the unrestricted visual and spatial access believed to boost business. Photograph by author.

Figure 3.15. Spillover display space in Blue Area. Photograph by author.

Figure 3.16. Sketch of the "temporary" bazaar in Karachi Company. The four-sided shapes in solid gray represent vendors' stalls.

and informal modes of commerce. Vendors enjoy the patronage of shop-keepers but also provide additional income to them. Their low-cost merchandise attracts more shoppers to the market. While different in their material forms and property rules, formally and informally planned businesses, where they coexist, share a symbiotic relationship.

Although the concept of long-term temporariness inheres in the policies of the state and routine modalities of street commerce in Islamabad, these

Figure 3.17. A view of the "temporary" bazaar in Karachi Company. Notice the UNHCR (United National High Commissioner for Refugees) logo on the stretched tarp. Vendors buy durable tarp from secondhand markets where refugee-relief goods like the UNHCR tents are also traded. Photograph by author.

Figure 3.18. The vendors' bazaar area in Karachi Company early in the morning before trading hours. Photograph by author.

informal arrangements do not enjoy complete immunity from removal or re-
ordering. Pressures from various citizen groups and government institutions result in pushes to clear encroachers from roads and sidewalks. During
my fieldwork, I witnessed one such reorganization of a vendors' market next
to the clothing stores in Karachi Company. Karachi Company's buildings
and sidewalks come under CDA's jurisdiction, while the police oversee the
management of service roads and parking areas. In this instance, an anti-
encroachment drive was carried out by the police to clear the service roads
and parking areas. Before the anti-encroachment action, stalls and stands
were built every day on two sides of the parking area with a pedestrian walk-
way in between. As seen in Figure 3.19, the police reorganized this bazaar by
clearing vendors' stalls on the side closer to the main avenue to make space
for motorcycle parking. They also installed steel railings to define entry points
for pedestrians and to protect these circulation spaces from future encroachments. While several hawkers and vendors operating on the service road
and sidewalks lost their spots, the bazaar itself survived the police campaign
to restore the G-9 markaz to its planned order. When I visited Karachi Company four years later, the informal bazaar had returned to its original size,
with stalls built around the steel railings on both sides of the parking area.
The flexibility and adaptability that sustain ordinary forms of informal commerce also ensure its continued existence. In this example, hawkers and
vendors were able to reorganize their businesses in a manner acceptable to
the concerned officials and reclaim their spot when the immediate threat was
over.

Conclusion

From the location of khokhas etched onto the sectoral plans maintained at
CDA's Maps and Record Unit to the provision of licensing encroachments
written into the *Municipal Bye-Laws of 1968–69*, informal spaces are deeply
entwined with Islamabad's formal planning framework. As the steward of a
capital city designed by a famed western architect, CDA has the difficult job
of ensuring Islamabad's legacy as a "planned" and "modern" city. The "clean-
slate" conception from which the city was supposedly developed places
stress on its managers to maintain fidelity to the official master plan. How
do city administrators bridge the gap between the abstract master plan and
real-world challenges of urban poverty and limited resources? In the case of

Before the "operation" (2013)

After the "operation" (2014)

Figure 3.19. Transformations after an anti-encroachment operation—showing hawkers removed from one side of the service road in order to create space for parking. Photographs by author.

ordinary encroachments like hawking and vending, the condition of temporariness is invoked to allow necessary functions to persist, often for long periods. The concept of long-term temporariness is evident in the bureaucratic procedures, everyday spatial practices, and social norms related to the sale of services and merchandise on greenbelts, streets, parking areas, building verandas, and sidewalks in Islamabad. Temporary spatial arrangements allow street and sidewalk vendors, as well as middle- and upper-class businesspeople in commercial markets, to create retail spaces in public areas.

The interconnected, complementary relationship between commercial buildings and vendors' stalls in Islamabad is based on a planning paradigm—characterized by dynamism, flexibility, and adaptability—in contrast to the rigidity and so-called comprehensiveness of high-modernist planning. This generative and relational aspect of city-making causes places like Karachi Company to be in a constant state of making and unmaking, never complete, always continually "coming-into-being."[29] Moreover, "fluid, densely used, and intensely contested" streetscapes based on everyday spatial practices transform "mundane" city spaces into communities and livelihoods.[30] In this chapter, I showed how this transformation of master-planned streets, sidewalks, and greenbelts is based on architectural forms and modalities of temporariness. The architectural strategies discussed here are not incidental to improvised city spaces but integral to their sustenance.

By deliberately avoiding structural permanence, temporary building practices bring "forms of resilient yet dynamic stability" to urban built environments and allow excluded and marginalized people to gain access to open public spaces.[31] Vendors and hawkers whose temporary structures are bulldozed, dismantled, or confiscated in a raid or demolition drive may relocate, retreat, or resume as soon as the immediate threat is over. Architectural forms and modalities of temporariness function as survival tactics for vendors and hawkers by helping them create spaces that appear to be *temporarily* encroaching on master-planned areas. These material practices and aesthetics define the terms (however inhumane and precarious) under which marginalized communities (like underprivileged citizens or undocumented immigrants) around the world create spaces of livelihoods in systems that exclude them. While strategic negotiations with city officials are essential for the long-term survival of ordinary informalities, the role of the aesthetics and material forms of temporary urbanism in this process cannot be underestimated.

CHAPTER 4

Elite Informality

n 2017, former cricketer and later prime minister of Pakistan Imran Khan approached the chief justice of Pakistan to take action against CDA. Khan's main contention was that CDA had been negligent in checking the "municipal lawlessness that reign[ed] supreme" in his scenic neighborhood of Bani Gala, where "encroachers, land mafias and anarchic builders" were carrying out "unplanned and unregulated" constructions, cutting down trees, and destroying the natural ecosystem.[1] Located toward the edge of the city, Bani Gala shelters some of Pakistan's most elite citizens in a scenic area that includes a beautiful lake, pristine streams, and forested hills. Khan lives in a sprawling residence built on top of a private hill as part of a thirty-seven-acre estate.[2] Other elite residents like him own elaborate mansions with lush green lawns that cluster around a beautiful lake. But built on parkland surrounding what is Islamabad's major water source, all these exclusive villas are in breach of the city's official master plan and were themselves once encroachments. Then why did Imran Khan—owner of an elite yet illegal residence in Bani Gala—complain to the chief justice about CDA's ineffectiveness against encroachers? The answer to this question reveals the paradoxical desire of elite homebuilders like Khan to preserve the master plan, in particular, the protected nature of the parkland on which they themselves built encroachments—that is, how they attend to the master plan even as they find ways to violate it.

This chapter examines the history of Bani Gala as an elite informal neighborhood, where a handful of influential homebuilders constructed lavish mansions and eventually initiated a process of revision to the city's official zoning regulations. Elite homebuilders chose this protected nature reserve as a building site precisely because of its designation in the master plan as an exclusive, scenic area close to Islamabad's urban sectors. By mobilizing their networks of monetary resources and political connections, developing unlikely alliances, and mimicking bureaucratic procedures, wealthy homebuilders were able to transform the undeveloped area of Bani Gala into an elite neighborhood. These elite homebuilders resisted CDA's anti-encroachment campaigns and were ultimately able to harness judicial power to legitimize their illegal building activities.

The legitimization of Bani Gala attracted many lower- and middle-class people who started moving to its less desirable, inexpensive locations. The arrival of the less affluent residents drastically changed the density and demographics of this exclusive neighborhood. In contrast to the elite homebuilders who bought acres of land on top of hills or along the shoreline of the lake, lower-middle-class residents started buying small plots along narrow streets without proper sewerage or renting apartments in jerry-built plazas. Even though Imran Khan's villa is located within a gated enclosure built on top of a hill accessible through a private road, the only two approaches to his sanctuary are full of potholes and offer unsightly views of garbage and sewage strewn about because of haphazard construction and lack of municipal oversight in the area. The problem for the elite residents of Bani Gala is that while they may have the ability to encroach beautifully on top of hills and along lakes, their less-privileged neighbors mostly encroach in an unassuming and, to the elites, unsightly manner. The elites bemoan and resent encroachments by lower- and middle-income people in Islamabad, yet they themselves use legally dubious mechanisms to self-segregate in urban peripheral areas like Bani Gala. They justify their actions with their claims that state institutions like CDA are corrupt and unstable.[3] But elite homebuilders in Bani Gala still enlist the help of CDA officials (along with other actors) to assist in their building practices because of an underlying sense of entitlement and exceptionalism shared by elites, not only in Pakistan but also worldwide.[4]

Despite their immense wealth and privilege, elite homeowners build and defend their lavish dwellings using accretive processes that have much in common with the ways ordinary squatter settlements are built. Though they work in drastically different material and political circumstances, both elite and ordinary encroachments are built with attention to the master plan and the bureaucratic procedures necessary to sustain encroachments. Participation in informal urban development, including the contentious legal process of reassigning an urban space to a purpose vastly different from its official conception, gave these urban elites a means to assert their existing positions of power and privilege.

At the heart of the Bani Gala story are the competing visions for the same peripheral urban space imagined respectively by Islamabad's architect-planner, Constantinos A. Doxiadis, and the wealthy homebuilders, who eventually determined the fate of the region. In this chapter, I look at the processes through which those elite homebuilders, spearheaded by the wealthy and enterprising "housewife" Mrs. Nabila Sheikh, were able to replan the scenic yet undeveloped area of Bani Gala.[5] During my interviews of longtime residents of Bani Gala, they repeatedly named Mrs. Nabila as one of the leading figures in its initial development as an elite neighborhood. An examination of court reports and news articles also verified her pivotal role in creating this residential community and legitimizing it through media campaigns and a pseudo-legal paper trail. Finally, Mrs. Nabila's perspective also helps illuminate the motivations of elite homebuilders who indulge in informal spatial practices despite their ability to afford formally developed land elsewhere.

The elite neighborhood of Bani Gala falls squarely within the expansive area designated as the National Park in Islamabad's official master plan. Doxiadis conceived the National Park area as a large, open green space of respite for the citizens (Figure 4.1). The master plan allowed for a select number of institutional buildings, recreational parks, and sports facilities in the National Park, but it strictly prohibited any residential use. Long before it transformed into an elite neighborhood, Bani Gala was one of the small village communities that had existed for generations on the site for Islamabad.[6] It is one of the most scenic parts of the city, blessed with forested hills, streams, and spectacular views of the adjacent Rawal Lake—an artificial water reservoir built in the 1960s. Doxiadis recognized the picturesque quality of the area around Rawal Lake and its potential as an attractive building site when he noted in a report submitted to CDA in the early 1960s, "It is understood that this area is one of the most beautiful areas of Islamabad and the adjacency of the Lake makes it more attractive. But the importance of the land use specified in both the above cases should not be diminished from the fact that a small number of people should have the privilege of enjoying the best area of Islamabad. This area should be left for use by all citizens of Islamabad in such a way as to fulfill also the requirements of proper treatment of the Lake."[7] Despite Doxiadis's early warnings, a small number of privileged people did end up staking claims to this scenic area for their personal enjoyment. They were able

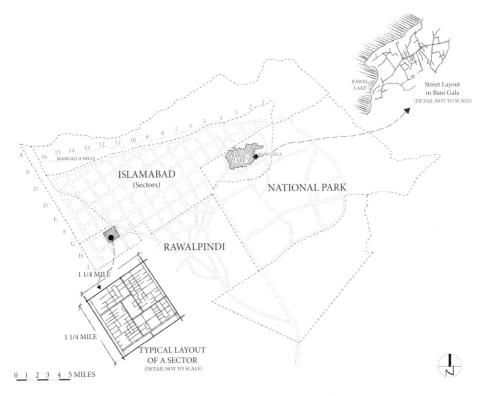

Figure 4.1. Master plan of Islamabad with details of a typical sector and street layout in Bani Gala.

to do so by mobilizing monetary resources and social connections with other elites, developing opportunistic alliances with nonelites, and creating a paper trail to legitimize their illegal building activities. I now turn to Mrs. Nabila Sheikh because her perspective illuminates each of these processes in detail.

Mrs. Nabila's Plan for Bani Gala

When Mrs. Nabila visited Bani Gala for the first time in 1984, it was a small village in an undeveloped area. What caught her immediate attention was the rare combination of water, trees, and mountains, all within easy physical and visual proximity. When speaking about the idyllic setting of her house in Bani Gala, Mrs. Nabila declared, "When you think of God and nature, this is what comes to mind. You have water, mountains, and jungle all together in one place!"[8] As a daughter of a middle-class army officer, Mrs. Nabila had always envisioned herself living on a large property with lush green lawns and gardens. The bucolic setting of Bani Gala and the absurdly low land prices in the area, compared to developed sectors in Islamabad, quickly motivated Mrs. Nabila to purchase undeveloped land for the construction of her dream project (Figure 4.2). Even though she was an outsider, Mrs. Nabila spoke the local language, Potohari, which she thinks helped bridge the social distance between her and the locals and hence helped her find the ideal piece of land.

The conversion of Bani Gala from a "jungle" to a comfortable modern neighborhood was not a simple feat as it involved setting up necessary utilities and infrastructure, including electricity, telephone lines, roads, and other amenities, without CDA's formal support and in contravention of the official master plan. But Mrs. Nabila used connections among her friends, some of whom also invested in land in Bani Gala, to get physical infrastructure to this undeveloped rural area. For instance, in order to get telephone lines, Mrs. Nabila's friend, whose daughter also bought land in Bani Gala, approached an influential minister who ordered that official funds be diverted to telephone line construction. When Mrs. Nabila met with the general manager of Pakistan Telecom Corporation Limited, he told her that, had it not been for the *sifarish*,[9] Bani Gala would not have gotten phone connections for another fifty years.

The development of Bani Gala into a residential neighborhood also entailed establishing a brand-new community of residents. The recruitment of an elite community who shared similar socioeconomic backgrounds and enjoyed political clout was an important step in the neighborhood's development. In addition to buying land for herself, Mrs. Nabila encouraged friends and family to invest in the area. When the construction of her house was completed in about 1988, Mrs. Nabila celebrated the occasion with a big housewarming dinner party. One of Mrs. Nabila's friends asked if he could bring his friend along to the party; this friend turned out to be Dr. Abdul Qadeer Khan, Pakistan's most celebrated yet controversial nuclear scientist, who became one of the first elite residents of Bani Gala to make their homes along the shores of Rawal Lake.[10] Dr. Khan came to Mrs. Nabila's house the morning after the party to have breakfast with her family. He enjoyed the beautiful views of the lake from her house and liked the place so much that he decided to buy land nearby for his own residence. What Dr. Khan brought with him, along with other early well-to-do settlers of Bani Gala, was immense

Figure 4.2. Lake-front residences in Bani Gala. Photograph by author.

political clout that helped in its development as an elite neighborhood and its legitimization through subsequent legal proceedings.

Mrs. Nabila bought over 70 kanals of land along the banks of Rawal Lake next to her property for her siblings and a friend to create a private residential gated compound (Figure 4.3).[11] Their residential compound currently comprises five mansions belonging to Mrs. Nabila, her two sisters, her brother, and a friend, with room for Mrs. Nabila's daughter to build her own house in the future if she so desires. The community is walled and can be accessed via two successive entry gates. A private security guard monitors the entry of visitors into the compound. The residential pattern of elite mansions in Bani Gala, resembling the architecture of private, gated enclaves, thus stands

Figure 4.3. Aerial view of Mrs. Nabila's residential compound in Bani Gala.

in sharp contrast to the Doxiadis sectors, which are designed as self-contained yet accessible neighborhood units.

It is no coincidence that one of the main actors in the establishment of Bani Gala as a high-end neighborhood was not a private professional developer or land speculator but an elite woman. While researching new residential constructions in Bani Gala, I encountered several female figures like Mrs. Nabila who were involved in the design and construction of lavish houses for themselves and their families; as Mrs. Nabila had, they encouraged friends to settle in this area. These women, some with professional careers, were mostly married to influential and wealthy men and shared the same desire to live on expansive properties in scenic locales in Islamabad.

While these elite women obviously enjoyed the support of their husbands and other male homebuilders in the area, they were able to transform their existing identities through participation in informal residential constructions and to develop effective strategies to legitimize their building projects. And while these elite women are typically called "housewives," their real-estate endeavors took them well beyond the realm of their homes.

Mrs. Nabila's involvement in the development of Bani Gala illustrates this well. Although an army of domestic servants and helpers assists in the routine of running her house, Mrs. Nabila is considered a "housewife" in the Pakistani sense, since she is not engaged in professional work. The house thus becomes her primary concern and represents her competence as a figurative homemaker; real-estate development in Bani Gala, in turn, became an important factor in Mrs. Nabila's quest for an ideal home for herself and her family. Mrs. Nabila considers her house in Bani Gala her dream project, her "child." "I like doing challenging things," Mrs. Nabila claimed in our first meeting. And so, instead of feeling apprehensive about the absolute wilderness in Bani Gala at the time she made her land purchase, she took on the development of the desolate yet promising site of her future house as a challenge. Mrs. Nabila's narration of events portrays her husband as an amused bystander, even though she deployed his money, name, and connections in the construction of her dream home. She fondly remembers that her husband, an influential retired army officer, thought she was mad when she declared her plans to build a house in this area. By taking the lead in the house construction and urban development process, Mrs. Nabila was able to both reinforce and transcend her identities as an elite "housewife," a sister, friend, and neighbor.

Mrs. Nabila's interactions with the villagers of Bani Gala over the course of its construction and legalization processes exemplify the multifaceted work of a so-called housewife. The place-based "sense of community" among long-term villagers and new elite residents of Bani Gala did not form easily, and Mrs. Nabila recalls several altercations with local villagers, whom she considers *muft khoray* (freeloaders) and frauds. During the late 1980s, when Mrs. Nabila's house was constructed, land prices in Bani Gala had just started to rise, as small-scale private developers and individual property owners began investing in the area.[12] Mrs. Nabila remembers harassment from local villagers who, after realizing the financial potential of this land, made multiple attempts to take over her large property. A neighboring villager, for instance, tried to encroach on her land and even sell it to other buyers. To deter her neighbor once and for all, Mrs. Nabila called the *tehsildar* and told

him to send his staff of *patwari* and *girdawar* to her property.[13] She also called
neighboring villagers and made the *patwari* and *girdawar* mark out their
property lines. She then directed her builders to shift the property line one
foot toward her side as a concession to the neighboring villagers. The villagers appeared not to appreciate her act of goodwill, as they fired shots at her
guard and builders during the night. Mrs. Nabila was fed up with the villagers' defiance. She called the local police officer and got more than fifty people
arrested on a fifteen-day remand, during which they were beaten daily.
Mrs. Nabila remembers that after the arrest of the villagers, village women
issued threats that they would "beat up the *begum*" (high-status lady) who
had gotten their menfolk arrested. When the news of the threats reached
Mrs. Nabila, she went up to the village and dared these women to come out
of their houses to make good on their threats.

Mrs. Nabila uses her narration of these events to demonstrate her resilience, benevolence, and power in the area. She presents herself as someone
who is not easily dissuaded even by attacks on her staff or personal threats
against her. She could be benevolent one moment, as she was when she gave
away part of her property to win over her neighbors, but ruthless the next, as
when she marshaled state violence to arrest and beat neighboring men to send
the clear message that her neighbors best not cross her. Mrs. Nabila's actions
attempted both to appease and to intimidate the village residents.

In this way, Mrs. Nabila took on the role of an unconventional elite *dalal-
cum-ghundah* (Urdu for "broker-cum-bully") for Bani Gala's informal development. These are essential figures involved in most spatial illegalities in
urban Pakistan: the *dalal* is a broker of illegal land subdivisions, while a *ghun-
dah* provides protection in land-related irregularities. Attracting new settlers is one of the main preoccupations of illegal land developers operating
in urban areas of Pakistan.[14] On the one hand, Mrs. Nabila understood the
importance of enrolling other stakeholders, such as her family members,
friends, and acquaintances, in the informal neighborhood of Bani Gala. On
the other, providing protection to friends and family she attracted to the area
was also a part of the role she crafted for herself.

For instance, when CDA launched an anti-encroachment operation in
Bani Gala in 1992, Mrs. Nabila was offered immunity if she were to sign an
agreement that CDA would not touch her property but would bulldoze all
the other houses in her compound. She refused to sign the agreement and
instead chose to defend the properties of her friends and family since she felt
responsible for their investments. At one point during the anti-encroachment

drive, Mrs. Nabila and her sister even placed themselves in front of a manned bulldozer to block it from moving forward with the demolition. Because of her status as a wealthy and influential woman, Mrs. Nabila also briefly took on the role of local community "leader" after the anti-encroachment drive; she remembers how the "whole village" came to her house to convince her to pursue legal cases against CDA in the High and Supreme Courts. Mrs. Nabila may have been motivated initially by the ostensibly "domestic" desire to live in a scenic setting in a modern city. But in the process of building her new house and a new neighborhood, she ultimately transcended the private realm of the domestic to enter the public domain of contestations and negotiations with other actors, much like France Colony's Faheema (discussed in Chapter 2).

In contrast to the popular media representations of elite housewives as self-indulgent, conspicuous consumers and frivolous spenders, elite housewives in different parts of the world play an integral, albeit less visible role in enabling and maintaining their privileges and in the accumulation of their husbands' wealth and power by effectively managing their large homes and domestic staff and coordinating their children's numerous school and extracurricular activities.[15] Parul Bhandari argues that elite housewives do not simply *spend* money; they *use* it for various purposes, including secret financial investments that both generate more wealth and help establish them as independent, self-reliant, and prudent wives, mothers, daughters, and friends.[16] The Bani Gala example corroborates Bhandari's insights and shows the kind of challenges that elite housewives face and overcome in the name of building "dream homes" for themselves and their families. In the process, they establish their status as enterprising women while contributing considerably to their families' wealth through real-estate development of undeveloped rural areas.

While this chapter mainly focuses on elite residential constructions in Bani Gala, it is important to note that the illegal building activities of elites like Mrs. Nabila had an uneven impact on local villagers. The biggest winners of Bani Gala's development process were the village landlords who accumulated a lot of wealth instantaneously by selling their farmland to elite homebuilders or property speculators. Some enterprising villagers started working as property dealers, brokering transactions between local landholders and outside buyers. In contrast to village landlords' and property dealers' sudden accumulation of wealth, several villagers lost their land and livelihoods. Land speculators looking to buy large tracts of land used various forms of harassment, threats, and pressure tactics to force small landholders to sell their land and relocate. For small landholders, the immediate monetary gain of selling agricultural land was short-lived and accompanied by a loss of livelihood and food insecurity. One successful property dealer claims that he knows people who now "work as domestic servants in the houses that are built on the land that they once owned."

I will illustrate the contrasting impact of Bani Gala's informal development using the examples of two village residents, Colonel Shahid and Nadia. Colonel Shahid is a retired army officer and the developer of a new, gated residential community in Bani Gala, which I will call Park View Residencia. Colonel Shahid calls his role as a real-estate developer a "coincidence." He lives in Malpur, a small village located right next to Bani Gala. CDA acquired Malpur village in the 1960s but allowed its residents to live in their houses until it needed the area for development purposes.[17] Still, Colonel Shahid and members of his family, worried about their future displacement, started looking for a suitable place to resettle several years ago. Colonel Shahid, his siblings, and cousins eventually decided on a beautiful site next to a stream in the neighboring village of Bani Gala where they bought 34 kanals (4.25 acres) of land for their future homes.

Colonel Shahid and his older brother saw an opportunity in real-estate development after the sudden increase in Bani Gala's property values in the 1990s. In the early 2000s, they purchased about 350 kanals (43.75 acres) of land next to their Bani Gala property to develop a "full housing society."[18] Colonel Shahid and his brother prepared a master plan for Park View Residencia by dividing the site into plots separated by 30-foot-wide streets. Colonel Shahid believes they were "lucky" in selling their plots to "educated, well-to-do people," including an architect, retired army and naval officials, police officers, and a sitting member of the National Assembly. Like Mrs. Nabila had, the developers and new elite homebuilders used their monetary resources and political connections to develop a modern and exclusive community in Park View Residencia.

I met Nadia, a teenage girl, during one of my visits to Park View Residencia. I came across three half-demolished houses in a part of the housing scheme that was under construction. The three houses stood on an elevated site that looked dangerously unstable. The land next to the houses had been cut and leveled to clear the way for residential plots, creating a sharp difference in level between the houses and the adjacent land (Figure 4.4). Nadia lived with her family in one of the three half-demolished houses, while the other two belonged to her uncles and their families.

Figure. 4.4. Sharp differences in level between Nadia's family's half-demolished houses and land owned by Colonel Shahid. Photograph by author.

Nadia remembered the time before the "Colonel" acquired land near their houses.[19] There were about sixty to seventy small houses in their area, which at the time was "only a jungle." People of this area would go and wash their clothes in a nearby ravine (that now runs right next to a lavish Park View Residencia residence built by an influential politician). Around the early 2000s, the Colonel started asking these people to sell their land to him. Nadia explained that only her family resisted selling their properties until the Colonel purchased land right next to their houses and started development there. Nadia's family finally was forced to relocate because of the cutting and leveling of adjacent land that literally cut them off completely from all sides (not to mention, structurally destabilized their property).

The Colonel offered each displaced family a plot of land in an area immediately outside the high concrete walls of Park View Residencia. In addition to a replacement plot, the Colonel promised 16-foot lanes, electricity and water connections, and the "choice" between a new 5-marla (about 1,125 square feet) house built by his contractor or 500,000 rupees (about $5,500 at the time) in cash. Nadia's family considered the contractor-built houses to be of inferior quality because concrete blocks instead of burnt bricks were being used as the main building material. So they decided to take the cash buyout option, even though building a new house was going to cost them more than twice the amount offered in the Colonel's "relocation package." At the time of my visit, Nadia's family members were busy carrying salvageable building materials and household items from their half-demolished houses to their new location.

Not surprisingly, Bani Gala's elite-driven development did not benefit the local villagers equally. While people like Colonel Shahid "coincidentally" amassed a lot of wealth, people like Nadia and her family not only lost their homes but also suffered financially because of their forced displacement. Before the elites discovered the real estate potential of Bani Gala, these remote settings were home to low-income communities. Ultimately, the village landowners and property dealers, who profited from the elite residential constructions in their area, emerged as important stakeholders in Bani Gala's development process. I now return to Mrs. Nabila's efforts to legitimize her illegal construction, but I will discuss in greater detail the place-based alliances and fallouts between Mrs. Nabila and local villagers later in the chapter.

Bureaucratic Devices

Wealthy prospective homebuilders like Mrs. Nabila were able to transform Bani Gala because of the unique configuration of land ownership and administration in Islamabad. CDA does not own all the land that falls within the capital region. Small rural communities, such as those in Bani Gala, have existed in the area for generations and occupy land that is privately owned.[20] Additionally, CDA does not hold complete administrative authority over the entire capital region.

Broadly speaking, the administration of urban areas in Pakistan is based on three tiers of government, namely, the federal, provincial, and local governments. For effective governance, provinces are subdivided into various geographical units with corresponding governing bodies: each province is subdivided into divisions, each division into districts, each district into *tehsils*, and each tehsil into union councils.[21] The administrative body at the lowest level in Pakistan, governing one or more villages, revenue estates, or census blocks, is the union council.[22]

Even though Islamabad geographically falls within Punjab province, as a federally administered area it remains independent of the provincial government and enjoys the same powers and roles as that of a provincial government.[23]

Islamabad District comprises the entire capital region, referred to as the Islamabad Capital Territory, and is further subdivided into two areas, urban and rural, each with its own governing body.[24] Urban areas are governed by CDA, which was formed as a municipal corporate body in 1960 to oversee the development and administration of the new capital city. All residential, commercial, industrial, and institutional areas within the urban sectors of Islamabad are under CDA's jurisdiction. These are the areas that were developed according to a grid of sectors planned under the Doxiadis master plan.

The administration of rural areas comes under a second administrative authority: Islamabad Capital Territory Administration (ICTA). ICTA administers the rural areas through various "union councils" that include elected councilors and a nominated chairman. In rural areas, a union council is the basic administrative unit, which administers a group of 5 to 23 villages. ICTA is administratively subdivided into 12 union councils governing about 133 villages located in Islamabad (Figure 4.5).[25] The National Park area is mainly composed of rural areas that come under ICTA jurisdiction. ICTA manages the day-to-day administration of rural areas in Islamabad, but CDA holds the power to plan and develop both rural and urban areas and controls the sale of developed land, which is a major source of its revenue.

Builders of informal spaces in Islamabad often successfully exploit this dual administrative structure. The elite homebuilders took advantage of the fact that Bani Gala, as an undeveloped village, came under ICTA's jurisdiction. They also recognized an opportunity in the fact that villagers and not CDA owned land in Bani Gala. They were successfully able to manipulate these lacunae in land administration and ownership structure in the capital region by buying land directly from local villagers. Moreover, they were able to challenge CDA's authority in exercising control over the use of the National Park area as a protected space by privileging ICTA's authority over CDA's. They fabricated a building approval process based on written permissions from officials who, while maintaining administrative jurisdiction over the National Park area, did not hold any authority over its planning and development. The unique urban administrative structure of urban and rural areas in Islamabad allowed these elite homebuilders not only to build informally but also to legitimize their mansions in a protected nature reserve through bureaucratic and legal procedures.

Elite homebuilders selectively documented their interactions with various state actors to help them make claims to legitimacy of their encroachments. For instance, after buying land directly from local villagers, Mrs. Nabila started

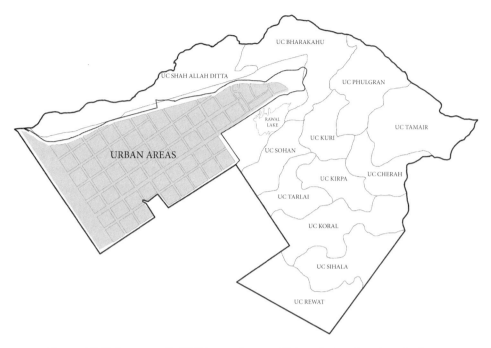

Figure 4.5. Union councils (UC) in rural areas of Islamabad under Islamabad Capital Territory Administration jurisdiction. Urban areas of Islamabad under Capital Development Authority jurisdiction are shown in gray. Drawn from a CDA map.

the process of collecting documentary evidence of official correspondence with various CDA and ICTA officials. The official master plan did not permit new residential construction in Bani Gala since it was part of the National Park area; yet Mrs. Nabila and other elite homebuilders received approval for the construction of their houses from Bani Gala's concerned union council. The approval process involved the submission of architectural drawings of their proposed houses to the chairman of the union council, who issued his permission in the form of a signature and an official stamp on the submitted drawings and other documents (Figure 4.6). As the lowest level of government in Pakistan, union councils are easily influenced to participate in this kind of approval process. But more to the point, the approval process itself was a pure fabrication (in anticipation of future legal prosecution by the state) since the union council did not have the authority to give permission for new construction in areas under its administrative control. Only CDA

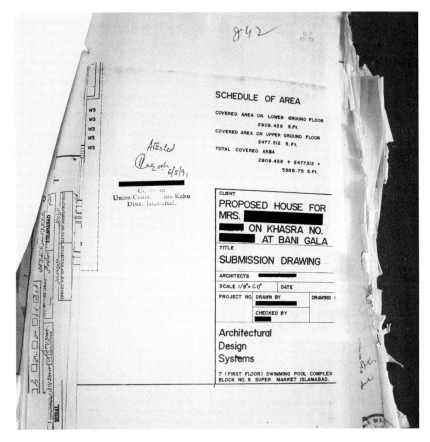

Figure 4.6. Photo of an approved submission drawing for the house of one of the petitioners bearing the stamp and signature of chairman of the Union Council Bahra Kahu, Islamabad. Photograph by author.

held the power to approve new construction in both urban and rural areas of Islamabad.

New residents of Bani Gala, like Mrs. Nabila, were thus able to receive "official" approval for houses designed in violation of the official building regulations of Islamabad on land reserved for nonresidential purposes according to the official master plan. By using fabricated documentary evidence, such as the union council chairman's approval stamp, Mrs. Nabila and others were able to create a gray area of legitimacy for their houses. These people did not seek approval from the concerned union council because they had any intention to follow existing building and zoning laws in Islamabad. Instead, they sought to create a falsified "official" paper trail to prove the legitimacy of their actions should they be challenged at a later stage. The union council that provided the fictitious approval for the construction, while exercising legitimate control over the area, was not ultimately responsible for its development. Even though Bani Gala's new residents violated the zoning regulations of Islamabad by building their houses in the National Park area, written building permissions from an executive authority gave their building activity the illusion of legitimacy.

CDA was nevertheless aware of the development of Bani Gala as an up-and-coming neighborhood in rural Islamabad, and along with other concerned authorities, it made feeble attempts to warn prospective homebuilders against purchasing land or carrying out any sort of new construction in a protected area.[26] At least six warning notices from CDA appeared in English and Urdu daily newspapers from 1987 to 1992.[27] In 1991, the Environmental Protection Agency of Punjab issued a notice in the newspapers warning against the pollution of Rawal Lake due to ongoing construction in the area.[28] In addition to warning the general public about prohibitions on construction in Bani Gala, CDA also issued two notices, in 1989 and 1991, to the chairmen of the union councils that controlled rural areas of Islamabad. These notices informed the union councils of ongoing construction in the Islamabad Capital Territory Area that lacked CDA's approval and directed the chairmen to ensure that such illegal construction was not allowed in their jurisdiction.[29] CDA also issued notices to new homebuilders, warning them not to initiate illegal construction in Bani Gala and ordering the immediate removal of these structures.

Mrs. Nabila received one such notice from CDA's Enforcement Directorate on June 9, 1988; it directed her husband to cease construction on his house immediately. Even though the property belonged to Mrs. Nabila and she was running the project, the concerned CDA official chose to correspond with her husband, which was indicative of the gender hierarchy and segregation norms prevalent in Pakistani society. Citing clauses from official regulations, the Enforcement Directorate contended that the house was illegal since its construction had not been approved by CDA. On June 29, 1988, Mrs. Nabila drafted a reply with the help of her friend and sent it on behalf of her husband. Citing two previous court cases, from 1967 and 1986, against persons carrying out construction in areas under various union councils, the letter noted that these cases found that CDA did not have authority over construction in the

Islamabad capital region.[30] The letter argued that CDA's notice for demolition of their property was in excess of its powers since these previous cases
established that the agency had no jurisdiction in Bani Gala; the letter also
criticized CDA's Enforcement Directorate for interfering in matters that
came under the jurisdiction of the union council and not CDA. The letter
demanded the director of enforcement to withdraw his notice and issue a
statement informing them of his remedial actions. Furthermore, as a pre-
caution, the letter concluded with the following, of course construed as
the words of Mrs. Nabila's husband: "In case I do not hear from you by 03,
July 1988 I will presume that you have accepted my stand as it is in the law
and will cause no further interference in the peaceful possession and construction of my property." On July 11, 1988, Mrs. Nabila and her husband sent
another letter declaring the validity of their stance and its acceptance by the
enforcement director. Silence on the part of CDA was seen as submission to
the arguments presented by Mrs. Nabila and her husband.

This official correspondence between Mrs. Nabila's husband and the enforcement director, and the latter's subsequent silence, reveal the intentions
of both sides in creating documentary paper trails for their activities.
Mrs. Nabila used a strategy of ostensibly open communication—responding
to the enforcement director in writing, citing legal precedents, and issuing a
deadline for his response—as a way to establish the legitimacy of her building project. For his part, the enforcement director issued written notices to
the general public and homebuilders to create the impression that he was
keeping checks on illegal construction activity. In actuality, his written notices were nothing more than an empty formality, as the Directorate purposely did not create too much of an obstacle in a complicated land irregularity
involving well-to-do and well-connected people.

The use of bureaucratic devices to create an impression of legitimacy is
not unusual in informally built housing, as poor squatters in South Asia (and
beyond) are routinely involved in collecting and preserving official forms of
documentation, such as ration cards, electricity bills, and affidavits as evidence of the legitimacy of their otherwise precarious claims to space. We need
only recall the discussion in Chapter 2 of a similar tendency to balance formal and informal practices and procedures in the land and property transactions among the residents of France Colony. In these situations, the state
will often recognize the dossier of documents collected by the residents of
informal communities, since the state itself actively participates in creating
ambiguities embodied in official records, files, and other forms of paper doc-

uments.[31] As Emma Tarlo's work on slum resettlement schemes during the Indian Emergency of 1975–77 has shown, official records and documents created "paper-truths" that were meant to manipulate and soften the reality of draconian government policies.[32] Similarly, Mrs. Nabila and others were able to establish "official truths" of their own through "official" paper documents that concealed and manipulated the reality of illegal constructions in Bani Gala.[33] The point is that elite informal urbanism involving powerful actors does not only involve a bold evasion of formal planning procedures. It also necessitates an active engagement with bureaucratic devices to create a dossier of "proofs" similar to that collected by poor people living in informal settlements.

The Anti-encroachment Drive of 1992

New construction in Bani Gala went on for a few years until June 1992, when the then chairman of CDA directed the seizure of land in Bani Gala through a hasty, military-style anti-encroachment operation. In the days leading up to CDA's operation, tensions rose between the residents of Bani Gala and CDA employees. CDA started to file cases against illegal encroachments in the Civil Court in the early 1990s. The court appointed various local commissions to carry out field inspections in Bani Gala and submit reports on the ongoing illegal construction in the Bani Gala area. In their reports, local commissioners mentioned the difficulty in verifying the ownership of new constructions being raised in the area.[34] All reports noted organized noncooperation demonstrations by local villagers who refused to assist the commissioners in collecting necessary information. The reports also claimed that local villagers had decided among themselves not to receive any notices or orders from CDA or courts about land that belonged to them. One of the local commissioners reported hostility from the Bani Gala villagers as follows:

> I visited the spot twice but due to mob resistence [sic] I was unable to inspect the suit property. It would not be out of place to mention that the local people gathered in dozens and issued open threats that in case I proceeded with the inspection of the spot I shall have to face dire consequences.
>
> Due to the extraordinary resistence [sic] and interference by the local people of the area I could not inspect the suit property in compliance of the orders of this learned court in spite of my two visits.[35]

In 1992, tensions between CDA and Bani Gala residents escalated to a point where banners prohibiting the entry of CDA personnel were boldly displayed in the village.[36] A senior officer from the Enforcement Directorate remembers that locals in Bani Gala would throw stones at CDA staff during their inspection visits to the area.[37]

After years of half-hearted attempts to stop the ongoing illegal residential construction in Bani Gala, CDA staff finally launched a formal anti-encroachment campaign under the direct orders and involvement of the CDA chairman, whom Mrs. Nabila calls "Hitler" based on his ruthlessness during the operation. According to Mrs. Nabila and a senior CDA official, the cause of this sudden escalation was one of Bani Gala's elite homebuilders, an influential lady nicknamed Seemi. While the details are vague, Seemi had allegedly offended many important people, including the then CDA chairman. In retaliation against Seemi and her illegal neighborhood, the CDA chairman directed the deputy commissioner to acquire land in Bani Gala in March 1992.[38] A senior official's personal grudge rather than the rectification of a land-use irregularity ultimately provided the impetus for CDA's acquisition and anti-encroachment action in Bani Gala.

The acquisition of private land for the construction of new areas of Islamabad is normally a slow process involving years of negotiation between CDA and landowners. In the case of the Bani Gala operation, senior government officials worked with remarkable speed and efficiency in seeking approvals to urgently acquire land and demolish illegal constructions, precisely because they sought to prevent influential residents from using their power and mechanisms of cronyism to delay the land-acquisition process. At about 3:30 P.M. on Thursday, June 25, 1992, a large contingent of CDA staff and police equipped with bulldozers and armored cars formally launched a military-style anti-encroachment operation in Bani Gala. CDA officials strategically selected the day and time for carrying out the operation—after official working hours and on a weekend—in order to deny its residents the ability to seek stay orders from a court of law.[39] Getting stay orders in land-related matters is a routine practice used by alleged elite encroachers to avert anti-encroachment raids. For instance, during my fieldwork, most owners of non-conforming commercial buildings (discussed in Chapter 5) had initiated court cases against CDA and received stay orders that remained effective, often for years, during which time business went on as usual.

The news of an operation did not come as a complete surprise to Mrs. Nabila, as she had previously heard rumors that CDA had called the Punjab Police to carry out a big operation for which they were practicing in the Margalla Hills. She did not take this news seriously, though. Mrs. Nabila remembers that around the time of the operation, electricity and phone lines to their houses were disconnected as she got word that an anti-encroachment raid was under way. Mrs. Nabila and her husband knew the deputy commissioner—the same official who had signed the land-acquisition order—and contacted him for help at the time of the operation. Because of his intervention, the CDA contingent moved their operation elsewhere in Bani Gala. Mrs. Nabila's phone lines and electricity connection were restored later that day as well. Once again, private connections with senior government officials prevailed in thwarting imminent disaster and the enforcement of law.

Other residents of Bani Gala were not so fortunate in averting CDA's anti-encroachment drive and the destruction it brought that day. Many houses belonging to new residents and existing villagers were either partially or fully demolished. The operation took a violent turn when gunfire was exchanged between the police and some residents of Bani Gala. The crossfire resulted in the deaths of two villagers and a policeman and several injuries on both sides. In the evening, the villagers came to meet Mrs. Nabila in order to devise a plan to stop CDA's demolition activities. For the villagers, Mrs. Nabila thus strategically transformed from an intruder in Bani Gala to a local community leader with the ability (and connections) to save the neighborhood from destruction.

Early the next morning, on June 26, 1992, Mrs. Nabila received news that the operation staff had returned to resume demolitions in her part of the neighborhood. Electricity and phone lines went down again. The police and CDA officials showed up at her gate that evening. The time bought by their call to the deputy commissioner had apparently run out. CDA staff parked two of their bulldozers inside her residential compound. Things took a dramatic turn as Mrs. Nabila and her sister stood in front of the bulldozer. Mrs. Nabila remembers that their mother started crying at this disturbing sight. CDA staff and police threatened Mrs. Nabila, saying they were going to take over the house and, if the family didn't leave the house voluntarily, they would use tear gas to force them out. Mrs. Nabila remembers that a couple of policemen even entered her premises. At this point, her husband used one of his connections to influential people and contacted the head of Inter-Services Intelligence, Pakistan's premier intelligence service.[40] At the time of the call, the head of intelligence happened to be with the prime minister of Pakistan, Nawaz Sharif. Apparently, Mr. Sheikh's call was effective:

shortly after, Sharif ordered the CDA chairman to immediately stop the Bani Gala operation.

The contested and contradictory actions of bureaucrats and other officials described in this chapter confirm that the state is not a homogeneous entity operating according to a single, coherent set of principles.[41] While the anti-encroachment drive was carried out by CDA staff and the police on the orders of the CDA chairman, many city officials directly assisted Mrs. Nabila in the construction and legitimization of her illegal home: by signing and stamping the architectural drawings for Mrs. Nabila's house, the union council chairman helped fabricate pseudo-legal documents, which Mrs. Nabila used as evidence that her house was officially approved. One of Mrs. Nabila's friends, who was CDA chairman at the time she started building her house, informed her about past court orders that challenged CDA's authority in rural areas like Bani Gala. She included this valuable information in her written response to the warning issued by the director of enforcement of CDA. The structural engineer who drafted Mrs. Nabila's house plan, designed the structure, and supervised the construction of her house was also a CDA employee. He advised her to inform the concerned union council of her construction plans and to get "diary numbers" for all her applications and letters to CDA as proof of her correspondence with various officials.[42] The fact that a city official had been directly involved in the construction of Mrs. Nabila's house was presented in the court case (discussed next) as evidence that CDA was aware of the ongoing residential constructions in Bani Gala.[43] The deputy commissioner who ordered the forced acquisition of land in Bani Gala also ordered CDA's anti-encroachment contingent to vacate Mrs. Nabila's compound on the first day of their demolition operation. The inconsistency in official response toward informal spaces, driven by the personal interests of officials within CDA, decidedly benefited Bani Gala's illegal development.

Taking CDA to Court

CDA's anti-encroachment operation lasted for two days, and Bani Gala residents were eventually able to register their case in the court and get a stay against further demolition. While CDA staff successfully demolished several houses in Bani Gala, those of Mrs. Nabila, Dr. Khan, and several other influential people were spared. Mrs. Nabila again used her connections to get a renowned senior law advocate to take on the Bani Gala residents' case. The advocate agreed to represent them for a hefty fee toward which they all contributed.

From 1992 to 1997, a total of sixteen petitions were filed with the High Court against CDA's ban on construction activities and the subsequent anti-encroachment operation in Bani Gala.[44] The petitioners formed two groups of residents in Bani Gala: those who had owned land in the village where they had been living for generations and those who had recently purchased land from local villagers to build their houses in this suburban area. The tone of petitions against CDA within these two groups of petitioners remained consistent, even if the grounds of the plea had variations.

All petitioners challenged CDA's authority to impose restrictions on construction in Bani Gala, which they argued legally fell under the jurisdiction of the local union council. Petitions from local villagers claimed that CDA had acted unjustly in imposing a ban on all construction in Bani Gala without acquiring land in the village or having any jurisdiction over it. They pleaded that by placing an absolute prohibition on all sorts of construction in Bani Gala, CDA had rendered their property valueless, since land over which such restrictions exist could not be sold in the market at a fair price. By failing to legally acquire Bani Gala land from the villagers after the payment of fair compensation, CDA had furthermore violated the constitutional rights of the villagers. The villagers could not exercise the right to use their land for dwelling purposes—the only function for which this land could be used, given the prevailing circumstances.[45] The petitions of recent arrivals, like Mrs. Nabila and Dr. Khan, similarly highlighted CDA's high-handedness in claiming jurisdiction over an area that fell under the control of the local union council. They presented letters and submission drawings proving that they had started the construction of their houses "legally" and only after getting permission from the concerned authority: ICTA's union council.

CDA argued that houses in Bani Gala had to be demolished because construction close to Rawal Lake was polluting the main source of water for the 1.5 million residents of Rawalpindi and Islamabad. CDA officials contended that these constructions were in direct violation of the official master plan, zoning regulations, and other laws prohibiting construction in the protected zones of Islamabad. But residents of Bani Gala did not see CDA's hasty attempt to seize Bani Gala as simply a matter of environmental concern or zoning violations, since it had approved a model village and recreational and other types of development in the vicinity of Rawal Lake. The case remained in the High Court for six years, during which old and new residents of Bani

Gala organized themselves for collective action to complement their legal battle against CDA.

Unlikely Strategic Alliances

Sensational news reports with vivid photos of the Bani Gala operation circulated in Urdu and English dailies for weeks after the 1992 anti-encroachment drive incident. Newspaper articles and letters by concerned citizens variously criticized and applauded CDA's anti-encroachment operation. In order to gain public sympathy after the anti-encroachment drive, residents of Bani Gala and their supporters carried out a media campaign against CDA and its chairman. For instance, a few days after the anti-encroachment drive, a newspaper published a photo of residents of Bani Gala setting fire to a copy of the CDA Ordinance, the law that established CDA as a municipal corporate body for the planning and development of Islamabad in 1960, as a dramatic act of protest against CDA's violence in Bani Gala.

Mrs. Nabila actively participated in meetings with important government and political representatives, including Pakistan's prime minister, to make a case for protecting built residences in Bani Gala. She organized public protests with her close female friends and family members but also invited village women from Bani Gala for added effect. For public anti-CDA demonstrations, Mrs. Nabila would rent Suzuki vans to transport local village women to various venues, as she found village women to be stronger and braver than her high-society friends and easier to handle than the village men.

The demonstration of "solidarity" across class lines evidenced during these anti-CDA protests provides insights into the nature of alliances created because of extraordinary spatial concerns. From the rift between the poor residents of France Colony and their well-off neighbors in sector F-7 discussed in Chapter 2, it is obvious that such associations between different socioeconomic groups do not form as an inevitable result of their proximal living arrangements in the same neighborhood. As Mrs. Nabila indicated in her narration of events, local villagers in Bani Gala initially did not accept her intrusion into their existing community. But they did recognize her high social status and position of power, based on her exhibition of force and influence during various altercations with them. In the aftermath of the anti-encroachment drive, Mrs. Nabila and her village allies strategically used the skills and resources each side brought to the movement to save Bani Gala and for the success of their public protests. Mrs. Nabila's personal connections and monetary wealth, and the Bani Gala village residents' apparently destitute yet resilient bodies, were each important assets to help garner public sympathy and political support against CDA's anti-encroachment operation.

The transactional nature of this alliance between rich and poor residents of Bani Gala was easily recognizable. The press coverage of this demonstration was unforgiving in its portrayal of Mrs. Nabila and her elite collaborators: "Coming in [Mitsubishi] Pajeroes and Toyota Cressidas these women also brought with them a few poor women who had not even seen such cars from inside all their lives. . . . There was an impression that these poor women, who deserved every sympathy, were brought on the scene to serve others' interests."[46] Earlier newspaper coverage of a press conference held by residents of Bani Gala in a hotel in Islamabad a few days after the anti-encroachment operation similarly reported, "The 'organisers' of the press conference were seemingly those who had purchased land at the picturesque Bani Gala near the Rawal Lake and built palatial houses there. They had brought the women of those poor families from whom they had purchased lands and who had been the actual victims of the operation, to narrate the stories of police excesses."[47]

The postoperation communal "solidarity" between old and new residents of Bani Gala turned out to be short-lived. About two months after the anti-encroachment operation, residents of Bani Gala (primarily local villagers) entered into an agreement with CDA, accepting among other things monetary compensation for the acquisition of their land.[48] The agreement between CDA and residents of Bani Gala also included monetary compensation for the injured and the families of those who were killed in the crossfire during the CDA operation. The families of the deceased were additionally given plots of land in Islamabad, and CDA offered employment to one member of each bereaved family. In return for these and other concessions, CDA asked those who entered the agreement to withdraw all legal proceedings against CDA. By September 1992, 156 residents of Bani Gala had accepted this agreement.

Mrs. Nabila was unhappy about the deal between CDA and Bani Gala villagers, as she felt it sabotaged her court case. In the agreement, the area of the old village was to be left unacquired by CDA. It was also decided that those local residents living outside of the old village area would either be relocated close to the old village area or given 20-by-60-foot plots in one of

CDA's model villages.[49] Mrs. Nabila believes that CDA crafted this deal for the benefit of local villagers and intended for the new elite residents to be forced out of Bani Gala. When she received news of the agreement, she told the villagers that they should be "ashamed of [themselves]" for entering into the deal. She reminded them that it was because of people like her that their land prices had increased: "Otherwise they would have lived miserably all their lives!"

In a study of the encounter between elite fashion designers and local inhabitants of Hauz Khas village in Delhi's metropolitan area, Emma Tarlo notes that the "commercial attitude of villagers was shocking to [elite] women . . . because it did not conform to the stereotype of the timeless village peasant."[50] Similarly, Mrs. Nabila's anger toward the Bani Gala villagers was because she failed to recognize that the villagers were "just as capable of asserting their subjecthood" as elites like her.[51] Village landowners in Bani Gala recognized elite homebuilders like Mrs. Nabila as valuable assets and allies in the development of their area. But they were also aware of the exploitative and transactional nature of their relationship with the elites. Landowners who sold premium land at throwaway prices to early elite settlers like Mrs. Nabila felt slighted and cheated, so Bani Gala's landholders became more careful about making profitable transactions with future buyers and investors. The villagers were also not afraid of breaking alliances with powerful people when they were offered a better deal by other powerful people or state institutions. The development of Bani Gala as a thriving neighborhood and its legal defense in Islamabad involved both partnerships and conflicts between the local and new landowners.

Legitimized Encroachments

After an arduous six-year legal battle, a High Court judge ruled in favor of the residents of Bani Gala in 1998.[52] The judge declared that CDA's actions violated the constitutional rights of the residents of Bani Gala by depriving them of proprietary rights and placing restrictions on the use of land legally owned by them. The justice also denounced as illegal CDA's haste in the forceful occupation of private property in Bani Gala without following prescribed land-acquisition procedures. The judge observed that unless a "proper scheme" for the National Park was prepared by CDA or the Central Government, acquisition of land for this purpose under the 1960 Ordinance could not be carried out. CDA could not simply acquire land under the pretext that it was a part of the protected National Park area. More planning was necessary to acquire land for the implementation of the Doxiadis master plan.

Mrs. Nabila's written correspondence with CDA officials was cited in nearly all the petitions filed by various Bani Gala landowners against CDA and quoted in the High Court's final judgment. These documents ultimately proved in court that CDA had for years been aware of the residential constructions that had been going on in Bani Gala next to the lake but had chosen not to take any corrective measures. The judgment challenged CDA's claim to unlimited powers in acquiring any land in the region earmarked for Islamabad. But it did not prohibit CDA from acquiring land in Bani Gala in the future after preparing a scheme for public purpose and following legal procedures. The court also stipulated that CDA could only acquire land by providing a suitable alternative to the residents of Bani Gala and after paying compensation for their properties according to prevailing market rates.

Soon after the High Court's judgment in favor of the residents of Bani Gala, CDA challenged the decision in the Supreme Court of Pakistan. Mrs. Nabila remembers that "the whole village landed again" in her house to convince her to pursue the case in the Supreme Court as well. They asked their advocate once again to take on the case, and after a few hearings the case was decided in favor of the Bani Gala residents on May 14, 1999.[53] Residents and city officials of Islamabad consider that these decisions have legitimized elite residential constructions in Bani Gala, as it is practically impossible for CDA to ever acquire this neighborhood at market rates given the high investments in housing and escalating land prices in the area.

James Holston argues that the "terms through which encroachments are reliably legalized" are set by peculiar land-law systems, which in certain societies intentionally produce complication and obscurity rather than resolution in land-related conflicts.[54] In the case of Bani Gala's mansions, it was not the laws' complication and irresolution that enabled the eventual legitimization of encroachments. Elite homebuilders in Bani Gala had purchased land legally, but they were using it in a way that violated the official master plan. It was the courts that upheld the residents' rights to private property ownership over the authority of the master plan and helped legitimize an encroachment. While the courts facilitated the legitimization of this neighborhood, the basis of this legitimized encroachment was the ability of elite homebuilders to bypass and challenge CDA's monopoly as the sole developer of Islamabad.

A petition filed by a new landowner (the wife of an influential lawyer-cum-politician) in Bani Gala illustrates this point. The petition claimed that CDA's objections, such as pollution of Rawal Lake, were "contrived" to mask its vested interest in maintaining a monopoly over the development of land in Islamabad.[55] The petition elaborated that CDA's normal practice for the development of residential sectors in the planned capital involves the acquisition of land from existing villagers at nominal rates; the acquired land is then developed and sold to prospective homebuilders at exorbitant prices, often out of the reach of even the middle-income group. In the past, the petition alleged, CDA had sold land it acquired for 500 rupees per kanal for about 1 to 1.5 million rupees per kanal.[56] It is worth noting here that the sale and auctioning of residential and commercial plots in Islamabad is the main source of revenue generation for CDA. Private development of land in the unacquired areas of Islamabad, the petition contended, therefore threatened CDA's monopoly of land and its vested interest in maintaining scarcity and artificially high prices for plots in the city. Elite homebuilders in Bani Gala felt confident about their ability to bypass CDA's authority to develop an exclusive site on the master plan for their private residential use. They balanced legal and illegal practices to create a semblance of legality and stoke conflict between CDA and the courts. "Intra-elite competition" thus emerges as an essential feature of the development and legitimization of elite informal spaces like Bani Gala.[57]

While the goals of the elite homebuilders in Bani Gala were limited and self-serving, the outcomes of their actions—specifically, the introduction of residential uses in a protected nature reserve—have had long-term consequences for Islamabad's master plan and regulations. As the next chapter shows, major revisions were made to the official zoning regulations of Islamabad to accommodate residential constructions in the protected National Park area after elite residents started building lavish yet illegal mansions there. These elite encroachments were legitimized through court proceedings in glaring contradiction to Islamabad's master plan and zoning regulations. Subsequent zoning changes in the National Park were an attempt to mediate Doxiadis's master plan with elite informal constructions and recuperate a sense of comprehensive order by incorporating non-conforming spaces. Changes in Islamabad's official regulations suggest that informal spaces like the Bani Gala mansions did not simply succeed in evading official zoning laws. The elite residents were able to mobilize their personal connections and monetary resources, publicize their violations, enlist the unlikely help of less affluent neighbors, and expose the inherent ambiguity in land ownership and administrative structure to such an extent that they all but forced the hand of jurists and bureaucrats in changing the very laws that the elites had violated in the first place.

Conclusion

Today Bani Gala is largely associated with the Pakistani elite as a symbol of their excess and penchant for flouting the rule of law.[58] But over the years, Bani Gala has opened its less scenic and less desirable areas to middle-class residents who seek affordable housing. The excessive constructions of smaller houses and jerry-built apartments along the main streets and lanes in the neighborhood has been a source of annoyance for Bani Gala's wealthy elites who pioneered this neighborhood for their exclusive use. The complaint of the former prime minister of Pakistan to the chief justice about CDA's incompetence mentioned at the beginning of this chapter illustrates the way elites like him view encroachments by others.[59] The ex–prime minister was not irritated by "municipal lawlessness" per se, because it was precisely CDA's ineffective municipal oversight that allowed wealthy elites like him to build their lavish mansions in violation of the master plan. He was mainly complaining about the unchecked development of middle-class houses and apartments in his once exclusive and scenic neighborhood. To get to their safe and scenic enclaves, Bani Gala's elite must drive through narrow streets often full of potholes and garbage, streets that are lined with unsightly, congested, and haphazard constructions. But it all appears to be a small price to pay to live on expansive properties, purchased at low prices, with breathtaking views of water, mountains, and trees.

The Bani Gala example highlights the contentious nature of elite informal urbanism that resulted in serious conflicts between the elite residents and city officials. Elite homebuilders used their positions of power and their monetary resources to undermine CDA's authority in order to develop a fully functional residential area on their own. The new homebuilders of Bani Gala did not simply flout the master plan and planning laws of Islamabad; they also deliberately balanced authorized and unauthorized actions to complicate the legal status of their neighborhood. They purchased their land legally but developed it for an illegal use. While they used personal connections to acquire physical infrastructure like electricity and telephone lines for their neighborhood, they legitimized their actions by paying the required initial installation fees and making monthly payments. This performance of conformity with rules played an important role in the legitimization process of Bani Gala.

In contrast to "the quiet encroachment of the ordinary," a term Asef Bayat uses to describe the politics of extremely vulnerable urban populations, elite practices are more accurately described as "the bold encroachment of the extraordinary."[60] By balancing legal and illegal spatial practices and mobilizing their connections with friends in government and politics, the elite homebuilders in the National Park area were able to create conflicts between CDA and the courts, prove the legitimacy of their actions via legal decisions, and initiate a process that instituted major structural changes in official planning frameworks. Elite informality thus demonstrates the confidence of the urban elite to infringe on existing planning laws and their ability to develop opportunistic, "community-based" strategies to legitimize spatial violations while maintaining social hierarchies and spatial divisions. As the next chapter shows, illegal elite mansions not only represent massive violations of official zoning laws or the difficulty in their implementation; they also illustrate how these violations ended up changing the very laws that declared this type of construction illegal.

CHAPTER 5

Non-conforming Uses

F-7, full house 10, 16, 18 beds [bedrooms] main location
best for Multinationals, NGO's, Embassies, reasonable
rent.

F-6/2 Excellent Margalla view house 11 beds [bedrooms]
D/D [drawing and dining room] TVL [TV lounge] S/qtr
[servant quarter] open parking nice location best for
only office purpose demand [Rs]225000.
                    —Classified ads, *News International* (2013)

Many elite houses in Islamabad accommodate nonresidential functions. During my fieldwork, the classified sections of local newspapers routinely featured advertisements for large houses available
for rent as offices. I held my first job as a junior architect in an architecture
firm located in a section of the principal architect's house, where he lived with
his family; another part of this house-office functioned as an art gallery. I
have also had dental appointments, haircuts, and visa interviews take place
in buildings originally intended to be houses. Private schools, high-end cafés, and expensive clothing boutiques are other nonresidential functions commonly found in large houses. The elevated land values and rental prices in
Islamabad place houses well beyond the reach of most people. For property
owners, the high costs of living coupled with the high rental potential for offices or retail space make it more profitable to rent their houses for commercial functions. High-end business owners find it less expensive to rent space in
a large house than in a comparable space in a commercial market. Moreover,

managers of high-end stores claim that houses offer more privacy, exclusivity, and imagined security, all of which appeal to their customers, which include wealthy Pakistani and foreign elites. All these factors have led to the trend of using large houses along busy streets, or next to markaz markets, for nonresidential functions.

But the use of residential buildings for commercial purposes is illegal in Islamabad. Official building regulations declare a legally owned property "non-conforming" if "the use of a plot or structure thereon [does] not conform . . . to the purpose authorized or permitted under th[e] regulation or the conditions of allotment."[1] In Chapter 3, I argued that ordinary encroachments flourish when their material forms and aesthetics are perceived to be temporary. Chapter 4 highlighted the bureaucratic and social processes involved in the development and defense of elite yet illegal mansions. In this chapter, I show how architectural strategies play an important role in sustaining elite commercialized houses by helping to create an impression of conformity to officially designated uses. Most commercialized houses look like houses, even if they are completely transformed on the inside. With the help of design professionals, wealthy homeowners deliberately avoid building structures that appear commercial on the outside, a strategy used to defer legal action. City officials also help perpetuate the practice of using residential buildings for commercial functions. By issuing written warnings and notices, officials maintain an outward appearance of monitoring non-conforming uses; in reality, they have no intention of disrupting businesses involving wealthy and influential people.

The first part of this chapter discusses how city officials and influential businesspeople participate in a well-established system that sustains elite non-conforming spaces by creating an impression of adherence to the law. This system of compliance without intent is based on bureaucratic and architectural practices and an aesthetics of conformity to the official use. But legal actions over elite non-conforming spaces in Islamabad have also resulted in changes to the city's planning laws. The second part of this chapter traces the history of Islamabad's zoning laws that were shaped by court cases related to elite buildings. In particular, the chapter connects the illegal development of lavish mansions on legally owned land in the protected National Park area with major revisions in zoning laws. While elite non-conforming spaces ended up challenging and changing the very laws that had initially declared them illegal, this does not mean that these spatial irregularities go unchallenged. This chapter on the making of non-conforming spaces concludes with a discussion of their recent unmaking in the aftermath of court decisions. These instances of unmaking reveal the contingency and unpredictability of informal urbanism.

The Making of Non-conforming Spaces

According to the Islamabad building codes, houses can accommodate businesses only if they fall under the "home occupation" category. The term *home occupation* refers to the approved use of a part of a house as a place of business by its owner. Self-employed professionals like architects, planners, lawyers, dentists, and engineers are allowed to open offices in their homes as long as it does not disturb their neighbors.[2] Architecturally, home occupation is authorized if "the overall residential character of the building/apartment is not changed" and if the office does not use "more than two rooms/not more than 25% of covered area of the floor on which it is located."[3] But there are offices and institutions that exceed the maximum area permitted under the home-occupation category, and they still are officially authorized. For instance, many government institutions and those foreign embassies that have not yet transitioned to the Diplomatic Enclave (a master-planned area for foreign diplomatic missions) use the entirety of a house as office space. In addition to violating the space restrictions, these non-conforming offices often disturb the tranquility of the neighborhood; the security apparatus of government and foreign institutions situated in residential buildings encroaches on adjacent sidewalks, greenbelts, and roads, creating a considerable nuisance for their neighbors and for pedestrians and motorists in the area. Because of their association with high-level government and foreign establishments, these authorized non-conforming spaces enjoy complete immunity from legal action.

CDA officials occasionally devise policies to regulate certain non-conforming spaces. For instance, Figure 5.1 shows a private kindergarten along a main road in Islamabad. The front gate of the house has been blocked by using movable concrete barriers; a slide, monkey bars, and an umbrella have been installed in the public greenbelt outside of the boundary wall. At the time of this study over 350 private schools were operating from very large houses in some of the most expensive sectors in Islamabad.[4] To curb the growing number of private schools in residential areas, which caused traffic congestion and inconvenience for adjacent homeowners, CDA developed a policy agreement with the Private Schools Association Islamabad around 2003. A court judgment in a petition filed by the director of a private school against CDA cited this policy:[5] "No new school shall be allowed to be opened in residential Sectors and in order to accommodate only those schools which were functioning prior to December, 1999 that it was decided that such schools which were located in internal streets may be allowed to be relocated to other houses situated along Dual Carriage way which has satisfactory accommodation and subject to obtaining of N.O.C. [No Objection Certificate] from the owner and the neighbours of the locality. Even this arrangement was purely temporary in nature."[6] For eligible non-conforming schools, CDA policy identified houses next to main thoroughfares because they were more suitable for the quick dispersal of students and vehicles at pick-up and drop-off times. Moreover, CDA's concessions to non-conforming schools were imagined to be "purely temporary in nature," while in reality the permanent elimination of non-conforming spaces may never happen. By invoking the notion of temporariness and finding suitable locations for non-conforming spaces according to the master plan, this policy shares many features with the way officials routinely regulate ordinary informal spaces like kiosks, tea stalls, and hawkers' stands in the city.

For monitoring all other unauthorized non-conforming uses, officers in the agency's Building Control Directorate are responsible for keeping a check on all violations of official building codes, regulations, and bylaws. Each building-control officer is assigned supervision of one or more sectors within the city and maintains detailed lists of non-conforming uses in residential buildings along with the status of the legal actions taken against each violating person or establishment. For instance, a building-control officer in 2012 showed me his list, which indicated there were some 80 schools, 202 offices, 75 guesthouses, 48 embassies, and 63 restaurants/clinics/beauty salons operating in the residential areas of the elite F-series sectors (F-6 to F-11).

On identification of a non-conforming use, the concerned building-control officer initiates a case against the violator by serving a written notice. The violator then has a fifteen-day grace period within which to discontinue the violation. If the non-conforming use continues despite written notices and warnings, which was the norm during the early 2010s, the case is referred for trial in the court of the deputy commissioner (DC) of Islamabad. The DC issues another notice that grants the violators a further fifteen-day grace period to discontinue their activities. If the non-conforming use persists after the DC's warning, the DC can decide to send a "show cause"

Figure 5.1. A private kindergarten along a main road in sector I-8/2 in Islamabad. Note how the homeowner on the right has privatized the greenbelt outside the boundary wall using a tall hedge and metal-pipe fencing. Photograph by author.

notice to the violator, who is either fined a lump sum or a per diem amount for as long as the violation continues. Once fined, violators can seek redress in the courts, typically in the form of a stay order to prevent further prosecution from city authorities. In rare cases, allotments of the plot owned by a violator were either canceled or the violating business sealed, but usually a fine marked the extent of legal action taken by CDA officials against elite nonconforming uses.

The practice of issuing notices and imposing fines to deal with violations of zoning regulations formed a well-established system of work-arounds rather than a deterrent against non-conforming uses. For CDA, it seemed more important to maintain the appearance of monitoring and accountability than to enforce zoning laws. The mechanisms of surveillance and prosecution were well understood by individuals and organizations who successfully undermined these mechanisms without openly disregarding them—by responding to notices, paying fines and bribes, getting stay orders, and fighting court cases. When I asked managers of non-conforming businesses how they dealt with CDA's notices, I received vague and sheepish responses that implied the use of political influence and bribes, such as: "We resolve chotay motay massallay" (small, trivial problems) with CDA staff "amicably." Confident in their ability to carry on their non-conforming businesses without any interference, elite business owners made daring investments in either adapting existing houses for commercial functions or building brand-new commercial spaces to replace existing houses.

An examination of the material conversion of large houses into commercial spaces reveals that architectural design has played an important role in sustaining elite non-conforming spaces by concealing their commercial intent. During my fieldwork, existing houses were refurbished as commercial and institutional spaces without losing their external identities as houses. A simple conversion involves a home-workplace combination in which the owner or renter of a house lives in one part and works in the other. This arrangement falls under the "home occupation" category described above and is considered legal as long as the business does not create a nuisance or exceed the permitted space for nonresidential use. When I conducted my research in the early 2010s, most architectural firms and beauty salons in Islamabad were located in the residences of the principal architect or salon stylist. But these firms and salons often did not respect space restrictions set for businesses in the "home occupation" category. The business owners claimed that CDA did not bother them as long as the house's exterior gave no indication of the commercial set-up within. In most cases, architects or stylists lived and worked in the same house, and the work areas were separated from the living areas by using independent entrances or closing off the residential parts with doors and screens.

The changes needed to outfit residential buildings for service-oriented businesses, such as dental clinics, offices, or schools, are relatively simple in comparison with those necessary for sales-oriented businesses, such as furniture showrooms and restaurants. Changes to service-oriented businesses are mostly cosmetic, such as placing signboards on the front façade; replacing existing windows with large, unobstructed display windows; and lowering or puncturing exterior boundary walls to improve curb visibility (Figure 5.2). Accommodating sales-oriented businesses in houses requires more serious interventions to existing structures to create open interior spaces for displaying merchandise. Existing houses are retrofitted through moderate structural changes, such as opening the interior space by taking down non-load-bearing walls between different rooms, upgrading all interior surfaces (walls, flooring, ceilings) and lighting, and performing the usual façade treatment for commercialized houses, which includes creating large windows for the display of merchandise and low and punctured boundary walls.

At the time of my research, large houses were particularly popular choices as venues for home-furnishing stores because they offered a domestic architectural setting for the display of furniture and other home decor items. Figures 5.3, 5.4, and 5.5 show the before and after images of a house that has been converted into a furniture showroom, across the street from the F-7 markaz market. The renovation was carried out from 2011 to 2012 at a total cost of about 10 million rupees (then $100,000). The interior and exterior structural changes needed to transform an existing residence into an open-concept showroom added to the high cost of this project. Moreover, because the renovation was intended for a high-end business, expensive and imported finishing materials were used for the interior transformation of this house, which involved removing doors and en suite bathrooms, widening openings, and taking out non-load-bearing walls, thus creating more openness and connectivity while improving the flow of movement. On the outside, the renovation included a major uplift of the front façade to give it a clean, contemporary look. Without altering the overall structure or building footprint, the business owner effectively changed this residential house into a commercial building.

Figure 5.2. Exterior view of a house used as a home-furnishing store. Photograph by author.

While most business owners accommodated non-conforming uses by retrofitting existing houses, the early 2010s saw a growing trend of customized commercial spaces built to replace existing houses. Many landowners in Islamabad started building large houses, using the maximum covered area permitted under existing building codes to create more rentable space.[7] The commercial intent of these houses was evident in their interior layout. Instead of containing rooms for various living functions, the interior spaces of these new commercial houses were characterized by open floor plans and large, doorless halls indicative of a retail environment. On the outside, these houses presented boxy masses with large, fixed windows meant for the display of merchandise. But these converted houses still retained their overall

1

2

3

Figure 5.3a.
Commercialization of an
existing house in sector F-7:
exterior view showing
transformation of the façade.
Photos by architect Faisal
Arshad.

Figure 5.3b. Commercialization of an existing house in sector F-7: interior view.
Photo by architect Faisal Arshad.

residential aesthetic by maintaining compulsory setbacks, boundary walls, gates, driveways, car porches, and front lawns. In contrast to ordinary informal spaces that are sustained because of their imagined temporariness (see Chapter 3), elite informal commercial spaces are designed to maintain the appearance of being highly "planned." Taking a cue from the "home-occupation" regulation, which requires that the "overall residential character of the building" must be maintained, elite businesspeople, aided by design professionals, deliberately preserve the outward appearance of residential architectural forms of their stores, cafés, boutiques, and salons to maintain an impression of conformity to the law.[8]

Since CDA's approval is required for all sorts of construction projects, from minor structural alterations and renovations to major reconstruction projects, hiding the commercial intent of residential spaces is an important step during the approval process for non-conforming buildings. For both renovation and new commercial-use home projects, project architects prepare two sets of drawings: one for the client's approval, which shows the actual intended commercial use of the building, and the other for CDA's approval. The drawings prepared for CDA camouflage the actual purpose of the building by mislabeling large interior open halls as living rooms, dining rooms, and bedrooms. In the words of a leading architect with experience in designing commercial buildings on residential plots, the practice is akin to *fileon k pet bharna* (filling the belly of files). Builders of non-conforming spaces, architects, and CDA officials all participate in the charade to fulfill a bureaucratic requirement, a practice popularly referred to as *kaghazi kar rawai* (literally "papery proceeding," meaning a proceeding with a lot of inconsequential paperwork and red tape).

Architects working in Islamabad have mixed views about this practice of evading building regulations. While most are aware of the ethical issues associated with aiding clients who intend to defy building codes, they present different rationales for the need to open residential areas to commercial uses. Some architects take a pragmatic approach and consider it unwise to turn away paying clients, while others prefer not to get involved in the approval process and leave the clients to their own devices to get official approval. Still others believe that uncontrolled rents in Islamabad, coupled with high land prices and construction costs, have necessitated the repurposing of residential areas for commercial use to lower rental costs relative to master-planned markets and to maximize returns on investments. Irrespective of their political position, architects retrofit existing houses or build new ones for high-end commercial uses while being sure to maintain the impression of conformity to the officially designated use.

While some influential homeowners employ architectural and bureaucratic strategies to sustain commercial uses in residential zones, other elites circumvent the intentions of Islamabad's master plan in the opposite direction, by building lavish villas and mansions on properties zoned for nonresidential purposes. Notably, some of these elite non-conforming villas built on farmland as ostensible "farmhouses" introduced major structural changes to Islamabad's master plan and regulations. Owners of extravagant yet illegal farmhouses were able to legitimize their constructions through favorable

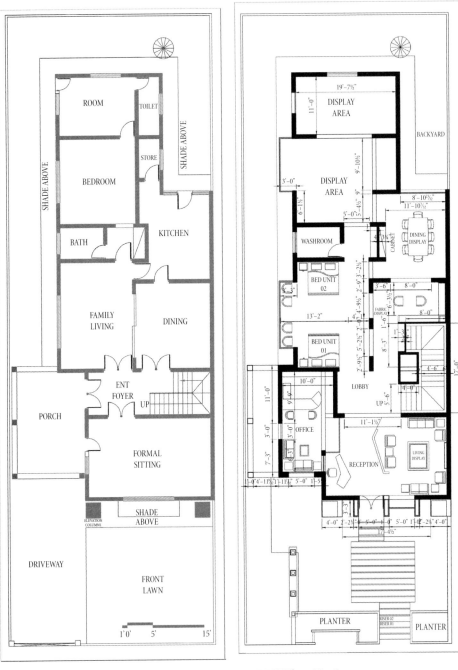

FIRST Floor- Original Layout   FIRST Floor- New Layout

Figure 5.4. Commercialization of an existing house in sector F-7: before and after first-floor plans. Drawings by architect Faisal Arshad.

Second Floor - Original Layout

Second Floor - New Layout

Figure 5.5. Commercialization of an existing house in sector F-7: before and after second-floor plans. Drawings by architect Faisal Arshad.

court orders that upheld the private-property rights of elite homebuilders over the master plan and municipal planning regulations. The legitimization of farmhouses reveals how non-conforming spaces do not only exist in disguise but can occasionally challenge and change the very laws that declare them illegal. In this process of certain elite non-conforming spaces becoming the rule, the courts emerge as an important force that shapes the planning and development of Islamabad.

Remaking Regulations

A few years before the elite homebuilders started purchasing land directly from local villagers in Bani Gala (discussed in Chapter 4), CDA started designating large plots of land in the National Park area as "agro-farms." These agro-farms were initially offered as compensation to existing villagers who had lost their cultivable land owing to construction projects. CDA imagined that the agro-farms would contribute toward the local production of fruits and vegetables. But these ostensible farms quickly became sites of elite non-conforming uses. Wealthy and influential people began purchasing agro-farms, either from people to whom CDA had allotted farmland or from CDA directly. Instead of farming, they used the farmland to build their "farmhouses."

The term *farmhouse* is deceptive because it implies a modest house built on land where a farmer lives and works. In many South Asian countries, farmhouses represent a new kind of periurban housing financially accessible only to the super elite: extravagant villas on large estates with gardens and orchards, all within a short driving distance from the main city. Islamabad's farmhouses are particularly desirable because they are located both in the National Park area and within city limits. Built on acres of farmland, these palatial, non-conforming farmhouses are home to influential residents like politicians, lawyers, civil servants, and senior military officials, including the former military dictator and president of Pakistan, General Pervez Musharraf. Additionally, some farmhouses are used as rental spaces to host concerts, weddings, and other exclusive events.

While the builders of the elite Bani Gala mansions and farmhouses were mainly interested in developing large estates within city limits, their building practices in a protected nature reserve have had serious consequences for Islamabad's master plan and zoning regulations. This is particularly true of the National Park area; ironically, this area is represented on the master plan displayed on CDA's website and on the walls of CDA planning offices in a solid green color. The green color on the master plan drawing misleadingly implies a large, protected parkland, free from built-up areas, as imagined in the 1960s Doxiadis master plan. In reality, the National Park is no longer a protected area; it is now home to many elite and middle-class residential schemes built by private developers and CDA itself in the form of sprawling gated communities, in urban patterns that are very different from Doxiadis's rectilinear sectors. The evolution of Islamabad's zoning laws, which have transformed the National Park from a protected parkland into a thriving residential area, can be directly linked to the elite illegal residential constructions that began in the region in the 1980s and 1990s.

The first zoning regulation of Islamabad was passed in 1992, a few months after CDA carried out its anti-encroachment operation in Bani Gala and the Bani Gala residents filed a court case against CDA's demolition activities (see Chapter 4). The 1992 zoning regulation subdivided Islamabad into five zones based on areas where urban development is either authorized or prohibited (Figure 5.6). Zones I and II correspond to the "Islamabad Proper" area in the Doxiadis master plan, where development takes the form of a grid of identically sized "sectors." Zone III is designated as a protected nature retreat that encompasses the Margalla Hills on the northwestern edge of the city and parts of the National Park area, including Rawal Lake.[9] Zone IV includes the rest of the National Park area, where only limited institutional and recreational development is authorized. Finally, Zone V is located to the south of Zone IV, on the southern edge of the city of Rawalpindi; the land in Zone V initially was not a part of the Doxiadis master plan.[10] Zone V allows large-scale residential schemes in the configuration of elite gated communities.

The 1992 zoning regulation preserved the overall organization of the Doxiadis master plan, except for Zone V, which was a new addition to Islamabad's territory and where development did not follow Doxiadis's grid of identical sectors. But in the early 2000s, major revisions were introduced into the official zoning regulations that appeared to benefit the development of elite non-conforming mansions in the supposedly protected Zone IV.

Consider a 2005 government order that introduced new laws for Zone IV's "unacquired areas." Unacquired areas are those areas that belong to local rural communities and that had not yet been purchased by CDA; according to the law at the time, no new construction was allowed in the unacquired areas in the National Park (Zones III and IV). This 2005 order gave private landowners

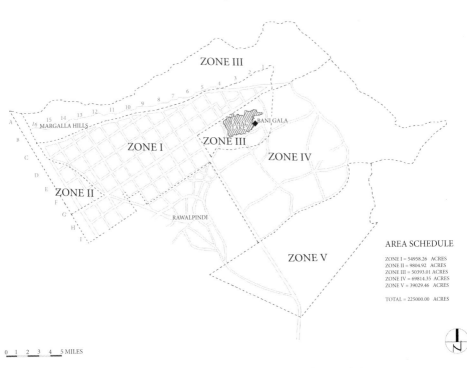

Figure 5.6. Zones of Islamabad according to the Islamabad Capital Territory Regulation of 1992.

access to the unacquired areas, allowing them to develop agro-farms or orchards (with permission from CDA) on at least 20 kanals (2.5 acres) of land. On each farm or orchard, the order authorized the building of a farmhouse with a maximum area of 2,250 square feet. Moreover, these farms could be either developed individually or as part of a scheme made up of at least 50 acres, which was less than the 100 acres minimum previously required for farming schemes in the National Park. These revisions made it legal to build larger farmhouses on relatively smaller plots in a zone that had previously been protected from all new construction.

A 2007 case initiated by a Supreme Court judge led to more comprehensive changes to land-use policy in Zone IV (National Park).[11] The case was spurred on by various news reports on the increase in prices of basic food items "due to the loose administration and week [sic] policy of the government regarding price control."[12] Broadly speaking, the case proceedings followed two main lines of inquiry: first, the presiding judge demanded reports from all provincial governments on the ongoing price inflation of food items in Pakistan; and second, he focused on the role of the agro-farming scheme in Islamabad in promoting the local supply of fresh fruits and vegetables. This second line of inquiry—into the agro-farming scheme—resulted in a legal decision that changed the designation of parts of Zone IV, removing them from the "protected parkland" category.

Noting the trend of non-conforming farmhouses in agro-farms, the Supreme Court judge first issued the following directive to CDA: "Take necessary steps with regard to Farm Houses [in existing agro-farms], inspect them and in case any Farm House is not producing vegetables/fruit etc., cancel its lease according to law and submit report."[13] But over the course of the case proceedings, the court shifted the blame for the misuse of agro-farms to CDA and its ineffectiveness. The final court ruling, for instance, identified CDA's failure to provide water for irrigation as one of the reasons for the construction of luxury "farmhouses":[14] "The use of the land leased out for Farming under Agro Farming Scheme for other purposes is due to the ineffective policy of CDA and lack of proper administration. It appears that due to the neglect of CDA to provide the basic facilities including source of irrigation water to develop the Farming Scheme, the lease holders instead of concentrating on Farming, preferred to built [sic] only a Farm-house for their residence without proper utilization of leased land."[15]

The court directed CDA to provide proper facilities to the leaseholders rather than send them lease-cancellation notices. The judgment took an even harsher turn for CDA when it came to those agro-farms that were developed on private, unacquired land in Zone IV. The judge noted that in the absence of proper facilities for irrigation, electricity, and agricultural loans for landowners in Zone IV, the regulation allowing only agricultural land use in the unacquired areas had placed extreme hardships on private-property owners. The final judgment criticized the unachievable requirements for agro-farms in zoning regulations particularly for owners of small plots (less than 2.5 acres), who were ineligible to participate in the agro-farming scheme yet were forbidden by the regulations from using their land for any purpose other than farming. This situation, according to the court, led such owners to engage in haphazard and illegal development in Zone IV. The court shifted blame from property owners to CDA, viewing its ineffective management of land and distribution of services as the main cause of encroachment in the protected Zone IV.

The judgment thus declared the existing bylaws for Zone IV "unjust, un-reasonableness [sic], . . . discriminatory" and consequently without legal force.[16] The judgment concluded by issuing detailed instructions to CDA for a major revision to the laws for Zone IV, which included a decrease in the minimum-area requirement for agro-farms in the privately owned, unac-quired areas. Notably, the Supreme Court judge ordered that privately owned land in Zone IV be opened up for residential and commercial building just "like other areas and zones of Islamabad." The judge thereby fundamentally changed the character of the National Park area as envisioned in the Doxi-adis master plan.[17]

The Cabinet of the Government of Pakistan in April 2010 approved an amendment to the zoning regulations, based on the Supreme Court's ruling. The 2010 amendment subdivided Zone IV into four subzones to accommo-date both existing and new land uses (Figure 5.7).[18] In addition to agro-farming, institutional buildings, and recreational facilities, residential uses are now authorized in three of the four subzones. The amendment also makes it easier to build larger farmhouses on much smaller plots: the minimum area of the agro-farm has been reduced from 20 kanals (2.5 acres) to 4 kanals (0.5 acres) in one of the subzones, and the maximum covered area for farmhouses has been increased from 2,250 square feet to 9,000 square feet (excluding basement area). Residential uses include both individual houses and multi-unit housing schemes, which are mostly built in the form of gated commu-nities, as opposed to Doxiadis's identical sectors. The 2010 amendment also includes provision for the regularization of previously illegal commercial and residential constructions after a payment of fees to CDA. No longer a protected zone, the National Park area is instead a site for new urban development, particularly housing schemes generated by CDA and private developers.

Since the 2010 zoning amendment, private developers have successfully launched several residential schemes in the former National Park area. As Figure 5.8 shows, the development of farmland into residential plots is nearly complete in most places. This accelerated pace of residential development has been facilitated by informal processes and practices, as many housing sub-divisions have been created without CDA's approval.

CDA's response to the violating developments has been predictable: it has diligently prepared a list of unauthorized housing schemes, and this list is regularly updated on its official website.[19] It is no surprise that the former Na-tional Park area (Zone IV) currently has the longest list of unauthorized residential projects (over eighty) in the city. Most of these illegal residential

ZONE IV

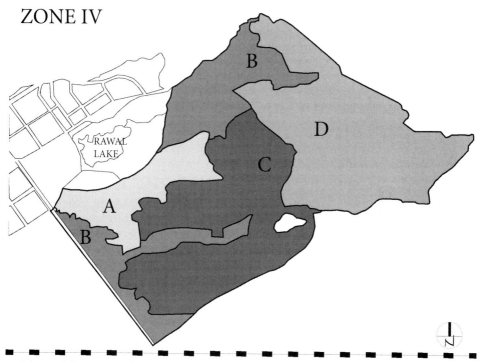

Subzone A (12,188 Acres) =   Orchard, Agro Farming (20 kanal per farm), Institutions, Model Villages

Subzone B (14,409 Acres) =   Mixed land uses, Residential and Commercial Buildings, Residential and Commercial Schemes in unutilized patches of land

Subzone C (19,811 Acres) =   Agro farms, Agro Farming Schemes (4 kanal per farm), Govt. Housing Schemes, Existing Model Villages

Subzone D (23,618 Acres) =   Reserved Forests, Sport and Recreation and I. T. Parks

Figure 5.7. Subzoning plan for Zone IV, Islamabad, according to the 2010 amendment. Source: Capital Development Authority, Urban Planning Directorate, Planning and Design Wing, Islamabad.

schemes in Zone IV are concentrated in subzones B and C, the areas where residential construction is authorized according to the amendment (see Figure 5.7). The housing area shown in Figure 5.8 is part of a highly successful yet unauthorized middle-class housing scheme in subzone B. Despite its illegal status, buyers continue to invest in properties here and in other illegal schemes

Figure 5.8. Google Earth images (from 2009 and 2021) show the transformation of a part of the National Park area from an agricultural farmland into a modern residential community.

in the area. Official zoning regulations for subzones B and C, which were modified by elite non-conforming residential constructions, now guide the development of new unauthorized residential schemes in the former National Park area. The interplay between regulations and encroachments is an ongoing feature of development in this area.

Court decisions on elite non-conforming constructions in the National Park area have legitimized subsequent zoning changes, in a glaring contradiction to the Doxiadis master plan. This trend of judicial interventions into urban policy is not exclusive to Islamabad. Scholars of twenty-first-century Delhi have highlighted the major role courts have played in the spatial restructuring of the city, especially by ordering mass evictions of ordinary informal settlements while allowing spatial violations by elites.[20] Gautam Bhan uses the term "judicial urbanism" to refer to a mode of contemporary urbanization based on a set of rationalities, technologies, and subjectivities that are shaped by judicial intervention.[21] The Islamabad court cases I consider here similarly reveal the considerable role of the judiciary in the city's planning and administration. These cases also highlight the judicial mechanisms that mediate between an official planning framework and elite informal constructions and how courts evaluate and treat elite informal spaces differently from those built by poor people.

The legal proceedings discussed in this chapter mostly recognize the rights of people who legally own property but use it for illegal purposes. In Chapter 4, I discussed the 1998 High Court decision on Bani Gala that declared CDA's anti-encroachment actions to be in violation of the constitutional rights of Bani Gala's residents. The 2007 Supreme Court ruling on Zone IV similarly declared Islamabad's official zoning regulations to be "unjust" toward owners of smaller parcels of unacquired land, since the regulations prohibited landowners from any kind of construction on their property. The only function for which the landowners could use their land was farming, but the regulations prohibited any agro-farms smaller than 20 kanals. The 1998 and 2007 court rulings on elite residential construction in the National Park area thus highlight the tension between planning rules and regulations on the one hand and the rights of property owners on the other. Private-property owners' rights are limited in highly regulated cities, as official planning rules control nearly every aspect of the building-use and construction processes. Yet the 1998 and 2007 court decisions not only upheld the proprietary rights of landowners in the National Park area but also created a legal basis for major changes in official regulations. In the case of elite non-conforming spaces, breaking the law created the conditions for its remaking.

Legal philosopher Lon L. Fuller asserts that the reality of law can be found in the mediation between law in words and law in action.[22] The role played by the courts in this mediation is critical as "the law cannot enforce itself. Some human agency must be charged with that responsibility."[23] In the case of Islamabad, the application of law does not necessarily involve its application by law-enforcement agencies like CDA. Because CDA is often involved in institutionalizing spatial irregularities, the mediation of the courts has resulted in both the enforcement and renunciation of the official planning framework. Exceeding their supervisory role, the judges encroached on the roles of the legislature and administration because they view bureaucratic and law-enforcement institutions to be incompetent and corrupt. But the leniency toward elite non-conforming spaces in the National Park court cases was also an instance of official mechanisms privileging people with extreme power and wealth by condoning their illegal actions. On the one hand, the judges blamed CDA as an ineffective and corrupt institution incapable of implementing the master plan. But on the other hand, the judges' decisions provided the legal mechanism of challenging official planning regulations to accommodate development patterns introduced by elite encroachers.

If this bureaucratic and legal support for elite non-conforming spaces functioned as a form of preferential treatment of the wealthy, it eventually met with resistance. While elite and ordinary informal spaces were thriving in Islamabad at the time I conducted this study, as I discuss in the final section of this chapter, the situation changed considerably a few years after. The same legal mechanisms that had once legitimized non-conforming spaces then provided the basis for curbing the "mess of non-conforming uses" in the planned capital city.[24]

The Unmaking of Non-conforming Uses

In 2001, well-to-do owners of several guest houses in Islamabad took CDA to the High Court for denying them their constitutional right to engage in lawful trade.[25] This case had been filed as part of a standard procedure at the time, which involved owners of non-conforming uses getting a court stay order against CDA's legal notices and actions. Because the purpose of going to the court was to delay legal action against elite non-conforming spaces, the case made no progress during its first thirteen years. From 2001 to 2014, there were a total of twenty-seven case hearings, which repeatedly mentioned the unavailability of the "learned counsel for the petitioners," followed by a request for adjournment and relisting of the hearing. Because CDA officials were also involved in under-the-table negotiations with owners of elite non-conforming uses in Islamabad, they showed little interest in driving the case toward a meaningful resolution.

But the case took a drastic turn in 2014 with the appointment of a new High Court judge, Shaukat Aziz Siddiqui. Justice Siddiqui heard the case for a few months in late 2014 and reached a final verdict against the petitioners by January 2015. He noted that the "mess of non-conforming use has disrupted civic fiber of the City, (and) manipulated master plan of the capital." While being skeptical of CDA officials' ability to enforce regulations to maintain the integrity of Islamabad as a "state of the art" city, Siddiqui declared non-conforming uses illegal and ordered CDA to take necessary actions to "bring the residential areas into original conditions" within a three-month period.

This was the second time that CDA officials had come under fire from this judge. At the time, Justice Siddiqui was also presiding over another court case filed by a resident of a katchi abadi in Islamabad. At the beginning of 2014, Amin Khan, resident of a katchi abadi in sector G-11, approached the High Court of Islamabad with a personal grievance.[26] Khan claimed in his petition that his basic citizenship rights were being violated by the National Database and Registration Authority (NADRA), which refused to issue him a Computerized National Identity Card because, as a Pashtun resident of a katchi abadi, he did not fulfill the official domicile requirement in Islamabad by providing a property title, lease document, or local domicile certificate.[27]

A court case filed by the resident of an informal settlement for the issuance of a government identification card quickly turned into an inquiry into the very existence of katchi abadis in Islamabad. In the first hearing, Justice Siddiqui summoned high-ranking government officials to explain "under which authority of law different Ka[t]chi Abadis have been allowed to emerge in different parts of ICT."[28] Subsequent proceedings similarly focused on the problem of removing informal settlements from Islamabad rather than on the right of a katchi abadi resident to a computerized national identity card. By questioning how someone like Amin Khan was even able to reside in a place like a katchi abadi in Islamabad, Justice Siddiqui dismissed Amin Khan's right to a national identity card. Moreover, the judge ordered the eviction of all katchi abadis in the city. This order resulted in the brutal, needless eviction of two large squatter settlements, but further evictions were halted after Islamabad's katchi abadi residents and their allies appealed to the Supreme Court against Siddiqui's mass eviction order.[29]

In contrast to the 1998 and 2007 court decisions that upheld the proprietary rights of landowners in the National Park area, the 2014 and 2015 High Court decisions on non-conforming uses and katchi abadis were cases where a judge restored the master plan of Islamabad and its status as a "state of the art city" by removing encroachments created by both elites and nonelites. The wide-scale anti-encroachment drive resulting from the 2015 court orders included the demolition of roadside cafés and tea stalls and the closure of high-end retail stores, salons, clothing boutiques, gyms, home-furnishing stores, and many other elite services operating out of commercialized residences. Most high-end businesses have now relocated from residential to various commercial markets, while many new houses that had been built exclusively for high-end retail purposes stand empty and abandoned (Figure 5.9).

Over the last six years, I have monitored the status of both elite and ordinary informal spaces of commerce that were respectively sealed and demolished in various anti-encroachment drives in the city. While non-conforming businesses in elite residential areas have taken a major hit, things go on as usual for many ordinary informal commercial spaces. In one case, for instance, I observed how the owner of a once-thriving roadside tea stall resumed his operation after CDA's drive. During my fieldwork in 2011, a tea stall thrived in a greenbelt next to a bus stop and road intersection across from the G-9 markaz market (Karachi Company). As shown in Figure 5.10, this tea stall began as a brick-and-steel structure with a tree-shaded eating area. When I visited the site in 2018, the tea stall had been demolished, but the owner was still carrying out his business in the half-demolished structure. As the gas meter located in the middle of Figure 5.11 shows, the tea-stall owner was able to secure a gas connection to continue his tea and food business despite the demolition of his structure. This arrangement went on until 2019, when the tea-stall owner was able to build a new kiosk in the same greenbelt a few feet from the original, demolished structure (Figure 5.12).

In various ways, roadside businesses in Islamabad have shown their extraordinary ability to adapt, improvise, and recover after being demolished. In all likelihood, the tea-stall owner was able to rebuild and resume his business after arriving at an amicable arrangement with the relevant CDA staff. But his strategy of continuing business in a half-demolished structure for

Figure 5.9. High-end retail stores in residential buildings that were closed after the 2015 court decision. Photographs by author.

Figure 5.10. Roadside tea stall thriving in sector G-9 in 2011. Photograph by author.

Figure 5.11. Roadside tea stall in sector G-9 in business in a half-demolished structure in 2018. Note the gas meter (for making tea and food) in the middle of the photo. Photograph by author.

Figure 5.12. Newly rebuilt roadside tea stall using brick masonry walls and steel roofing near the original location in sector G-9 in 2019. Photograph by author.

about a year before rebuilding on the same site confirms the importance of maintaining an aesthetic of temporariness in defending an earlier informal claim to space. The material form of the half-demolished structure played an important role in signaling the temporary status of this tea stall and prevented unwanted attention from its critics. In contrast, the high-quality and permanent architecture of elite informal businesses remain materially intact but are more vulnerable to long-term closures after the 2015 court decision. In elite sectors of F-6 and F-7, many large houses that were previously being used for commercial purposes have been sitting vacant since their businesses were sealed in 2015. This strategy of leaving property in prime areas unused could be explained by the owners' capacity to wait it out until more favorable conditions are created for non-conforming businesses to continue as before. Of course, this strategy is only feasible for the wealthy elites who are well-equipped to sustain financial setbacks caused by the sealing of their businesses. Even in the unmaking of encroachments, architectural forms and aesthetics determine whether a business can bounce back after it has been sealed or demolished: temporary, ordinary, and flexible architecture rather than its elite permanent counterpart shows higher resiliency and adaptability to anti-encroachment drives.

Conclusion

Elite non-conforming spaces represent massive violations of official zoning and building laws, and highlight the practical difficulties CDA has faced in implementing Islamabad's master plan and regulations. They are a kind of spatial irregularity based on the unauthorized use of legally owned properties. Wealthy businesspeople make substantial monetary investments and take a calculated risk in developing non-conforming properties because they recognize that under favorable conditions, the payoffs may be substantial. They try to mitigate the risk with the use of their money, power, and influence. With the help of architects and other design professionals, elite businesspeople create buildings that appear to conform to official regulations from the outside but that in actuality are used for unauthorized functions. But participating in the system of compliance without intent through architecture design does not make non-conforming activities invisible to the state. Building-control inspectors and other CDA officials are well aware of the ongoing commercial activities in residential areas, and they participate in creating an impression of compliance to rules by sending out notices while carrying out under-the-table negotiations with the owners of illegal businesses.

Building non-conforming spaces is more than an evasion of the law; it can lead to substantial changes in the laws that declare non-conforming spaces illegal. The transformation of the National Park area from a protected nature reserve into a thriving middle-class and elite residential community illustrates this phenomenon well. The master plan adapted to these changes retroactively because the city's layout had already been changed by non-conforming spaces. The instantiation of Islamabad's planning laws takes place in the complex, ongoing processes through which the citizens, judiciary, and CDA mediate between laws as written on paper and laws as realized (and challenged) through human actions. This chapter showed how conflicts among actors within the judicial and administrative institutions have facilitated the making of encroachments in Islamabad. On the contrary, the unmaking of elite non-conforming spaces in the aftermath of the 2014 and 2015 court decisions revealed that the courts can also demand the restoration of aspects of the master plan via the removal of both ordinary and elite encroachments.

The making and unmaking of elite and ordinary informality represent more than a story of the boom-and-bust cycles of encroachments in Islamabad. They confirm that the uncertainty and the contingency of both master plans and encroachments are integral features of contemporary city-making. What causes encroachments to emerge and fade in places like Islamabad are shifts in governmental attitudes toward violations. Master planning in such contexts is not about controlling and eliminating uncertainty about future urban developments; it is about setting in motion practices that are unanticipated and non-conforming but are in fact essential to how planning works. Because of the reconciliation between plans and violations, uncertainty and contingency emerge as important elements of the planning process.

Conclusion

Contingent Plans

Last year I started the challenging process of searching for a home in Los Angeles, the city where I live and work and where the median home price is about one million dollars. Los Angeles is a city of extreme inequalities: it is home to some of the world's wealthiest people who live in over-the-top, unnecessarily large "McMansions" and mega mansions, but it is also where thousands of unhoused men, women, and children sleep in their cars or on sidewalks under blankets and tents. My search of single-family houses in Los Angeles on online real-estate sites like Zillow and Redfin generated many listings that referred to "unpermitted" additions like bedrooms and bathrooms or garage conversions. Visits to some of these listings revealed that unpermitted work is mostly sited in backyards, which makes it difficult to spot from the street. Similarly, unpermitted conversions of garages into granny flats or rental units are carried out without removing garage doors from the exterior wall, even if they have been blocked with drywall on the inside.[1] These deliberate architectural decisions are meant to maintain the exterior appearance of a house or garage in accordance with zoning laws in order to avoid unwanted attention from building inspectors. Houses with unpermitted constructions are sold through complex legal systems that include licensed real-estate agents, building inspectors, appraisers, and lenders. While transacting the sale of houses with unpermitted constructions is completely legal, there are companies that offer services to help homeowners obtain retroactive building permits for their unpermitted work. From Los Angeles's low-income region of South Central to the elite neighborhoods of Bel Air and Pacific Palisades, an entire system of legal and illegal building practices legitimizes different kinds of unpermitted residential construction and their transactions by strategically using architectural forms and bureaucratic procedures.[2]

I bring up my recent experiences of Los Angeles to argue that most of the processes and practices I describe in the main chapters of this book are not unique to Islamabad. The numerous examples of informal spaces in the Southern California city, from elite mansions to unlicensed sidewalk vendors' stalls, refute the idea that informal construction only thrives in supposedly dysfunctional, "developing" countries where rules are not obeyed. The interplay between official regulations and violations is common in urban settings around the world, where low-, middle- and upper-income people engage with official plans and regulations to build constructions to meet their particular needs under changing economic and political conditions. *Master Plans and Encroachments* shows the pervasiveness of this relationship in one city, but a consideration of land development and property exchange in cities like Los Angeles reveals that regulations and violations—facilitated by architectural forms and bureaucratic procedures—frequently work in mutually constituted relationships.

New cities like Islamabad are based on the myth that comprehensive modernist planning can address and eliminate all existing and future urban challenges related to poverty, congestion, and dilapidated infrastructure, to name only a few. But this imagined view of centralized master planning fails to acknowledge the role of contingency—of both the master plan and its violations—in actual city-making. One of my primary goals in this book has been to argue that factors that contribute to this contingency in urban development are not based on random actions of various individuals and institutions but often involve their careful consideration and understanding of both formal and informal systems. I have taken pains to show that many of these unanticipated spaces are not divorced from planning frameworks or the everyday functioning of a city. The residents and businesspeople of Islamabad regularly, and with some form of official permission, create spaces in violation of the master plan. Moreover, CDA functionaries are often responsible for devising revocable bureaucratic mechanisms that allow certain spatial irregularities to continue for long periods. But conflicts between state actors and institutions as well as local politics may contribute to the withdrawal of the same allowances on short notice. In such situations, city officials violate the terms of their own rules concerning encroachments; in effect, they make city planning both contingent and contentious.

Consider one final example of the bureaucratized trend of authorizing elite homeowners to encroach on adjacent open public areas and greenbelts in Islamabad. At the time of my fieldwork, CDA issued NOCs to allow those (mostly influential) residents who showed interest in adopting larger open areas in existing sectors near their houses for "beautification purposes."[3] The "beautification" process in Islamabad involved the transformation of open spaces in residential areas from their natural state into lawn-like expanses by leveling or clearing the site and planting grass, flowers, and trees. In some cases, residents "beautified" public open spaces, often larger than the lawns within their boundary walls, not for the benefit of the general public but for their personal enjoyment, even going so far as to enclose the spaces within fences and walls.[4]

In 2014, a High Court judge ordered the removal of all such encroachments from Islamabad. In one instance, CDA's enforcement squad removed vegetation and structures in a public area that Mr. Ijaz Chaudhary, a wealthy politician, had "beautified" next to his house. The politician owned a house on a cul-de-sac in the elite sector of F-7. According to news reports, he not only had fenced in the open public space next to his house but had also built a barrier, a guardroom, and an aviary, and installed benches and children's play equipment. Chaudhary maintained that he had not done anything illegal: "I have permission since 2003 to develop and beautify some 10 kanals [1.25 acres] of land lying vacant adjacent to my house, they [CDA] should at least have given me a formal notice . . . before rampaging."[5] This example illustrates how permissions and violations often go hand in hand; written permission from CDA did not limit Chaudhary's ambitions to beautify and privatize the open public space. Written permissions give an impression of legality, but in practice what people do with those permissions may be in violation of the terms of the permission.

After the court instructed CDA to demolish all encroachments in Islamabad, CDA canceled the NOC it had issued to Chaudhary on the grounds that he had violated its terms and conditions by privatizing the beautified area and blocking a public thoroughfare. A newspaper reported that CDA carried out the anti-encroachment raid under the pretext of a complaint filed by some residents of France Colony who claimed that the politician was "encroaching into the *katchi abadi*."[6] This complaint and the consequent official action provide an ironic development after the earlier attempts made by the influential homeowners of sector F-7 to stop further expansion of France Colony into their neighborhood, as discussed in Chapter 2. Rather than the usual complaints by elite homeowners about poor squatters' encroachments onto the public space of elite neighborhoods, here were reports that residents of a squatter settlement had complained to the city about encroachments into their settlement by a wealthy homeowner.

CDA's withdrawal of its bureaucratic concession transformed Mr. Chaudhary's "lawn" from a green vacant space "beautified" with official permission into a public area that had been illegally encroached on and privatized. Protesting the brutality with which CDA staff demolished the beautified lawn, Chaudhary said, "But the worst thing is that the CDA staff destroyed trees that were fruiting."[7] As is evident in his accusation, the politician used the destruction of the trees as evidence of CDA's ruthlessness against harmless, natural things. Chaudhary felt betrayed by CDA because they had violated their own general practice of bending rules for wealthy encroachers.

Elite and nonelite homeowners and businesspeople with official permissions often use informal strategies to claim additional adjacent space. They may receive licenses or NOCs to build encroachments on open public spaces but in practice occupy more than the permitted area. Moreover, city officials in Islamabad routinely help to make plans and regulations contingent by tolerating or authorizing informal spaces. Bureaucratic devices like NOCs and licenses—created specially to regulate encroachments—reveal that the contingency in planning is not an unintended consequence of building actions that ignore the laws; the contingency is instead very much an integral feature of planning itself and of how individuals and institutions use existing planning laws selectively and strategically to fulfill their goals.

This apparent disintegration of centralized planning systems does not mean that Islamabad's powerful corporate municipal authority, CDA, lacks power and control over the city's overall planning and development. On the contrary, CDA continues to be a powerful entity, but the actions of its staff and officials are ambivalent about Doxiadis's master plan and design philosophy. Their vested interests and priorities are better suited by ad hoc development practices; their policies must reconcile with the global and local economic and political pressures as well as the realities of extreme power and destitution. Pakistan has a serious "VIP culture," which makes it acceptable to prioritize and bend rules to meet the needs and priorities of influential people. High costs of living, low literacy levels, unchecked population growth, unemployment, low incomes, and limited space and resources often make it necessary for low-income people to live and work in illegally developed and operated spaces. CDA officials and staff break and adapt planning rules to benefit the affluent and tolerate the destitute; their actions reveal an approach of making things work for different interest groups under different terms and pressures.

Proponents of high-modernist planning believed that scientifically calculated and rational planning principles were universal and could be applied successfully in diverse contexts like Latin America, West Africa, the Middle East, and South Asia. Thus, the master plans of the high-modernist cities of Islamabad, Brasilia, Chandigarh, and Tema all feature a grid of identical communities, distinct zones that maintain functional segregation, and efficient traffic circulation. One of the design strategies employed to isolate different functions was to separate distinct functional zones with vast expanses of open space. These generously sized, open public spaces, which became a characteristic feature of high-modernist cities, serve as sites for encroachments in Islamabad: squatter settlements in the irregular gaps between the gridded streets and existing nalas; small, informal kiosks and tea stalls in roadside greenbelts; and elite, lavish mansions in the National Park area. The design principles of rational organization and functional clarity work in unexpected ways to accommodate spaces of informality in places like Islamabad.

Encroachments can impact planning laws and regulations in profound ways, by forming the basis for changing the laws that declare the encroachments illegal in the first place. The retroactive legalization of informal constructions in Islamabad (and beyond) shows us that carefully calculated breaches of the law are very much a part of the law itself; the law often exists because of its widespread violations. For instance, the Building Control Department of CDA developed the bureaucratic category of "compounding area" specifically to legalize illegal construction. A compounding area is that part of an existing building that, though exceeding the total permissible area according to building bylaws, can be regularized by paying a fine. Wealthy homeowners routinely build over the permitted covered area with the intention of paying fines and legalizing the compounded area after its completion. Some version of this practice of retroactive legalization of construction exists in other cities around the world. But encroachments are not simply legalized by existing laws; encroachments can also occasionally create new laws. The farmhouses and Bani Gala mansions I discuss in this book are but two examples of an alternative legal framework used to facilitate elite suburban developments of dubious legal status in contemporary cities throughout South Asia.[8] Bani Gala was developed by a handful of interested homebuilders like Mrs. Nabila who possessed extraordinary wealth and influence. They identified an ideal site on the master plan for personal residential use and developed it without CDA's direct involvement. Using tactics typical of poor squatters, they physically occupied and developed an undeveloped region and eventually legitimized their constructions through favorable court decisions. Elite mansions and farmhouses in the National Park areas are not legal exemptions to Islamabad's official master plan; they formed a basis of changing the master plan and zoning regulations for the once-protected National Park area.

Without the possibilities offered by informal living and working arrangements, Islamabad would have been even more unlivable for the urban poor. The difficulties and challenges of living in katchi abadis and working as street hawkers and vendors are undeniable; still, inhabitants of underprivileged communities make deliberate use of ordinary material forms to sustain spaces of shelter and livelihood. City officials recognize, however grudgingly, the necessity of squatter settlements and vendors' stalls in meeting the essential housing and livelihood needs of low-income populations. They devise bureaucratic procedures that allow low-income residents and businesspeople to sustain themselves under precarious conditions. It would be simplistic to assume that encroachments in Islamabad represent a failure of the master plan or CDA's ineffectiveness; it is more accurate to see encroachments as part of the concessions and negotiations that must take place to make a city both livable and functional.

The same mechanisms that make cities more accessible to marginalized communities are manipulated by wealthy people to further their self-serving interests, which go beyond basic needs for shelter and livelihood. Elite homebuilders violate zoning laws because they see the laws as an intrusion into their private-property rights. The elite homebuilders of Bani Gala felt justified in their actions because they felt entitled as legal property owners to use the land as they wished. Contestation over the zoning laws in the National Park area resulted in revisions and amendments once officials recognized that the existing laws would be unenforceable due to competing notions of urban living and governance. These competing notions have helped decentralize urban planning power from CDA and distribute it among people and institutions (like the courts). But this redistribution of power is not equitable, as low-income communities are displaced to make way for the new development patterns envisioned by elite actors.

What is the future of centralized planning in places like Islamabad, where informality thrives despite—and because of—plans and regulations? Modern architecture and planning principles are based on the false belief that they can avoid unanticipated spaces by foreseeing and "planning for" all desires and needs in advance. This approach to city-making fails to recognize that plans and regulations actually work in unpredictable and contradictory ways. But this unpredictability does not result in a complete disregard for official planning systems. As I show in this book, Islamabad's master plan serves as a blueprint both for spaces on the plan and for those in violation. Instead of imposing an abstract idea onto geographic and social space and projecting confidence about its future outcomes, design professionals and official planning authorities must be willing to accept flexibility and contingency as inherent conditions of official planning paradigms. This may mean a reorientation of the official planning framework, which is not premised on a specific vision but that willingly adjusts to unanticipated pressures and expects multiple outcomes.

As I write these words in early 2023, the world has entered the third year since the COVID-19 outbreak was declared a global pandemic. The human response to COVID-19 has shown that centralized city-planning authorities have the ability, in varying degrees, to function in nimble ways to introduce temporary programs that provide relief during uncertain times. Institutional actors like architects, urban designers, policy makers, and city officials could also tap into the generative nature of our current crisis by learning from contingency-planning approaches rooted in quick response to evolving and unprecedented situations. It may also require learning from the ordinary, everyday practices of people and developing flexible policies that allow for manifold opportunities rather than singular solutions to address complex problems.

Cities are not manifestations of the vision of designers, bureaucrats, and leadership; top-down, centralized master plans and regulations conceived on paper are often "distorted" in practice.[9] It would be too simplistic to view such "distortion" in the world's most rapidly urbanizing regions as the result of corruption and incompetence. While bribes and favors are an important part of the politics of urban development, encroaching processes and informal spaces do important work to make cities functional.[10] Cities that work are not necessarily cities that follow the plan. They are places where people want to live, places that sustain various social and spatial aspirations of their inhabitants. The architectural and bureaucratic practices I have examined in this book allow people to meet their unfulfilled essential needs; these practices are based on the adaptive nature of the formal planning framework. But the democratic aspects of contingent and flexible city-making, which contribute to the livability and inclusivity of cities, can also be coopted by elites in efforts to accumulate more wealth and power. The challenge is to devise contingent ways of city-making and flexible planning systems that address the unmet needs and aspirations of underprivileged people without falling prey to exploitative real estate practices.

NOTES

Introduction

1. David G. Epstein, *Brasilia, Plan and Reality: A Study of Planned and Spontaneous Urban Development* (Berkeley: University of California Press, 1973); and Madhu Sarin, *Urban Planning in the Third World: The Chandigarh Experience* (London: Mansell, 1982).

2. James Holston, *The Modernist City: An Anthropological Critique of Brasilia* (Chicago: University of Chicago Press, 1989), 5.

3. About 2,500 houses were being used for non-conforming purposes in 2015. Civil Petition No. 1328 of 2014, Supreme Court of Pakistan, date of hearing: February 4, 2015.

4. Danish Hussain, "Illegal Kiosks: CDA Top Brass at a Loss to Tackle the Menace," *Express Tribune*, March 22, 2013, https://tribune.com.pk/story/524457/illegal-kiosks-cda-top-brass-at-a-loss-to-tackle-the-m nace/.

5. Jonathan S. Anjaria, "Ordinary States: Everyday Corruption and the Politics of Space in Mumbai," *American Ethnologist* 38, no. 1 (January 1, 2011): 58–72; Asef Bayat, *Life as Politics: How Ordinary People Change the Middle East* (Stanford, CA: Stanford University Press, 2013); Seth Schindler, "Producing and Contesting the Formal/Informal Divide: Regulating Street Hawking in Delhi, India," *Urban Studies* 51, no. 12 (2014): 2596–612; and Dolf Te Lintelo, "Enrolling a Goddess for Delhi's Street Vendors: The Micro-politics of Policy Implementation Shaping Urban (In)formality," *Geoforum* 84 (August 2017): 77–87.

6. Manish Chalana and Jeffrey Hou, eds., *Messy Urbanism Understanding the "Other" Cities of Asia* (Hong Kong: Hong Kong University Press, 2016); D. Asher Ghertner, "Nuisance Talk and the Propriety of Property: Middle Class Discourses of a Slum-Free Delhi," *Antipode* 44 (2012): 1161–87; and James Holston, *Insurgent Citizenship: Disjunctions of Democracy and Modernity in Brazil* (Princeton, NJ: Princeton University Press, 2009).

7. Colin McFarlane, "Rethinking Informality: Politics, Crisis, and the City," *Planning Theory & Practice* 13, no. 1 (2012): 89–108; Eugenie L. Birch, Shahana Chattaraj, and Susan M. Wachter, eds., *Slums: How Informal Real Estate Markets Work* (Philadelphia: University of Pennsylvania Press, 2016); and te Lintelo, "Enrolling a Goddess."

8. Holston, *Insurgent Citizenship*.

9. Paula Meth, "Informal Housing, Gender, Crime and Violence: The Role of Design in Urban South Africa," *British Journal of Criminology* 57 (2017): 408.

10. Shubhra Gururani, "Flexible Planning: The Making of India's 'Millennium City,' Gurgaon," in *Ecologies of Urbanism in India: Metropolitan Civility and Sustainability*, ed. A. M. Rademacher and K. Sivaramakrishnan (Hong Kong: Hong Kong University Press, 2013), 119–44; D. Asher Ghertner, *"Rule by Aesthetics: World-Class City Making in Delhi* (New York: Oxford University Press, 2015); Pow Choon-Piew, "Elite Informality, Spaces of Exception and

the Super-Rich in Singapore," in *Cities and the Super-Rich: Real Estate, Elite Practices, and Urban Political Economies*, ed. R. Forrest, Sin Yee Koh, and Bart Wissink (New York: Palgrave Macmillan, 2017), 209–28.

11. Bas Van Heur and David Bassens, "An Urban Studies Approach to Elites: Nurturing Conceptual Rigor and Methodological Pluralism," *Urban Geography* 40, no. 5 (2019): 594.

12. Ananya Roy, "Why India Cannot Plan Its Cities: Informality, Insurgence and the Idiom of Urbanization," *Planning Theory* 8 (2009): 76–87.

13. Gururani, "Flexible Planning"; and Ghertner, *Rule by Aesthetics*.

14. Vilfredo Pareto, *The Rise and Fall of Elites: An Application of Theoretical Sociology* (New Brunswick, NJ: Transaction, 1991); Gaetano Mosca, *The Ruling Class (Elementi di scienze politica)*, trans. Hannah D. Kahn (New York: McGraw-Hill, 1939); and Charles W. Mills, *The Power Elite* (New York: Oxford University Press, 1956).

15. Bruno Cousin, Shamus Khan, and Ashley Mears, "Theoretical and Methodological Pathways for Research on Elites," *Socio-Economic Review* 16, no. 2 (2018): 225–49; and Van Heur and Bassens, "Urban Studies Approach to Elites."

16. Van Heur and Bassens, "Urban Studies Approach to Elites"; and Ray Forrest, Sin Yee Koh, and Bart Wissink, *Cities and the Super-Rich: Real Estate, Elite Practices and Urban Political Economies* (New York: Palgrave Macmillan, 2017).

17. Gururani, "Flexible Planning"; and Ghertner, *Rule by Aesthetics*.

18. Leela Fernandes, "The Politics of Forgetting: Class Politics State Power and the Restructuring of Urban Space in India," *Urban Studies* 41 (2004): 2415–30; and Partha Chatterjee, *The Politics of the Governed: Popular Politics in Most of the World* (New York: Columbia University Press, 2004).

19. Amita Baviskar, "Between Violence and Desire: Space, Power, and Identity in the Making of Metropolitan Delhi," *International Social Science Journal* 55, no. 1 (January 1, 2003): 89–98.

20. Gururani, "Flexible Planning"; Ghertner, *Rule by Aesthetics*; and Choon-Piew, "Elite Informality."

21. In 1971, English anthropologist Keith Hart introduced the term "informal sector" to explain the irregular self-employment patterns of Northern Ghanaian low-income migrant populations in the urban center of Accra. See Hart, "Informal Income Opportunities and Urban Employment in Ghana," *Journal of Modern African Studies* (March 1973): 61–89; International Labour Office, *Employment, Incomes and Inequality: A Strategy for Increasing Productive Employment in Kenya* (Geneva: International Labour Office, 1972); Dipak Mazumdar, "The Urban Informal Sector," *World Development* 4, no. 8 (1976): 655–79; Caroline O. N. Moser, "Informal Sector or Petty Commodity Production: Dualism or Dependence in Urban Development?" *World Development* 6 (1978): 1041–64; and Ray Bromley, *The Urban Informal Sector: Critical Perspectives on Employment and Housing Policies* (Oxford: Pergamon, 1979).

22. International Labour Office, *Employment, Incomes and Inequality.*

23. Mazumdar, "Urban Informal Sector"; and Moser, "Informal Sector or Petty Commodity Production."

24. Ananya Roy and Nezar AlSayyad, *Urban Informality: Transnational Perspectives from the Middle East, Latin America, and South Asia* (Lanham, MD: Lexington, 2004), 148, 159.

25. Roy, "Why India Cannot Plan Its Cities," 80, 81.

26. Gautam Bhan, "Planned Illegalities: Housing and the 'Failure' of Planning in Delhi: 1947–2010," *Economic and Political Weekly* 48, no. 24 (June 15, 2013): 58–70.

27. Jayaraj Sundaresan, "Urban Planning in Vernacular Governance: Land Use Planning and Violations in Bangalore, India," *Progress in Planning* 127 (2019): 1–23.

28. Francesco Chiodelli and Stefano Moroni, "The Complex Nexus Between Informality and the Law: Reconsidering Unauthorised Settlements in Light of the Concept of Nomotropism," *Geoforum* 51 (2014): 161–68.

29. These material tactics informed by official planning are subsequently accompanied by discursive measures involving filing of petitions and employing pressure tactics from high-level people to aid the legalization efforts of the concerned mosque group. To discourage these clandestine squatting tactics, planning officials in Islamabad often disguise sites for mosques as schools and parks on official planning drawings for newly planned yet undeveloped areas of the city. See Matthew Hull, *Government of Paper: The Materiality of Bureaucracy in Urban Pakistan* (Berkeley: University of California Press, 2012), 241, 243.

30. Daanish Mustafa and Amiera Sawas, "Urbanisation and Political Change in Pakistan: Exploring the Known Unknowns," *Third World Quarterly* 34, no. 7 (2013): 1293–304.

31. Sanaa Alimia, *Refugee Cities: How Afghans Changed Urban Pakistan* (Philadelphia: University of Pennsylvania Press, 2022).

32. Aasim S. Akhtar, "Patronage and Class in Urban Pakistan: Modes of Labor Control in the Contractor Economy," *Critical Asian Studies* 43, no. 2 (2011): 159–84; and Rashid Amjad, M. Irfan, and G. M. Arif, "How to Increase Formal Inflows of Remittances: An Analysis of the Remittance Market in Pakistan—Working Paper," International Growth Center, London, May 2013, https://www.theigc.org/wp-content/uploads/2014/09/Amjad-Et-Al-2013-Working-Paper.pdf.

33. Farooq Tirmizi, "Why (and How Much) Pakistanis Overinvest in Real Estate," *Profit: Pakistan Today*, July 11, 2020, https://profit.pakistantoday.com.pk/2020/07/11/why-and-how-much-pakistanis-overinvest-in-real-estate/; and Muhammad A. Rauf and Olaf Weber, "Urban Infrastructure Finance and Its Relationship to Land Markets, Land Development, and Sustainability: A Case Study of the City of Islamabad, Pakistan," *Environment, Development and Sustainability* 23, no. 4 (2021): 5016–34.

34. Ayyaz Mallick, "Urban Space and (the Limits of) Middle Class Hegemony in Pakistan," *Urban Geography* 39, no. 7 (2018): 1113–20.

35. Aasim S. Akhtar and Ammar Rashid, "Dispossession and the Militarised Developer State: Financialisation and Class Power on the Agrarian-Urban Frontier of Islamabad, Pakistan," *Third World Quarterly* 42, no. 8 (2021): 1866–84; and Nausheen H. Anwar, "State Power, Civic Participation and the Urban Frontier: The Politics of the Commons in Karachi," *Antipode* 44, no. 3 (2012): 601–20.

36. Preeti Sampat, "The 'Goan Impasse': Land Rights and Resistance to SEZs in Goa, India," *Journal of Peasant Studies* 42, no. 3–4 (2015): 765–90; and Juan Du, *The Shenzhen Experiment: The Story of China's Instant City* (Cambridge, MA: Harvard University Press, 2020).

37. Du, *Shenzhen Experiment*, 310, 304.

Chapter 1

1. These numbers and letters refer to the placement of various neighborhoods on the x- and y-axes of the grid, as explained in detail later in the chapter.

2. Lawrence J. Vale, *Architecture, Power, and National Identity* (New Haven, CT: Yale University Press, 1992).

3. Arif Hasan, *Seven Reports on Housing: Government Policies and Informal Sector and Community Response* (Karachi Orangi Pilot Project, Research and Training Institute for the Development of Katchi Abadis, 1992), 1.

4. The population of Karachi in 1947 was a little over 400,000. From 1947 to 1951, more than 600,000 refugees migrated to Karachi. An additional 5 percent of the total population influx included civil servant and migrants from within Pakistan. See Hasan, *Seven Reports*, 3.

5. In 1948, an Australian town-planning consultant to the Government of Sindh, Lieutenant Colonel G. Swayne Thomas, developed an unrealized proposal for a new administrative satellite city outside of Karachi. See Hull, *Government of Paper*, 37. In 1952, a Swedish consultancy firm, Merz Rendel Vatten (MRV), was asked to prepare a master plan for Karachi known as the Greater Karachi Plan or simply the MRV plan. See Hasan, *Seven Reports*, 3. The MRV plan proposed a new capital with a large gathering place; new administrative, commercial, educational, and residential areas in a preselected site in the northeast of Karachi; and "linking the core of the old town and the Capital together as intimately as possible" using an efficient communication system. See S. Lindstrom and B. Ostnas, *Report on the Greater Karachi Plan* (Karachi: Merz Rendel Vatten for Government of Pakistan, [1952] 1967), 36. In 1953, French architect-planner Michel Ecochard was invited to develop a scheme to settle the refugee population in a satellite city. See Ijlal Muzaffar, "Boundary Games: Ecochard, Doxiadis, and the Refugee Housing Projects Under Military Rule in Pakistan, 1953–59," in *Governing by Design: Architecture, Economy, and Politics in the Twentieth Century*, ed. Aggregate (Pittsburgh, PA: University of Pittsburgh Press, 2012), 153–162. In 1958, Greek architect and planning consultant, Constantinos Doxiadis—who was eventually commissioned to design Islamabad—was asked to prepare a scheme for Karachi, known as the Greater Karachi Resettlement Plan. See Hasan, *Seven Reports*, 6. Doxiadis proposed two new satellite residential townships about fifteen to twenty miles outside of Karachi and large industrial areas to provide employment opportunities to the residents of these townships. The Greater Karachi Resettlement Plan was ultimately abandoned because of property speculation, financial recovery, and failure to generate local employment opportunities. See Hasan, *Seven Reports*, 6–7. For a detailed analysis of a Doxiadis refugee settlement scheme that was built near Karachi see Markus Daechsel, "Sovereignty, Governmentality and Development in Ayub's Pakistan: The Case of Korangi Township," *Modern Asian Studies* 45, no. 1 (2011): 131–57.

6. To placate the eastern wing, Dhaka was declared the second capital of Pakistan in 1959 and received approval to develop a new capitol complex, which was designed by another celebrated western modern architect, Louis Kahn. See Sten Nilsson, *The New Capitals of India, Pakistan, and Bangladesh*, Scandinavian Institute of Asian Studies Monograph Series no. 12 (Lund, Sweden: Studentlitteratur, 1973); and Anupam Banerji, *The Architecture of Corbusier and Kahn in the East: A Philosophical Inquiry* (Lewiston, ME: E. Mellon, 2001). But growing discontent among people in East Pakistan because of policies of discrimination over language, culture, economic opportunities, and political representation mainly formulated in West Pakistan resulted in the liberation of East Pakistan as the independent nation-state Bangladesh in 1971. Kahn's capitol complex was eventually built after 1971, when Dhaka became the new capital of Bangladesh.

7. Markus Daechsel, *Islamabad and the Politics of International Development in Pakistan* (Cambridge: Cambridge University Press, 2015), 148–92.

8. See Markus Daechsel, "Misplaced Ekistics: Islamabad and the Politics of Urban Development in Pakistan," *South Asian History and Culture* 4, no. 1 (2013): 90. The Ford Foundation

was established in 1936 by the heir of the American Ford Motor Company as a public welfare organization with global philanthropic projects aimed at advancing human welfare. See Khwaja Zahir-ud Deen, *Memoirs of an Architect* (Lahore: Ferozesons, 1998), 70. For an overview of Ford Foundation projects in Pakistan see George Gant, "The Ford Foundation Program in Pakistan," *Annals of the American Academy of Political and Social Science* 323, no. 1 (May 1959): 150–59; and D. Ensminger and Ford Foundation, *The Ford Foundation: Self-Study of the India Program* (New Delhi: Ford Foundation, 1966).

9. Zahir-ud Deen, *Memoirs*, 70; and Daechsel, "Sovereignty, Governmentality and Development in Ayub's Pakistan."

10. Daechsel, "Sovereignty, Governmentality and Development in Ayub's Pakistan."

11. Daechsel, *Islamabad and the Politics of International Development in Pakistan.*

12. Constantinos and Emma Doxiadis Foundation, "Constantinos A. Doxiadis: The Man and His Work—Biographical Note," 2003, http://www.doxiadis.org/ViewStaticPage.aspx?ValueId=4276.

13. Doxiadis Foundation, "Constantinos A. Doxiadis."

14. Doxiadis used the term *ekistics* as early as the 1940s. During World War II, Doxiadis participated in underground resistance activities and served as the chief of Greece's national resistance group Hephaestus, which published the only underground technical magazine in the occupied territories, called *Regional Planning, Town Planning, and Ekistics*. See Doxiadis Foundation, "Constantinos A. Doxiadis"; and Constantinos A. Doxiadis, "Ekistics: The Science of Human Settlements," *Science* 170, no. 3956 (1970): 393.

15. Constantinos A. Doxiadis, *Architecture in Transition* (New York: Oxford University Press, 1963), 96.

16. Constantinos A. Doxiadis, *Ekistics: An Introduction to the Science of Human Settlements* (London: Hutchinson, 1968), 57.

17. Constantinos A. Doxiadis, "Islamabad: The Creation of a New Capital," *Town Planning Review* 36, no. 1 (April 1965): 1.

18. Zone I: 222.4081 square kilometers (85.87 square miles); Zone II: 39.6791 square kilometers (15.32 square miles); Zone III: 203.9333 square kilometers (78.74 square miles); Zone IV: 282.5287 square kilometers (109.08 square miles); Zone V: 157.9466 square kilometers (60.98 square miles). Zone V area was added later in the 1990s (Capital Development Authority, "Islamabad Capital Territory Map," http://www.cda.gov.pk/housing/ictmap.asp [accessed March 12, 2019]).

19. Doxiadis proposed the development of new areas in Rawalpindi along the same pattern of "sectors" used to organize Islamabad in order to reduce the differences between the urban forms of the new modernist city of Islamabad and the historically evolved city of Rawalpindi.

20. Doxiadis Associates, "Islamabad: Programme and Plan," Report No. 32, DOX-PA 88, September 30, 1960a, 46. CDA Library, Islamabad.

21. Doxiadis Associates, "Islamabad," Report No. 32.

22. The development of Islamabad and Rawalpindi as twin cities also marks a point of departure from the conception of the modernist cities of Brasilia and Chandigarh, which were developed as complete wholes in themselves in isolation from existing cities.

23. Other noteworthy projects where Doxiadis applied the principles of ekistics include master plans for the cities of Baghdad in Iraq, Tema in Ghana, and Riyadh in Saudi Arabia.

24. The fifteen ekistical units are man, room, dwelling, dwelling group, small neighborhood, neighborhood, small town, town, large city, metropolis, conurbation, megalopolis, urban region, urbanized continent, and ecumenopolis.

25. Congrès internationaux d'architecture moderne, or CIAM, was a consortium of influential modern western architects who deliberated over modern principles of architecture and urbanism from the early to mid-1900s.

26. Eric P. Mumford, *The CIAM Discourse on Urbanism, 1928–1960* (Cambridge, MA: MIT Press, 2000), 73.

27. Doxiadis, "Ekistics," 393.

28. Doxiadis, *Architecture in Transition*.

29. Constantinos A. Doxiadis, *Building Entopia* (New York: W. W. Norton, 1975), 31–33.

30. Doxiadis, *Building Entopia*, 32.

31. Doxiadis, *Building Entopia*, 33.

32. Doxiadis, *Building Entopia*, 34.

33. Doxiadis, *Building Entopia*, 37.

34. Doxiadis, *Building Entopia*, 36.

35. Mark Wigley, "Network Fever," *Grey Room* 1, no. 4 (July 1, 2001): 88.

36. Doxiadis Associates, "Islamabad," Report No. 32, 108.

37. Doxiadis Associates, "The Spirit of Islamabad," Report No. 61, DOX-PA 127, July 21, 1961, 18. CDA Library, Islamabad.

38. Each sector is also known as a community class V (20,000 to 40,000). It is composed of four smaller class IV communities (approximately 10,000 people each). Each community class IV comprises four class III communities (around 2,500 people each). Each class III community is further subdivided into several class II communities (100 or more people each). A class II community is composed of multiple class I communities (a family or a group of two or more individuals).

39. Clarence Perry, "The Neighborhood Unit," [1929], in *The City Reader*, ed. R. T. LeGates and F. Stout (New York: Routledge, 2011), 486–98.

40. Perry, "Neighborhood Unit," 488.

41. Perry, "Neighborhood Unit," 488.

42. Sanjeev Vidyarthi, "'Inappropriate' Appropriations of Planning Ideas: Informalizing the Formal and Localizing the Global," PhD dissertation, University of Michigan, Ann Arbor, 2008, 52–93.

43. Lindstrom and Ostnas, *Report on the Greater Karachi Plan*, 51, 54.

44. Muzaffar, "Boundary Games," 153–162.

45. Mayer-Nowicki's association with the Chandigarh project was prematurely terminated after Nowicki's unexpected death in a plane crash and the subsequent removal of Mayer from the city-building project.

46. Maxwell Fry, "Chandigarh: The Capital of Punjab," *Royal Institute of British Architects Journal* 62 (January 1955): 87–94; and Ravi Kalia, *Chandigarh: In Search of an Identity* (Carbondale: Southern Illinois University Press, 1987).

47. Norma Evenson, *Chandigarh* (Berkeley: University of California Press, 1966), 45.

48. Matthew Hull, "Communities of Place, Not Kind: American Technologies of Neighborhood in Postcolonial Delhi," *Comparative Studies in Society and History* 53, no. 4 (2011): 757–758.

49. Hull, "Communities of Place," 758.

50. Constantinos A. Doxiadis, "Islamabad the Capital of Pakistan," http://www.doxiadis .org/Downloads/Islamabad_project_publ.pdf (accessed on May 13, 2021), 9.

51. British prime minister William Pitt the Elder (1766–1768) is claimed to have used the term "the lungs of London" for the first time in the eighteenth century. See Theodore S. Eisenman, "Frederick Law Olmsted: Green Infrastructure and the Evolving City," *Journal of Planning History* 12, no. 4 (November 2013): 305 (note 16); and Catharine W. Thompson, "Linking Landscape and Health: The Recurring Theme," *Landscape and Urban Planning* 99, no. 3–4 (2011): 189.

52. The "Contemporary City of Three Million People" was Le Corbusier's first design for a utopian city where nature, man, and machine would be perfectly integrated. The design featured a symmetrically and efficiently organized city according to distinct functions, with elevated highways and tall towers set in an expansive parklike setting. See Robert Fishman, *Urban Utopias in the Twentieth Century: Ebenezer Howard, Frank Lloyd Wright, and Le Corbusier* (Cambridge, MA: MIT Press, 1977).

53. Doxiadis Associates, "Islamabad: Development of the Area North of Rawal Lake," Report No. 20, DOX-PA 20, February 1, 1962a, 2. CDA Library, Islamabad.

54. Speech made by Jawaharlal Nehru while visiting the site for Chandigarh on April 2, 1952. Cited in Ravi Kalia, *Chandigarh: In Search of an Identity* (Carbondale: Southern Illinois University Press, 1987), 21.

55. Federal Capital Commission, "Report on Preliminary Master Plan and Programme of Islamabad," ed. President's Secretariat (Islamabad: Government of Pakistan, 1960), 3.

56. Federal Capital Commission, "Report on Preliminary Master Plan," 29.

57. Federal Capital Commission, "Report on Preliminary Master Plan," 12. I calculated the number of *mouzas* from a "Tehsil Map of Specified Area Islamabad," available at CDA's Revenue Directorate, Iqbal Hall, Islamabad.

58. Panayiota Pyla, "Ekistics, Architecture and Environmental Politics, 1945–1976: A Prehistory of Sustainable Development," PhD dissertation, Massachusetts Institute of Technology, Department of Architecture, Cambridge, MA, 2002, 66–67.

59. Huma Gupta, "Migrant Sarifa Settlements and State-Building in Iraq," PhD dissertation, Massachusetts Institute of Technology, Department of Architecture, Cambridge, MA, 2020.

60. Gupta, "Migrant Sarifa Settlements," 219, 236–65.

61. According to the regulation, in exchange for every four kanals (roughly 2,000 square yards) of undeveloped acquired land, an affectee is eligible to receive "one developed plot of 500 sq yards, or two developed plots of measuring 35×70 feet (272 sq yards), or four developed plots of measuring 25×50 feet (139 sq yards) [sic]" in Islamabad. See Naeem A. Dar and Muhammad A. Basit, *The Islamabad Laws* (Lahore, Pakistan: Federal Law House, 2010), 684; and Farid Sabri, "CDA Deputy Commissioner Finalises Sector C-15 Award," *Daily Times,* August 17, 2016, https://dailytimes.com.pk/63032/cda-deputy-commissioner-finalises -sector-c- 15-award/.

62. Personal interview with *naib-tehsildar* (revenue officer at CDA), July 20, 2019. See Shahzad Anwar, "CDA Awards over 700 'Built-up' Property Cases in Islamabad," *Express Tribune,* October 7, 2017, https://tribune.com.pk/story/1524513/cda-awards-700-built-property -cases-islamabad/.

63. Personal interview with a local landowner, August 28, 2012.

64. Muhammad Anis, "CDA Directorates Trying to Include 700 Fake Claims of BuP in Award of Land for Medical University," *News International,* May 29, 2017, https://www .thenews.com.pk/print/207322-CDA-directorates-trying-to-include-700-fake-claims-of -BuP-in-award-of-land-for-medical-university.

65. While officially designated as model villages, the new residential communities are mostly referred to as towns. Residents prefer the word *town* for their model communities because it implies that they live in towns and not villages. See Aileen Qaiser, "Not in My Backyard," *Dawn,* June 4, 2008, https://www.dawn.com/news/1071245.

66. Sites-and-services schemes were popularized in the 1970s around the world as an effective housing approach for low-income people. Each sites-and-services project includes small, affordable, subdivided plots with basic infrastructure that can be upgraded later. People are allotted the plots on monthly installments and allowed to build their houses incrementally, as resources become available. MUSP is one of CDA's only attempts to build a new community to resettle the residents of the eligible existing squatter settlements in the city.

67. Capital Development Authority, "Information of the General Public for Awareness," July 26, 2019, https://www.cda.gov.pk/documents/publicnotices/475.pdf.

68. Capital Development Authority Planning Wing, Katchi Abadi Cell, "Upgradation and Rehabilitation of Katchi Abadis in Islamabad," 1999–2000, 11–12. In author's possession.

69. Zulfiqar A. Kalhoro, "Hindu and Sikh Architecture in Islamabad and Rawalpindi," *Journal of Asian Civilizations* 33, no. 1 (July 2010): 88–115.

70. Rizwan Shehzad, "Land Compensation Case: Report on Pending, Disbursed Payments Due on Jan 11,"*Express Tribune,* January 10, 2017, https://tribune.com.pk/story/1290633 /land-compensation-case-report-pending-disbursed-payments-due-jan-11/.

71. "Bheka Syedan Villagers Reject CDA Offer," *Dawn,* April 24, 2003, https://www .dawn.com/news/97878/bheka-syedan-villagers-reject-cda-offer.

72. Shah N. Mohal, "Sector G-12: Capital's 'No-Go area' for CDA, District Admin," *Pakistan Today,* March 30, 2018, https://archive.pakistantoday.com.pk/2018/03/30/sector-g-12 -capitals-no-go-area-for-cda-district-admin/.

73. Epstein, *Brasilia, Plan and Reality;* Sarin *Urban Planning in the Third World;* and James Holston, *Modernist City.*

74. Daechsel, "Misplaced Ekistics."

75. Daechsel, "Misplaced Ekistics."

76. James Holston, "The Misrule of Law: Land and Usurpation in Brazil," *Comparative Studies in Society and History* 33, no. 4 (October 1991): 695.

Chapter 2

1. The Embassy of France has relocated to the Diplomatic Enclave—a master-planned area for the offices and residences of foreign diplomatic missions.

2. This neighborhood is sometimes called French Colony, but the residents of this neighborhood refer to it as France Colony; hence my preference for the latter name.

3. While these neighborhoods are labeled as katchi abadis both in everyday and official discourses, this term does not accurately describe the nature of some of these early settlements, which were granted permission by the CDA and hence cannot be considered strictly illegal. The locations of the six settlements are in subsectors F-6/2, F-7/4, F-9, G-7/1, G-7/2, and G-8/1.

4. Akhter Hameed Khan Resource Center, "Shelter for the Poor: Legislation and Enforcement—a Case Study of Islamabad," Poverty Alleviation Policy Papers Series Monograph no. 1 (March 2010).

5. "CDA ne Labour Colony par phir bulldozer chala diye [CDA ran bulldozer again on Labour Colony]," *Tameer*, August 30, 1979.

6. See *Jang*, August 27, 1979. An earlier demolition operation was reported in *Nawa-i-Waqt*, October 23, 1977. CDA's anti-encroachment operations are military-style actions that often involve a heavy contingent of police, CDA staff, and bulldozing equipment.

7. *Tameer*, August 30, 1979.

8. *Daily Muslim*, August 28, 1979.

9. *Nawa-i-Waqt*, August 30, 1979.

10. *Daily Muslim*, August 28, 1979; and *Nawa-i-Waqt*, August 30, 1979.

11. While interviewing older residents of France Colony, I found out that not all who were allowed to settle here were laborers or low-income CDA employees. Some were engaged in employment elsewhere.

12. Theodore Gabriel, *Christian Citizens in an Islamic State: The Pakistan Experience* (Farnham, U.K.: Ashgate, 2008); and John O'Brien, *The Construction of Pakistani Christian Identity* (Lahore: Research Society of Pakistan, 2006).

13. The recent census results reported a decline in the Christian population. They have been challenged by the Christian leadership for undercounting members of their religious community. See Pakistan Bureau of Statistics, Government of Pakistan, "Population by Sex, Religion and Rural/Urban," 2017, https://www.pbs.gov.pk/sites/default/files/population/2017/tables/pakistan/Table09n.pdf (accessed on June 29, 2022).

14. Jeffrey Cox, *Imperial Fault Lines: Christianity and Colonial Power in India, 1818–1940* (Stanford, CA: Stanford University Press, 2002); Christopher Harding, *Religious Transformation in South Asia: The Meanings of Conversion in Colonial Punjab* (New York: Oxford University Press, 2008); and O'Brien, *Construction of Pakistani Christian Identity*.

15. Sara Singha, "Dalit Christians and Caste Consciousness in Pakistan," PhD dissertation, Georgetown University, Graduate School of Arts and Sciences, Washington, D.C., 2015.

16. Pieter Streefland, *The Sweepers of Slaughterhouse: Conflict and Survival in a Karachi Neighbourhood* (Assen, Netherlands: Van Gorcum, 1979); and Surinder S. Jodhka and Ghanshyam Shah, "Comparative Contexts of Discrimination: Caste and Untouchability in South Asia," *Economic & Political Weekly* 45, no. 48 (November 27, 2010): 99–106.

17. *Jang*, January 7, 1979; *Nawa-i-Waqt*, August 23, 1979; and *Muslim*, August 30, 1979.

18. While this policy was compiled after the decision to resettle the affectees of the labor colony eviction, it is indicative of the official attitude toward allowing different types of low-income populations into the new capital city. See Capital Development Authority, "Settlement Policy for Katchi Abadis in Islamabad," 1988, 3, CDA Secretariat, Islamabad.

19. Capital Development Authority, "Settlement Policy for Katchi Abadis," 3.

20. Capital Development Authority, "Settlement Policy for Katchi Abadis," 7.

21. Doxiadis Associates, "Islamabad: Plots and Houses for Labour Force," DOX-PI 28, June 25, 1962c, Constantinos A. Doxiadis Archives, Athens.

22. Doxiadis Associates, "Islamabad: Plots and Houses," 3.

23. Doxiadis Associates, "Islamabad: Plots and Houses," 3.

24. F-6/2 and G-7/2 settlements are two of the six settlements that also accommodated some of the evicted residents from the G-8/3 labor camp. The location of 100-quarters is in F-6/2, 66-quarters is in G-7/2, and 48-quarters is in G-7/3.

25. The name Jinnah Super is derived from the term *supermarket* even though each *markaz* market is a collection of independent stores.

26. Singha, "Dalit Christians and Caste Consciousness in Pakistan," 71–72.

27. Mr. Ahmed, personal interview with the author, March 4, 2013.

28. Different residents' associations in F-7 have filed several complaints against France Colony (Official file on F-7/4 squatter settlement, Katchi Abadi Cell, CDA Secretariat, Islamabad).

29. "Attempt to Erect Wall in Squatter Settlement France Colony: Residents Protest," *Daily Khabrain*, April 7, 2004.

30. "France Colony Residents Flay Closing of Main Entrance," *Nation*, March 2, 2004.

31. Capital Development Authority Planning Wing, Katchi Abadi Cell, "Upgradation and Rehabilitation of Katchi Abadis in Islamabad," 1999–2000, 9, CDA Secretariat, Islamabad.

32. F-6/2, F-7/4 (France Colony), G-7/1, G-7/2, G-7/3, and G-8/1 were selected for on-site upgrading while sectors I-9, I-10/4, I-11/1, I-11/4, and Muslim Colony (next to the model village of Nurpur Shahan) were to be relocated to alternate sites. See Capital Development Authority Planning Wing, "Upgradation and Rehabilitation."

33. Sanjeev Routray, "The Postcolonial City and Its Displaced Poor: Rethinking 'Political Society' in Delhi," *International Journal of Urban and Regional Research* 38, no. 6 (2014): 2292–308.

34. There were 163 households in France Colony according to a survey carried out by CDA in 1984–85 (Official file on F-7/4 squatter settlement, Katchi Abadi Cell, CDA). In 1995, the number increased to about 321 housing units as documented by a nonprofit called PIEDAR (Katchi Abadi Cell files on squatter settlements in Islamabad, CDA Secretariat, Islamabad).

35. An NOC is a legal document often required by government departments in the Indian subcontinent to process requests related to many things like land, money, and amenities. NOCs are permissions issued either by institutions or individuals stating that they do not object to the contents of the certificate.

36. Hameeda K. Naqvi, *Urbanisation and Urban Centres Under the Great Mughals, 1556–1707: An Essay in Interpretation*, vol. 1 (Simla: Indian Institute of Advanced Study 1, 1972), 14.

37. Wafaqi Mohtasib (Federal Ombudsman) Secretariat Islamabad, Case No. REG. H/19359/96, date of registration: October 30, 1996, name and address of the complainant: Mr. Mushtaq Masih S/O Piran Ditta, G-8/1, Katchi Abadi Islamabad, agency: Capital Development Authority, subject: Discrimination in Allotment of 2 Marla Plot.

38. Wafaqi Mohtasib, Case No. REG. H/19359/96; and Wafaqi Mohtasib Secretariat Islamabad, Complaint No. Reg.H/11946/2003, date of registration: December 16, 2003, name and address of the complainant: Mr. Sabir Hussain S/O Muhammad Amir Khan, H.No. C-11, Halqa No. 1, Muslim Colony, Noor Pur Shahan, Islamabad, name of the agency complained against: Capital Development Authority, subject of complaint: Discrimination in Allotment of Plot Being Affectee of Katchi Abadi.

39. Wafaqi Mohtasib Secretariat Islamabad, Case No. REG. H.12717/98 etc., decided on: October 11, 1998, name and address of the complainant: (1) Younus Masih, (2) James Masih, (3) Tariq Masih, Charles Colony, G-8/1 Katchi Abadi, Islamabad, agency: Capital Development Authority, subject: Discrimination in Allotment of Plot in Katchi Abadi G-8/1 Islamabad.

40. Haider K. Nizamani, "The Planned City That Forgot the Poor," *The News*, February 25, 1991.

41. Ijlal Naqvi, "Contesting Access to Power in Urban Pakistan." *Urban Studies* 55, no. 6 (2018): 1252.

42. Ursula Rao, "Tolerated Encroachment: Resettlement Policies and the Negotiation of the Licit/Illicit Divide in an Indian Metropolis," *Cultural Anthropology* 28 (2013): 768.

43. *Baji* is a title in Urdu used for older sister. Names of all individuals have been anonymized using pseudonyms throughout the book.

44. Wafaqi Mohtasib, Complaint No. Reg. H/11946/2003.

45. This is the reason why Faheema keeps her property documents safe, away from her alcoholic and abusive husband, with one of the *begums* (rich ladies) she used to work for and with whom she is still in touch.

46. Zameen blog, "Know About the Key Differences Between a Plot and a Plot File," Zameen.com, 2021, https://www.zameen.com/blog/difference-between-plot-and-plot-file.html (accessed January 15, 2022).

47. The English word *possession* is used in property transactions. See eProperty, "Pakistan Property Frequently Asked Questions," 2021, https://eproperty.pk/faq/ (accessed January 16, 2022).

48. Diary No. CDA/PLW-KAC-2(21)/195/426, November 4, 2010, CDA Planning Wing, Katchi Abadi Cell, CDA Secretariat, Islamabad.

49. "Ex-MNA Accused of Swindling Poor," *Muslim*, May 14, 1989.

50. Anthony James, personal interview with the author, November 10, 2012.

51. Michael Lipsky, *Street-Level Bureaucracy: Dilemmas of the Individual in Public Services* (New York: Russell Sage Foundation, 2010).

52. According to government policy, students residing in a particular neighborhood must attend the nearby government school. This rule does not apply to the more expensive private schools.

Chapter 3

1. *Markaz* is Urdu for "center." The shopping area designed in the middle of each sector is called a markaz (e.g., F-7 markaz, G-9 markaz).

2. Tariq, personal interview with the author, June 25, 2018.

3. Tariq used the word *illegal* in English in his response.

4. This translation of the original relocation certificate is published in a report by Akhter Hameed Khan Resource Center in Islamabad. See Akhter Hameed Khan Resource Center, "Shelter for the Poor: Legislation and Enforcement," 12. While many older residents of France Colony have confirmed the possession of relocation certificates, I have not been able to see these documents. Whenever the subject of relocation certificates came up in my interviews of France Colony residents, I would get the same response every time; I was always told that they would have to look for it, as they did not remember where they had kept the certificate given to them such a long time ago. I suspect their reluctance may have to do with CDA's desire to keep these documents concealed.

5. Oren Yiftachel, "Critical Theory and 'Gray Space': Mobilization of the Colonized," *City* 13 (2010): 89.

6. Yiftachel, "Critical Theory and 'Gray Space,'" 89.

7. Pamphlet published by the Khokha Association.

8. "Kiosk" and "tea stall" are terms used (in their English-language forms) by CDA offi-cials and vendors to refer to approved vendors' stalls. "Khokha" is mostly reserved for unli-censed stalls.

9. According to a news report from 2009, owners of khokhas located in prime locations, such as next to large public parks, earn as much as 30,000 to 35,000 rupees per day against a monthly license cost of only 2,000 rupees. See Syed D. Hussain, "CDA to Auction Khokhas, Signboards," *Nation*, October 21, 2009, https://nation.com.pk/21-Oct-2009/cda-to-auction-khokhas -signboards.

10. "Court Orders CDA to Seal Kiosk," *Dawn*, November 2, 2012, https://www.dawn .com/news/761117/court-orders-cda-to-seal-kiosk.

11. Enforcement Directorate official, personal interview with the author, November 6, 2012.

12. DMA official, personal interview with the author, March 22, 2013.

13. Jonathan S. Anjaria, "Ordinary States: Everyday Corruption and the Politics of Space in Mumbai," *American Ethnologist* 38, no. 1 (January 1, 2011): 59.

14. Naeem A. Dar and Muhammad A. Basit, *The Islamabad Laws* (Lahore: Federal Law House, 2010), 188.

15. Dar and Basit, *Islamabad Laws*, 188.

16. Dar and Basit, *Islamabad Laws*, 188.

17. Dar and Basit, *Islamabad Laws*, 221.

18. Dar and Basit, *Islamabad Laws*, 194.

19. A plan, elevation, and section are two-dimensional architectural representations of a three-dimensional building; they are drawn to represent the design and construction details of a building. In simplest terms, a plan is a view of the building from above, an elevation is a view of one of the façades, and a section is a view of the inside of the building drawn from a vertical plane slicing through the building.

20. Danish Hussain, "Illegal Kiosks: CDA Top Brass at a Loss to Tackle the Menace," *Ex-press Tribune*, March 22, 2013, https://tribune.com.pk/story/524457/illegal-kiosks-cda-top -brass-at-a-loss-to-tackle-the-m%20nace/.

21. Rana G. Qadir, "CDA Demolishes Bahria Dastarkhwan," *The News*, April 10, 2013, http://www.thenews.com.pk/Todays-News-13-22176-CDA-demolishes-Bahria-Dastarkhwan.

22. "An Operation Cleanup or a Raid on Enemy's Post: CDA Demolishes Tuck Shops, Kiosks in Front of PIMS," *City News: The News*, February 23, 2013.

23. "CDA Demolishes 11 Kiosks in Front of Pakistan Institute of Medical Sciences (PIMS)," *Pakedu.net*, February 24, 2013.

24. "An Operation Cleanup or a Raid on Enemy's Post."

25. "CDA Focuses on Roads, but Ignores Residential Sectors!" *Nation*, October 9, 2012.

26. CDA officer, personal interview with the author, March 20, 2013.

27. Amjad, personal interview with the author, September 8, 2012.

28. Waseem, personal interview with the author, September 8, 2012.

29. Colin McFarlane, "The City as Assemblage: Dwelling and Urban Space," *Society and Space* 29 (2011): 668.

30. Jonathan S. Anjaria, *The Slow Boil: Street Food, Rights and Public Space in Mumbai* (Stanford, CA: Stanford University Press, 2016), 162, 166.

31. Kim Dovey, "Informal Urbanism and Complex Adaptive Assemblage," *International Development Planning Review* 34 (2012): 377.

Chapter 4

1. Imran Khan was elected as the prime minister of Pakistan in 2018 and was ousted from power in 2022. Letter to Honorable Mian Saqib Nisar, Chief Justice Supreme Court of Pakistan, dated March 20, 2017. See Mahmood Idrees, "SC Issues Notice to CDA on Imran Khan's Application Against Encroachments in Bani Gala," *Daily Pakistan*, March 20, 2017, https://en.dailypakistan.com.pk/20-Mar-2017/sc-issues-notice-to-cda-on-imran-khan-s -application-against-encroachments-in-bani-gala.

2. Numerous news articles report the size of Imran Khan's property to be around 300 kanals (approximately 37.5 acres). See Saqib Virk, "PM Imran Owns Assets Worth over Rs108m: ECP," *Express Tribune*, July 2, 2019, https://tribune.com.pk/story/2004647/asset -details-pm-imran-owns-assets-worth-rs100m.

3. Rosita Armytage, *Big Capital in an Unequal World: The Micropolitics of Wealth in Pakistan* (New York: Berghahn, 2020).

4. Isabelle Bruno and Grégory Salle, "Before Long There Will Be Nothing but Billionaires! The Power of Elites over Space on the Saint-Tropez Peninsula," *Socio-Economic Review* 16, no. 2 (April 2018): 435–58.

5. "Nabila Sheikh" is a pseudonym. Her status as a "housewife" represents the term's common usage in Pakistan to refer to women who do not work professionally. I also call her "Mrs. Nabila," in keeping with the general practice in Pakistan of referring to a person using a title (in English) and first name. It implies respect given to women who belong to the middle and upper classes.

6. According to a villager who now works as a successful property dealer in Bani Gala, the history of this area goes back about 300 to 350 years ago, when a saint, Baba Shah Hussain Sharti, moved to the area to make it his home. The villager elaborated that at that time there was no source of water for the village cattle, so Baba Shah Hussain Sharti built a pond, which in local language is called a *bun* or *bunni*. Close to the pond were hills enclosing a plain, which is locally termed *galla* or *gala*. Hence, the village was named Bani Gala. Baba Shah Hussain Sharti's shrine, mosque, and *madrasah* (Islamic school) complex stand today near a pond in the Bani Gala village.

7. Doxiadis Associates, "Islamabad: Development of the Area North of Rawal Lake," Report No. 20, DOX-PA 20, February 1, 1962a, 6, CDA Library, Islamabad.

8. Nabila Sheikh, personal interview with the author, March 7, 2013.

9. *Sifarish* is Urdu for recommendation, favoritism, partiality toward friends.

10. While Dr. Khan held an important position in the national imagination as one of the critical figures in the development of Pakistan's atomic-bomb project, his celebrated image received a serious blow in 2004, when evidence proved his involvement in the illicit proliferation and trafficking of nuclear technology to other countries, including North Korea, Libya, and Iran. He later publicly confessed to this involvement.

11. Seventy kanals are equivalent to approximately 8.75 acres.

12. While the area had been earmarked on paper for the National Park, CDA had not made any strict arrangements to prohibit the sale and purchase of property within the protected area.

13. A *tehsildar* is a revenue administrative officer, while *patwari* and *girdawar* are record-keepers of Pakistan's national revenue department.

14. Jan van der Linden, "Dalalabad: An Inquiry into Illegal Subdivision in Karachi," in *Karachi, Migrants, Housing and Housing Policy,* ed. J. van der Linden and F. Selier (Lahore: Vanguard, 1991), 389; and Akhtar H. Khan, *Orangi Pilot Project: Reminiscences and Reflections* (Karachi: Oxford University Press, 1996), 72.

15. Luna Glucksberg, "A Gendered Ethnography of Elites: Women, Inequality, and Social Reproduction," *Focaal* 81 (2018): 16–28.

16. Parul Bhandari, "The Secret Lives of Money," in *Mapping the Elite: Power, Privilege, and Inequality,* ed. J. Naudet and S. S. Jodhka (Delhi: Oxford University Press, 2019), 274–300.

17. Even though CDA acquired Malpur in the 1960s, it has not yet displaced most of the local villagers, including Colonel Shahid, who continue to hold their residential properties in the village.

18. Colonel Shahid, personal interview with the author, September 13, 2012.

19. Nadia, personal interview with the author, February 27, 2013.

20. Local villagers–cum–property dealers consider Bani Gala's unacquired status a blessing of God or their local saint Baba Shah Hussain Sharti. Despite CDA's many unsuccessful attempts to acquire land in the area, most of Bani Gala village still remains in the hands of the local population, who are free to sell their land for a profit according to higher market rates in contrast to the residents of the neighboring villages of Lakwal and Malpur whose property was acquired in the 1960s for a marginal amount.

21. The administrative reforms of the year 2000 abolished divisions as an administrative unit between province and district. In the new system, provinces were subdivided into districts, districts into tehsils, and tehsils into union councils. Since 2008, divisions have been restored as an administrative tier between provinces and districts in some provinces of Pakistan.

22. Since 1959, various efforts have been made under different military and elected governments to make urban governance in Pakistan more democratic by giving powers to elected representatives rather than appointed bureaucrats. For instance, in 2001 General Pervez Musharraf instituted major changes in urban governance that came to be known as the Devolution of Local Government. The new system replaced the existing Commissionerate system, which was based on the civil bureaucracy and introduced in the region during the British colonial era. After the creation of Pakistan in 1947, the Commissionerate system was subsequently accepted with minor modifications as a model of governance. In this system, municipal control was under provincial government and its appointed officials (such as commissioners, deputy commissioners, and so on) belonging to the elite cadres of civil bureaucracy from the Pakistan Administrative Service (at the time called the District Management Group) of the Central Superior Services (then the Civil Service of Pakistan). The 2001 Local Bodies system, in contrast, was conceived as a democratic model in which municipal control was devolved from provincial to local governments or bodies headed by democratically elected representatives (called *Nazim*/supervisor/mayor, *Naib-Nazim*/deputy *Nazim*). This new system was partially implemented in some provinces of Pakistan until it was replaced by the Local Government Acts of 2010 and 2013 in various provinces. These acts gave strong control over local governance and funds to provincial governments.

23. In addition to the federal territory of Islamabad, there are four provinces (Balochistan, Punjab, Sindh, and North-West Frontier Province) and two autonomous territories (Azad Jammu and Kashmir, Gilgit Baltistan) in Pakistan.

24. Islamabad was initially a part of the Rawalpindi District, but in 1981 the Islamabad District was created to give independent status to the city. See ICTA, "Islamabad Capital Territory Administration," 2007, http://www.ictadministration.gov.pk/ (accessed April 13, 2014).

25. ICTA, "Islamabad Capital Territory Administration."

26. Report/Parawise comments in response to Writ Petition No. 599 of 1992 on behalf of CDA and others, submitted on September 17, 1992, to the Lahore High Court Rawalpindi Bench, Lahore High Court Rawalpindi Bench Record Room, Rawalpindi.

27. Public notices in Urdu and English dailies published on October 16, 1987; February 11, 1988; January 9, 1990; November 4, 1990; July 30, 1991; and February 7, 1992.

28. "Environmental Protection Agency Punjab Notice," *Muslim,* October 30, 1991.

29. Report/Parawise comments in response to Writ Petition No. 599 of 1992. Lahore High Court Rawalpindi Bench Record Room, Rawalpindi.

30. Mrs. Nabila learned about these court cases from a friend who held the position of chairman of CDA at the time of this written correspondence.

31. Hull, *Government of Paper.*

32. Emma Tarlo, "Paper Truths: The Emergency and Slum Clearance Through Forgotten Files," in *The Everyday State in Modern India*, ed. C. J. Fuller and B. Veronique (London: C. Hurst, 2001), 77–79.

33. Tarlo, "Paper Truths."

34. Suit for permanent injunction in the Court of the Senior Civil Judge Islamabad, *CDA v. Chairman Union Council Bara Kahu and others.* Commission report submitted by S. Ziaul Hasnain Shamsi on December 22, 1991. Lahore High Court Rawalpindi Bench Record Room, Rawalpindi.

35. Commission report submitted by S. Ziaul Hasnain Shamsi on December 22, 1991.

36. Mobarik Virk, "Violation of Law: A Prerogative of the Elite," *Muslim,* January 14, 1992.

37. Ex-enforcement (CDA) director, personal interview with the author, November 9, 2012.

38. Through its deputy commissioner, CDA has the legal right to acquire any land in areas earmarked for the construction of the new capital city. See Report/Parawise comments in response to Writ Petition No. 599 of 1992, Lahore High Court Rawalpindi Bench Record Room, Rawalpindi.

39. "Operation" refers to any military-style raid on encroachments in Islamabad. For instance, CDA carried out a similar operation in the late 1970s to evict residents of the G-8/3 labor colony, as mentioned in Chapter 2. Small-scale routine operations include demolition of illegal kiosks and stalls in the city.

40. ISI is the main intelligence agency in Pakistan. It is a powerful organization known for its central role in the Soviet-Afghan war, support of the Taliban, and the U.S. war on terror, as well as being actively involved in domestic politics and staging multiple military coups in Pakistan.

41. See James Ferguson and Akhil Gupta, "Spatializing States: Toward an Ethnography of Neoliberal Governmentality," *American Ethnologist* 29 (January 1, 2002): 981–1002; C. J. Fuller and John Harriss, "For an Anthropology of the Modern Indian State," in *The Everyday State and Society in Modern India*, ed. C. J. Fuller and Veronique Bénéï (London: Hurst, 2001), 1–30.

42. All kinds of documents received or sent by government organizations in Pakistan are given a diary number for recordkeeping purposes. These numbers are assigned by hand by the

receiving clerk. Diary numbers serve to track documents and record their receipt by the concerned department.

43. Writ Petition No. 599 of 1992, filed on August 9, 1992, *Dr. Shirin Bajwa v. CDA*, Lahore High Court, Rawalpindi Bench, Lahore High Court Rawalpindi Bench Record Room, Rawalpindi.

44. The cases were filed with the Rawalpindi Bench of the Lahore High Court.

45. Writ Petition No. 298 of 1992, filed on April 14, 1992, *Mr. Muhammad Rafiq v. CDA*, Lahore High Court, Rawalpindi Bench, Lahore High Court Rawalpindi Bench Record Room, Rawalpindi.

46. Arif Jamal, "Bani Gala Leaders to Continue Struggle," *Muslim*, July 2, 1992.

47. "Bani Gala Victims Call for Dismissal of CDA Chairman," *Dawn*, June 30, 1992.

48. C. M. No. 1504 of 1992 in Writ Petition No. 599 of 1992, October 1992, *Dr. Shirin Bajwa and others v. Federation of Pakistan and others*, Lahore High Court, Rawalpindi Bench. "Application under section 151 of C.P.C. on behalf of respondents no. 1 to 3 for production of additional documents and clarification of stay order." Lahore High Court Rawalpindi Bench Record Room, Rawalpindi.

49. C. M. No. 1504 of 1992 in Writ Petition No. 599 of 1992, Lahore High Court Rawalpindi Bench Record Room, Rawalpindi.

50. Around the same time that Mrs. Nabila found Bani Gala as a scenic idyllic setting for her dream house, Delhi's fashion designers (mostly elite women) "discovered" the Hauz Khas village in the metropolitan area as the "authentic" rural setting for their businesses based on ethnic fashion. They started renting rooms in existing village houses for their boutiques and workshops for a throwaway price. But recognizing the rental potential of their houses, local villagers started to maximize their profits through rent increases and new construction. See Emma Tarlo, "Ethnic Chic: The Transformation of Hauz Khas Village," *India International Centre Quarterly* 23, no. 2 (1996): 49.

51. Tarlo, "Ethnic Chic," 47.

52. 1999 YLR 247 [Lahore], *Abdul Qadeer Khan and others v. Chairman, CDA and others*, Writ Petition No. 513 of 1992, decided on October 23, 1998.

53. 1999 SCMR 2636 [Supreme Court of Pakistan], *Capital Development Authority and others v. Dr. Abdul Qadeer Khan and others*, Civil Petition Nos. 496 and 695 to 709 of 1999, decided on May 14, 1999.

54. Holston, "Misrule of Law," 695.

55. Writ Petition No. 791 of 1992, *Mrs. Bushra Aitzaz Ahsan and others v. CDA and others*, Lahore High Court, Rawalpindi Bench, 2, Lahore High Court Rawalpindi Bench Record Room, Rawalpindi.

56. Writ Petition No. 791 of 1992, 5. One kanal = 1/8 acre.

57. Van Heur and Bassens, "Urban Studies Approach to Elites," 597.

58. For example, the lavish mansions of Dr. Abdul Qadeer Khan and cricketer turned prime minister Imran Khan are regularly cited by their critics as evidence of their corruption and high-handedness.

59. Letter to Honorable Mian Saqib Nisar, Chief Justice Supreme Court of Pakistan, dated March 20, 2017. See Idrees, "SC Issues Notice."

60. Asef Bayat introduces the term "quiet encroachment of the ordinary" to explain the (non)politics of the urban subaltern in the Middle East based on their noncollective, local-

ized, silent, and pervasive struggles for everyday survival. See Bayat, *Life as Politics: How Ordinary People Change the Middle East* (Stanford, CA: Stanford University Press, 2013), 80–85.

Chapter 5

1. Dar and Basit, *Islamabad Laws*, 903.

2. Dar and Basit, *Islamabad Laws*, 910.

3. Dar and Basit, *Islamabad Laws*, 910.

4. Kashif Abbasi, "Private Schools Cannot Be Allowed in Residential Areas, CDA Board Decides," *Dawn,* August 3, 2018, https://www.dawn.com/news/1424504.

5. The petitioner claimed that even though the school relocated to a larger house in 2003, it had been operating in a smaller house since 1997. The petition argued that because the school had been established before the 1999 cut-off date, it was covered under CDA's agreement with the Private Schools Association Islamabad. The petition was dismissed in the court on many grounds, including the fact the petitioner could not provide proof that the school had been operating in a smaller house before 1999.

6. Muhammad A. Khokhar, et. al., editors. *All Pakistan Legal Decisions* (Lahore: PLD, 2004), 308.

7. This trend has been supplemented by the changes in permitted floor area ratio (FAR) in the 2005 Islamabad Residential Sectors Zoning (Building Control) Regulations, which superseded the 1993 Islamabad Residential Sectors Zoning (Building Control) Regulation. FAR is the ratio of the total area of a building to the plot size on which it is built. In 1993 regulations stipulated different FARs according to the type of dwelling (detached or terraced). In the 2005 zoning regulations, FAR calculations were eliminated as long as minimum setback requirements were observed. New homes built with the intention of being rented thus have boxy shapes intended to make maximum use of the permitted FAR according to the current regulations.

8. Dar and Basit, *Islamabad Laws*, 910.

9. According to a notification issued by the Federal Government of Pakistan in 1980, the area falling within two kilometers from the highest watermark of Rawal Lake was declared a part of the Margalla Hills National Park, which falls under Zone III where all forms of construction are strictly prohibited. The Islamabad Wildlife Ordinance, 1979, additionally protects any type of clearing of land within Margalla Hills National Park without CDA's permission.

10. Political pressure from military officials is often cited as the reason for including Zone V in Islamabad's territory. In the early 1990s, land in this area was being developed as a housing scheme by a military housing authority mainly for retired army officials. The inclusion of this area in Islamabad (as opposed to Rawalpindi) was meant to increase the status and prices of land in the military housing scheme.

11. The case was a *suo motu*, which refers to a legal proceeding on any matter of public and national interest that a judge starts on his or her own initiative without being moved by anyone else.

12. Suo Motu Case No. 10 of 2007 (Increased Prices of Daily Commodities), Supreme Court of Pakistan, Islamabad, judgment on January 24, 2008, by Justice Muhammad Nawaz Abbasi, ACJ [Acting Chief Justice], 2.

13. Suo Motu Case No. 10 of 2007, 6.

14. These lavish bungalows built on large properties meant for farming would come under public scrutiny once again in 2009, when Pakistan chief justice Iftikhar M. Chaudhry took a *suo motu* notice against the misuse of agro-farm schemes by influential people, including the former military dictator and president of Pakistan, General Pervez Musharraf. It is important to note here that in 2007, General Musharraf had dismissed Chief Justice Chaudhry, who was reinstated in 2009 following Musharraf's departure after the general elections in 2008. Chaudhry's efforts to cancel the lease of non-conforming farmhouses failed because of the power and influence enjoyed by the people who built these violations.

15. Suo Motu Case No. 10 of 2007, 15.

16. Suo Motu Case No. 10 of 2007, 21.

17. Suo Motu Case No. 10 of 2007, 22–23.

18. Amendment in ICT Zoning Regulation, 1992, approved on April 21, 2010, by the Cabinet, Government of Pakistan, Cabinet Secretariat, Cabinet Division.

19. Capital Development Authority, "Illegal/Un-Authorised Housing Schemes in Islamabad," 2021, https://www.cda.gov.pk/housing/unauthorised_schemes.asp (accessed January 10, 2022).

20. Bhan, "Planned Illegalities"; Gururani, "Flexible Planning"; and Ghertner, *Rule by Aesthetics*.

21. Bhan, "Planned Illegalities."

22. L. Lon Fuller, *Anatomy of the Law* (New York: Praeger, 1968), 20–21.

23. Fuller, *Anatomy of the Law*, 31.

24. Writ Petition No. 337/2014, *Amin Khan v. Federation of Pakistan and others*, date of order/proceeding January 28, 2014, Islamabad High Court, Islamabad.

25. Writ Petition No. 1337/2001, *Col. (R) Javed Agha and others v. Arshad Mahmud (CDA) and others*, Islamabad High Court, Islamabad.

26. Writ Petition No. 337/2014.

27. Amin Khan had migrated to Islamabad about forty years ago with his family from South Waziristan, previously a semiautonomous tribal region and now a part of the North-West Frontier Province in Pakistan. Amin Khan is one of the many low-income Pashtun migrants in Islamabad who are often treated as linguistic and cultural "outsiders" because of their different ethnicity from the Punjabi majority population in the city. Based on my research, NADRA has issued national identity cards to some residents of informal settlements in Islamabad. What this case makes apparent is the discretionary powers used by NADRA officials in the issuance of identity cards to the dwellers of katchi abadis in Islamabad. Applicants like Amin Khan were turned away because they could not verify their residency status based on property documents in Islamabad. According to NADRA's rules at the time, applicants could only apply for the identity card from their places of origin. Amin Khan's petition states that the reason he could not apply for a card in his native town was because the enemy tribe was not allowing the local office to register him there. NADRA's rule has been changed as it is now possible to apply for an identity card from anywhere in Pakistan.

28. Writ Petition No. 337/2014.

29. The evicted abadis (called Afghan Basti and Haq Bahu) were located in low-lying areas next to a nala (ravine) in sector I/11.

Conclusion

1. See also Vinit Mukhija and Anastasia Loukaitou-Sideris, *The Informal American City: Beyond Taco Trucks and Day Labor* (Cambridge, MA: MIT Press, 2014), 39–57.

2. Two iconic examples of elite informality in Los Angeles include American reality TV personality and luxury real-estate developer Mohamed Hadid's mega-mansion (which was built on twice the approved covered area) in the upscale neighborhood of Bel Air and the against-code mansion of wealthy developer Mehr Beglari in the upscale Pacific Palisades neighborhood. See William Stadiem, "Mohamed Hadid's Fight to Become the King of Bel Air Real Estate," *Town and Country*, February 3, 2017, https://www.townandcountrymag.com /society/money-and-power/a9120/mohamed-hadid-los-angeles-real-estate/; and Martha Groves, "Supersizing of Home Spurs Cries of Foul," *Los Angeles Times*, May 18, 2006, https://www .latimes.com/archives/la-xpm-2006-may-18-me-teardown18-story.html.

3. An NOC is a legal document often required by government departments to process requests related to many things like land, money, and amenities. NOCs are permissions issued either by institutions or individuals stating that they do not object to the contents of the certificate.

4. Umar Cheema, "Greenbelt of College Faces Demolition to 'Please an Influential,'" *News International*, June 27, 2019, https://www.thenews.com.pk/print/490422-greenbelt-of -college-faces-demolition-to-please-an-influential.

5. "CDA Clears Five Lawns Developed on Encroached Land," *Dawn*, December 12, 2014, http://www.dawn.com/news/1150392/cda-clears-five-lawns-developed-on-encroached-land.

6. "CDA Clears Five Lawns."

7. "CDA Clears Five Lawns."

8. Gurgaon, a satellite city of Delhi, exhibits an elite informal urbanism similar to that seen in Bani Gala. A city of shiny towers, expensive condominiums, and high-end shopping malls and the corporate home to over two hundred Fortune 500 companies, Gurgaon was once a village located just outside Delhi's federal area. The development of Gurgaon was made possible when a private land-developing company called Delhi Lease and Finance began speculative investment in the area during the 1970s. The company bought vast tracts of land from local villagers and developed the area as an affluent city just outside Delhi, attracting both local elites and foreign investors. To facilitate Gurgaon's planning and development, official exemptions were written in various planning acts established in the 1960s and 1970s. See Gururani, "Flexible Planning."

9. Shahana Chattaraj and Michael Walton, "Functional Dysfunction: Mumbai's Political Economy of Rent Sharing," *Oxford Review of Economic Policy* 33, no. 3 (2017): 438–56.

10. Chattaraj and Walton, "Functional Dysfunction."

BIBLIOGRAPHY

Abbasi, Kashif. "Private Schools Cannot Be Allowed in Residential Areas, CDA Board Decides." *Dawn*, August 3, 2018. https://www.dawn.com/news/1424504.

Akhtar, Aasim S. "Patronage and Class in Urban Pakistan: Modes of Labor Control in the Contractor Economy." *Critical Asian Studies* 43, no. 2 (2011): 159–84.

Akhtar, Aasim S., and Ammar Rashid. "Dispossession and the Militarised Developer State: Financialisation and Class Power on the Agrarian-Urban Frontier of Islamabad, Pakistan." *Third World Quarterly* 42, no. 8 (2021): 1866–84.

Akhter Hameed Khan Resource Center, Islamabad. "Shelter for the Poor: Legislation and Enforcement—a Case Study of Islamabad." Poverty Alleviation Policy Papers Series Monograph no. 1. March 2010.

Alimia, Sanaa. *Refugee Cities: How Afghans Changed Urban Pakistan*. Philadelphia: University of Pennsylvania Press, 2022.

Amjad, Rashid, M. Irfan, and G. M. Arif. "How to Increase Formal Inflows of Remittances: An Analysis of the Remittance Market in Pakistan." Working paper. International Growth Center, London. 2013. https://www.theigc.org/wp-content/uploads/2014/09/Amjad-Et-Al -2013-Working-Paper.pdf (accessed August 7, 2022).

Anderson, Benedict. *Imagined Communities: Reflections on the Origin and Spread of Nationalism*. New York: Verso, 1983.

Anis, Muhammad. "CDA Directorates Trying to Include 700 Fake Claims of BuP in Award of Land for Medical University." *News International*. May 29, 2017. https://www.thenews.com .pk/print/207322-CDA-directorates-trying-to-include-700-fake-claims-of-BuP-in -award-of-land-for-medical-university.

Anjaria, Jonathan S. "Ordinary States: Everyday Corruption and the Politics of Space in Mumbai." *American Ethnologist* 38, no.1 (January 1, 2011): 58–72.

———. *The Slow Boil: Street Food, Rights and Public Space in Mumbai*. Stanford, CA: Stanford University Press, 2016.

Anwar, Nausheen H. "State Power, Civic Participation and the Urban Frontier: The Politics of the Commons in Karachi." *Antipode* 44, no. 3 (2012): 601–20.

Anwar, Shahzad. "CDA Awards over 700 'Built-up' Property Cases in Islamabad." *Express Tribune*. October 7, 2017. https://tribune.com.pk/story/1524513/cda-awards-700-built-property -cases-islamabad/.

Armytage, Rosita. *Big Capital in an Unequal World: The Micropolitics of Wealth in Pakistan*. New York: Berghahn, 2020.

Arnstein, Sherry. "A Ladder of Citizen Participation." *Journal of the American Institute of Planners* 35, no. 4 (1969): 216–24.

"Attempt to Erect Wall in Squatter Settlement France Colony: Residents Protest." *Daily Khabrain*. April 7, 2004.

Banerji, Anupam. *The Architecture of Corbusier and Kahn in the East: A Philosophical Inquiry*. Lewiston, ME: E. Mellon, 2001.

"Bani Gala Victims Call for Dismissal of CDA Chairman." *Dawn*. June 30, 1992.

Baviskar, Amita. "The Politics of the City." *Seminar* 516 (2002): 40–42.

———. "Between Violence and Desire: Space, Power, and Identity in the Making of Metropolitan Delhi." *International Social Science Journal* 55, no. 1 (January 1, 2003): 89–98.

Bayat, Asef. *Life as Politics: How Ordinary People Change the Middle East*. Stanford, CA: Stanford University Press, 2013.

Benevolo, Leonardo. *The Origins of Modern Town Planning*. Cambridge, MA: MIT Press, 1963.

Benjamin, Solomon. "Occupancy Urbanism: Radicalizing Politics and Economy Beyond Policy and Programs." *International Journal of Urban and Regional Research* 32, no. 3 (2008): 719–29.

———. "Occupancy Urbanism as Political Practice." In *The Routledge Handbook on Cities of the Global South*, edited by S. Parnell and S. Oldfield, 309–20. London: Routledge, 2014.

Berman, Marshall. *All That Is Solid Melts into Air: The Experience of Modernity*. New York: Viking Penguin, 1988.

Bhan, Gautam. "Planned Illegalities: Housing and the 'Failure' of Planning in Delhi: 1947–2010." *Economic and Political Weekly* 48, no. 24 (June 15, 2013): 58–70.

Bhandari, Parul. "The Secret Lives of Money." In *Mapping the Elite: Power, Privilege, and Inequality*, edited by J. Naudet and S. S. Jodhka, 274–300. Delhi: Oxford University Press, 2019.

"Bheka Syedan Villagers Reject CDA Offer." *Dawn*. April 24, 2003. https://www.dawn.com/news/97878/bheka-syedan-villagers-reject-cda-offer.

Birch, Eugenie L., Shahana Chattaraj, and Susan M. Wachter, eds. *Slums: How Informal Real Estate Markets Work*. Philadelphia: University of Pennsylvania Press, 2016.

Boo, Katherine. *Behind the Beautiful Forevers*. London: Portobello, 2013.

Bowater, Donna. "Rio's 'Wall of Shame' Between Its Ghettos and Shiny Olympic Image." *Sunday Telegraph*. July 24, 2016. https://www.telegraph.co.uk/news/2016/07/23/rios-wall-of-shame-between-its-ghettos-and-shiny-olympic-image/.

Bromley, Ray. *The Urban Informal Sector: Critical Perspectives on Employment and Housing Policies*. Oxford: Pergamon, 1979.

Bruno, Isabelle, and Grégory Salle. "Before Long There Will Be Nothing but Billionaires! The Power of Elites over Space on the Saint-Tropez Peninsula." *Socio-Economic Review* 16, no. 2 (April 2018): 435–58.

Caldeira, Teresa P. R. "Fortified Enclaves: The New Urban Segregation." *Public Culture* 8, no. 2 (1996): 303–28.

Capital Development Authority. "Settlement Policy for Katchi Abadis in Islamabad." 1988. CDA Secretariat, Islamabad.

———. "Board Members." (2007–2014a). http://www.cda.gov.pk/about_us/board (accessed April 17, 2014).

———. "Wings and Directorates: Estate Wing." (2007–2014b). http://www.cda.gov.pk/about_us/wings_directorates/?wing_id=Estate&objid=3. (accessed October 15, 2013).

———. "Islamabad Capital Territory Map." (2007–2017). http://www.cda.gov.pk/housing/ictmap.asp (accessed March 12, 2019).

———. "Illegal/Un-Authorised Housing Schemes in Islamabad." 2021. https://www.cda.gov.pk/housing/unauthorised_schemes.asp (accessed January 10, 2022).

Capital Development Authority Planning Wing, Katchi Abadi Cell. "Upgradation and Rehabilitation of Katchi Abadis in Islamabad." 1999–2000. CDA Secretariat, Islamabad.

———. "Information of the General Public for Awareness." July 26, 2019. https://www.cda.gov.pk/documents/publicnotices/475.pdf.

"CDA Allows 'Katchi Abadi' in Capital Amid Protests from Residents. *News International*. August 29, 2012.

"CDA Clears Five Lawns Developed on Encroached Land." *Dawn*. December 12, 2014. http://www.dawn.com/news/1150392/cda-clears-five-lawns-developed-on-encroached-land.

"CDA Demolishes 11 Kiosks in Front of Pakistan Institute of Medical Sciences (PIMS)." Pak-edu.net. February 24, 2013.

"CDA Focuses on Roads, but Ignores Residential Sectors!" *Nation*. October 9, 2012.

"CDA ne Labour Colony par phir bulldozer chala diye [CDA ran bulldozer again on Labour Colony]." *Tameer*. August 30, 1979.

Certeau, Michel, de. *The Practice of Everyday Life*. Translated by S. Rendall. Berkeley: University of California Press, 1984.

Chalana, Manish, and Jeffrey Hou, eds. *Messy Urbanism: Understanding the "Other" Cities of Asia*. Hong Kong: Hong Kong University Press, 2016.

Chattaraj, Shahana, and Michael Walton. "Functional Dysfunction: Mumbai's Political Economy of Rent Sharing." *Oxford Review of Economic Policy* 33, no. 3 (2017): 438–56.

Chatterjee, Partha. *The Politics of the Governed: Popular Politics in Most of the World*. New York: Columbia University Press, 2004.

Chattopadhyay, Swati. *Representing Calcutta: Modernity, Nationalism, and the Colonial Uncanny*. London: Routledge, 2005.

Cheema, Umar. "Greenbelt of College Faces Demolition to 'Please an Influential.'" *News International*. June 27, 2019. https://www.thenews.com.pk/print/490422-greenbelt-of-college-faces-demolition-to-please-an-influential.

Chiodelli, Francesco, and Stefano Moroni. "The Complex Nexus Between Informality and the Law: Reconsidering Unauthorised Settlements in Light of the Concept of Nomotropism." *Geoforum* 51 (2014): 161–68.

Choay, Françoise. *The Modern City: Planning in the 19th Century*. New York: George Braziller, 1969.

Choon-Piew, Pow. "Elite Informality, Spaces of Exception and the Super-Rich in Singapore." In *Cities and the Super-Rich: Real Estate, Elite Practices, and Urban Political Economies*, edited by R. Forrest, Sin Yee Koh, and Bart Wissink, 209–28. New York: Palgrave Macmillan, 2017.

Chopra, Preeti. *A Joint Enterprise: Indian Elites and the Making of British Bombay*. Minneapolis: University of Minnesota Press, 2011.

"Classified Ads." *News International*. 2013.

Constantinos and Emma Doxiadis Foundation. "Constantinos A. Doxiadis: The Man and His Work—Biographical Note." 2003. http://www.doxiadis.org/ViewStaticPage.aspx?ValueId=4276 (accessed April 2, 2011).

Correa, Charles. *The New Landscape: Urbanisation in the Third World*. Sevenoaks, U.K.: Butterworth Architecture, 1989.

"Court Orders CDA to Seal Kiosk." *Dawn*. November 2, 2012. https://www.dawn.com/news/761117/court-orders-cda-to-seal-kiosk.

Cousin, Bruno, Shamus Khan, and Ashley Mears. "Theoretical and Methodological Pathways for Research on Elites." *Socio-Economic Review* 16, no. 2 (2018): 225–49.

Cox, Jeffrey. *Imperial Fault Lines: Christianity and Colonial Power in India, 1818–1940.* Stanford, CA: Stanford University Press, 2002.

Crinson, Mark. *Modern Architecture and the End of Empire.* London: Ashgate, 2003.

Daechsel, Markus. "Sovereignty, Governmentality and Development in Ayub's Pakistan: The Case of Korangi Township." *Modern Asian Studies* 45, no. 1 (2011): 131–57.

———. "Misplaced Ekistics: Islamabad and the Politics of Urban Development in Pakistan." *South Asian History and Culture* 4, no. 1 (2013): 87–106.

———. *Islamabad and the Politics of International Development in Pakistan.* Cambridge: Cambridge University Press, 2015.

Daily Muslim. August 28, 1979.

Dar, Naeem A., and Muhammad A. Basit. *The Islamabad Laws.* Lahore, Pakistan: Federal Law House, 2010.

Davidoff, Paul. "Advocacy and Pluralism in Planning." In *Readings in Planning Theory,* edited by S. Campbell and S. S. Fainstein, 305–22. Malden, MA: Blackwell, 1998.

Dickens, Charles. *Master Humphrey's Clock.* Leipzig: B. Tauchnitz, 1846.

Dovey, Kim. "Informal Urbanism and Complex Adaptive Assemblage." *International Development Planning Review* 34 (2012): 349–68.

Doxiadis Associates. "Islamabad: Programme and Plan." Report No. 32, DOX-PA 88. September 30, 1960a. CDA Library, Islamabad.

———. "Summary of Final Programme and Plan." Report No. 37, DOX-PA 93. September 30, 1960b. CDA Library, Islamabad.

———. "The Spirit of Islamabad." Report No. 61, DOX-PA 127. July 21, 1961. CDA Library, Islamabad.

———. "Islamabad: Development of the Area North of Rawal Lake." Report No. 20, DOX-PA 20. February 1, 1962a. CDA Library, Islamabad.

———. Report No. 73, DOX-PA 159. February 16, 1962b. CDA Library, Islamabad.

———. "Islamabad: Plots and Houses for Labour Force." DOX-PI 28. June 25, 1962c. Constantinos A. Doxiadis Archives, Athens.

———. Report No. 83, DOX-PA 197. September 25, 1962d. CDA Library, Islamabad.

Doxiadis, Constantinos A. *Architecture in Transition.* New York: Oxford University Press, 1963.

———. "Islamabad: The Creation of a New Capital." *Town Planning Review* 36, no. 1 (April 1965): 1–28.

———. *Ekistics: An Introduction to the Science of Human Settlements.* London: Hutchinson, 1968.

———. "Ekistics: The Science of Human Settlements." *Science* 170, no. 3956 (1970): 393–404.

———. *Building Entopia.* New York: W. W. Norton, 1975.

———. "Islamabad the Capital of Pakistan." http://www.doxiadis.org/Downloads/Islamabad_project_publ.pdf (accessed May 13, 2021).

Du, Juan. *The Shenzhen Experiment: The Story of China's Instant City.* Cambridge, MA: Harvard University Press, 2020.

Eames, Edwin, and Judith G. Goode, eds. *Anthropology of the City: An Introduction to Urban Anthropology.* Englewood Cliffs, NJ: Prentice Hall, 1977.

Eisenman, Theodore S. "Frederick Law Olmsted: Green Infrastructure and the Evolving City." *Journal of Planning History* 12, no. 4 (November 2013): 287–311.

"Electricity for French Colony Demanded." *Pakistan Times*. May 1, 1989.

Engels, Friedrich. *The Condition of the Working Class in England*. New York: Macmillan, 1958.

Ensminger, D., and Ford Foundation. *The Ford Foundation: Self-Study of the India Program*. New Delhi: Ford Foundation, 1966.

"Environmental Protection Agency Punjab Notice." *Muslim*. October 30, 1991.

eProperty. "Pakistan Property Frequently Asked Questions." 2021. https://eproperty.pk/faq/ (accessed January 16, 2022).

Epstein, David G. *Brasilia, Plan and Reality: A Study of Planned and Spontaneous Urban Development*. Berkeley: University of California Press, 1973.

Evenson, Norma. *Chandigarh*. Berkeley: University of California Press, 1966.

"Ex-MNA Accused of Swindling Poor." *Muslim*. May 14, 1989.

Federal Capital Commission. "Report on Preliminary Master Plan and Programme of Islamabad." Edited by President's Secretariat. Islamabad: Government of Pakistan, 1960.

Ferguson, James, and Akhil Gupta. "Spatializing States: Toward an Ethnography of Neoliberal Governmentality." *American Ethnologist* 29 (January 1, 2002): 981–1002.

Fernandes, Leela. "The Politics of Forgetting: Class Politics, State Power and the Restructuring of Urban Space in India." *Urban Studies* 41 (2004): 2415–30.

Ferraro, Vincent. "Dependency Theory: An Introduction." In *The Development Economics Reader*, edited by Giorgio Secondi, 58–64. London: Routledge, 2008.

Fishman, Robert. *Urban Utopias in the Twentieth Century: Ebenezer Howard, Frank Lloyd Wright, and Le Corbusier*. Cambridge, MA: MIT Press, 1977.

Forrest, Ray, Sin Yee Koh, and Bart Wissink. *Cities and the Super-Rich: Real Estate, Elite Practices and Urban Political Economies*. New York: Palgrave Macmillan, 2017.

Foucault, Michel. *Discipline and Punish: The Birth of the Prison*. New York: Random House, 1975.

"France Colony: A Lagoon Without Water—Dwellers Are Deprived of Basic Amenities." *Frontier Post*. May 1, 1989.

"France Colony Residents Flay Closing of Main Entrance." *Nation*. March 2, 2004.

"France Colony Underlines Contempt for Poor." *Muslim*. April 30, 1989.

"French Colony Deaths: CDA Pays Compensations." *Pakistan Times*. May 1, 1989.

"French Colony Incident: Findings Not Being Disclosed by CDA." *Pakistan Times*. August 9, 1989.

Fry, Maxwell. "Chandigarh: The Capital of Punjab." *Royal Institute of British Architects Journal* 62 (January 1955): 87–94.

Fuller, C. J., and John Harriss. "For an Anthropology of the Modern Indian State." In *The Everyday State and Society in Modern India*, edited by C. J. Fuller and Veronique Bénéï, 1–30. London: Hurst, 2001.

Fuller, L. Lon. *Anatomy of the Law*. New York: Praeger, 1968.

Fuller, Mia. "Building Power: Italy's Colonial Architecture and Urbanism, 1923–1940." *Cultural Anthropology* 3, no. 4 (November 1988): 455–87.

Gabriel, Theodore. *Christian Citizens in an Islamic State: The Pakistan Experience*. Farnham, U.K.: Ashgate, 2008.

Gant, George. "The Ford Foundation Program in Pakistan." *Annals of the American Academy of Political and Social Science* 323, no. 1 (May 1959): 150–59.

Ghertner, D. Asher. "Nuisance Talk and the Propriety of Property: Middle Class Discourses of a Slum-Free Delhi." *Antipode* 44 (2012): 1161–87.

———. *"Rule by Aesthetics: World-Class City Making in Delhi.* New York: Oxford University Press, 2015.

———. "When Is the State? Topology, Temporality, and the Navigation of Everyday State Space in Delhi." *Annals of the American Association of Geographers* 107, no. 3 (2017): 731–50.

Glover, William J. *Making Lahore Modern: Constructing and Imagining a Colonial City.* Minneapolis: University of Minnesota Press, 2007.

Glucksberg, Luna. "A Gendered Ethnography of Elites: Women, Inequality, and Social Reproduction." *Focaal* 81 (2018): 16–28.

Groves, Martha. "Supersizing of Home Spurs Cries of Foul." *Los Angeles Times.* May 18, 2006. https://www.latimes.com/archives/la-xpm-2006-may-18-me-teardown18-story.html.

Gupta, Huma. "Migrant Sarifa Settlements and State-Building in Iraq." PhD dissertation, Massachusetts Institute of Technology, Department of Architecture, Cambridge, MA, 2020.

Gururani, Shubhra. "Flexible Planning: The Making of India's 'Millennium City,' Gurgaon." In *Ecologies of Urbanism in India: Metropolitan Civility and Sustainability,* edited by A. M. Rademacher and K. Sivaramakrishnan, 119–44. Hong Kong: Hong Kong University Press, 2013.

Gutheim, Frederick A. *Worthy of the Nation: The History of Planning for the National Capital.* Washington, DC: Smithsonian Institution Press, 1977.

Hackney, Rod, and Fay Sweet. *The Good, the Bad, and the Ugly: Cities in Crisis.* London: F. Muller, 1990.

Hall, Peter. *Cities of Tomorrow: An Intellectual History of Urban Planning and Design in the Twentieth Century.* Oxford: Blackwell, 1988.

Hamdi, Nabeel. *Housing Without Houses: Participation, Flexibility, Enablement.* New York: Van Nostrand Reinhold, 1991.

Hamdi, Nabeel, and Reinhard Goethert. *Action Planning for Cities: A Guide for Community Practice.* New York: J. Wiley, 1997.

Harding, Christopher. *Religious Transformation in South Asia: The Meanings of Conversion in Colonial Punjab.* New York: Oxford University Press, 2008.

Harper, Anne. *The Idea of Islamabad: Unity, Purity and Civility in Pakistan's Capital City.* PhD dissertation, Yale University, New Haven, CT, 2010.

Hart, Keith. "Informal Income Opportunities and Urban Employment in Ghana." *Journal of Modern African Studies* 11, no. 1 (March 1973): 61–89.

Harvey, David. *Rebel Cities: From the Right to the City to the Urban Revolution.* London: Verso, 2012.

Hasan, Arif. *Seven Reports on Housing: Government Policies and Informal Sector and Community Response.* Karachi: Orangi Pilot Project, Research and Training Institute for the Development of Katchi Abadis, 1992.

———. *The Scale and Causes of Urban Change in Pakistan.* Karachi: Ushba Publishing International, 2006.

Hazareesingh, Sandip. "Colonial Modernism and the Flawed Paradigms of Urban Renewal in Bombay, 1900–1925." *Urban History* 28, no. 2 (2001): 235–55.

Holston, James. *The Modernist City: An Anthropological Critique of Brasilia.* Chicago: University of Chicago Press, 1989.

———. "The Misrule of Law: Land and Usurpation in Brazil." *Comparative Studies in Society and History* 33, no. 4 (October 1991): 695–725.

———. *Insurgent Citizenship: Disjunctions of Democracy and Modernity in Brazil.* Princeton, NJ: Princeton University Press, 2009.

———. "Insurgent Citizenship in an Era of Global Urban Peripheries." *City and Society* 21, no. 2 (January 1, 2009): 245–67.

Hosagrahar, Jyoti. *Indigenous Modernities: Negotiating Architecture, Urbanism, and Colonialism in Delhi.* London: Routledge, 2005.

Hughes, Jonathan, and Simon Sadler. *Non-Plan: Essays on Freedom Participation and Change in Modern Architecture and Urbanism.* New York: Routledge, 2000.

Hull, Matthew. "Ruled by Records: The Appropriation of Land and the Misappropriation of Lists in Islamabad." *American Ethnologist* 34, no. 4 (2008): 501–18.

———. "Communities of Place, Not Kind: American Technologies of Neighborhood in Postcolonial Delhi." *Comparative Studies in Society and History* 53, no. 4 (2011): 757–90.

———. *Government of Paper: The Materiality of Bureaucracy in Urban Pakistan.* Berkeley: University of California Press, 2012.

Hussain, Danish. "Illegal Kiosks: CDA Top Brass at a Loss to Tackle the Menace." *Express Tribune.* March 22, 2013. https://tribune.com.pk/story/524457/illegal-kiosks-cda-top-brass-at-a-loss-to-tackle-the-m%20nace/.

———. "Misuse of Agro-Farms: SC Scuttles Move to Legalise Violations." *Express Tribune.* April 19, 2013. https://tribune.com.pk/story/537489/misuse-of-agro-sfarms-sc-scuttles-move-to-legalise-violations/.

Hussain, Syed D. "CDA to Auction Khokhas, Signboards." *Nation.* October 21, 2009. https://nation.com.pk/21-Oct-2009/cda-to-auction-khokhas-signboards.

Hyatt, Ishrat. "A Tale of Two Cities: They Also Need Attention." *Muslim.* July 26, 1992.

ICTA. "Islamabad Capital Territory Administration." 2007. http://www.ictadministration.gov.pk/ (accessed April 13, 2014).

Idrees, Mahmood. "SC Issues Notice to CDA on Imran Khan's Application Against Encroachments in Bani Gala." *Daily Pakistan.* March 20, 2017. https://en.dailypakistan.com.pk/20-Mar-2017/sc-issues-notice-to-cda-on-imran-khan-s-application-against-encroachments-in-bani-gala.

International Labour Office. *Employment, Incomes and Inequality: A Strategy for Increasing Productive Employment in Kenya.* Geneva: International Labour Office, 1972.

"Islamabad's Population Surges." *Dawn.* April 22, 2011. http://dawn.com/2011/04/23/islamabads-population-surges/.

Jacobs, Jane. *The Death and Life of Great American Cities.* New York: Random House, 1961.

Jadoon, Amira. "Tenure Legalization: The Way Forward for Squatter Settlement Development?" MSc thesis, London School of Economics and Political Science, 2006.

Jamal, Arif. "Bani Gala Leaders to Continue Struggle." *Muslim.* July 2, 1992.

Jang. January 7, 1979.

———. August 27, 1979.

Jencks, Charles. *The Language of Post-Modern Architecture.* New York: Rizzoli, 1977.

Jodhka, Surinder S., and Ghanshyam Shah. "Comparative Contexts of Discrimination: Caste and Untouchability in South Asia." *Economic & Political Weekly* 45, no. 48 (November 27, 2010): 99–106.

Kalhoro, Zulfiqar A. "Hindu and Sikh Architecture in Islamabad and Rawalpindi." *Journal of Asian Civilizations* 33, no. 1 (July 2010): 88–115.

Kalia, Ravi. *Chandigarh: In Search of an Identity*. Carbondale: Southern Illinois University Press, 1987.

"Katchi Abadi." *Muslim*. September 23, 1989.

Katz, Peter, Vincent Scully, and Todd W Bressi. *The New Urbanism: Toward an Architecture of Community*. New York: McGraw-Hill, 1993.

Khan, Akhtar H. *Orangi Pilot Project: Reminiscences and Reflections*. Karachi: Oxford University Press, 1996.

Khokhar, Muhammad A., et. al., eds. *All Pakistan Legal Decisions*. Lahore: PLD, 2004.

King, Anthony D. *Colonial Urban Development: Culture, Social Power, and Environment*. London: Routledge, 1976.

Koenigsberger, Otto H. "New Towns in India." *Town Planning Review* 23, no. 2 (1952): 95–131.

"Kutchi Abadi Residents Hold Protest Demo." *Dawn*. March 2, 2004.

"Labour Colony Demolition: CDA States Its Case." *Muslim*. August 30, 1979.

Langewiesche, William. "The Wrath of Khan: How A. Q. Khan Made Pakistan a Nuclear Power—and Showed That the Spread of Atomic Weapons Can't Be Stopped." *Atlantic*. November 1, 2005. http://www.theatlantic.com/magazine/archive/2005/11/the-wrath-of-khan/304333/.

Lawrence, Roderick J. "High-Rise Housing Reconsidered from an Integrated Perspective." In *Evolving Environmental Ideals: Changing Ways of Life, Values and Design Practices*, edited by M. Gray, 428–36. Stockholm: Royal Institute of Technology, 1997.

Lefebvre, Henri. *The Urban Revolution*. Minneapolis: University of Minnesota Press, 2003.

Linden, Jan van der. "Dalalabad: An Inquiry into Illegal Subdivision in Karachi." In *Karachi, Migrants, Housing and Housing Policy*, edited by J. van der Linden and F. Selier, 385–419. Lahore: Vanguard, 1991.

Lindstrom, S., and B. Ostnas. *Report on the Greater Karachi Plan*. Karachi: Merz Rendel Vatten for Government of Pakistan, [1952] 1967.

Linge, G. J. R. "Canberra After Fifty Years." *Geographical Review* 51, no. 4 (October 1961): 467–86.

Lintelo, Dolf Te. "Enrolling a Goddess for Delhi's Street Vendors: The Micro-politics of Policy Implementation Shaping Urban (In)formality." *Geoforum* 84 (August 2017): 77–87.

Lipsky, Michael. *Street-Level Bureaucracy: Dilemmas of the Individual in Public Services*. New York: Russell Sage Foundation, 2010.

Liscombe, Rhodri W. "In-dependence: Otto Koenigsberger and Modernist Urban Resettlement in India." *Planning Perspectives* 21 (2006): 157–78.

Low, Setha M. "The Edge and the Center: Gated Communities and the Discourse of Urban Fear." *American Anthropologist* 103, no. 1 (March 2001): 45–58.

Lydon, Mike, and Anthony Garcia. *Tactical Urbanism: Short-Term Action for Long-Term Change*. Washington, DC: Island Press, 2015.

Lydon, Mike, et al. *Tactical Urbanism: Short-Term Action, Long-Term Change, Vol. 2*. March 2012. http://issuu.com/streetplanscollaborative/docs/tactical_urbanism_vol_2_final.

Mahsud, Ahmed Z. K. "Representing the State: Symbolism and Ideology in Doxiadis' Plan for Islamabad." In *The Politics of Making: Theory, Practice, Product*, edited by Mark Swenarton, Igea Troiani, and Helena Webster, 61–74. London: Routledge, 2007.

Mallick, Ayyaz. "Urban Space and (the Limits of) Middle Class Hegemony in Pakistan." *Urban Geography* 39, no. 7 (2018): 1113–20.

Marcuse, Peter. "The Enclave, the Citadel, and the Ghetto: What Has Changed in the Post-Fordist U.S. City." *Urban Affairs Review* 33, no. 2 (January 1, 1997): 228–64.

Masood, Alauddin. "Reducing Housing Deficit Demand and Supply Gap on the Increase." *News—Business and Finance Review.* August 4, 2008. http://jang.com.pk/thenews/aug2008-weekly/busrev-04-08-2008/p8.htm.

Mazumdar, Dipak. "The Urban Informal Sector." *World Development* 4, no. 8 (1976): 655–79.

McFarlane, Colin. "The City as Assemblage: Dwelling and Urban Space." *Society and Space* 29 (2011): 649–71.

———. "Rethinking Informality: Politics, Crisis, and the City." *Planning Theory & Practice* 13, no. 1 (2012): 89–108.

Mehrotra, Rahul, and Felipe Vera. *Ephemeral Urbanism: Cities in Constant Flux.* Santiago, Chile: ARQ Ediciones, 2016.

Meth, Paula. "Informal Housing, Gender, Crime and Violence: The Role of Design in Urban South Africa." *British Journal of Criminology* 57 (2017): 402–21.

Mills, Charles W. *The Power Elite.* New York: Oxford University Press, 1956.

Mohal, Shah N. "Sector G-12: Capital's 'No-Go Area' for CDA, District Admin." *Pakistan Today.* March 30, 2018. https://archive.pakistantoday.com.pk/2018/03/30/sector-g-12-capitals-no-go-area-for-cda-district-admin/.

Mosca, Gaetano. *The Ruling Class (Elementi di scienze politica).* Translated by Hannah D. Kahn. New York: McGraw-Hill, 1939.

Moser, Caroline O. N. "Informal Sector or Petty Commodity Production: Dualism or Dependence in Urban Development?" *World Development* 6 (1978): 1041–64.

Mukhija, Vinit, and Anastasia Loukaitou-Sideris. *The Informal American City: Beyond Taco Trucks and Day Labor.* Cambridge, MA: MIT Press, 2014.

Mumford, Eric P. *The CIAM Discourse on Urbanism, 1928–1960.* Cambridge, MA: MIT Press, 2000.

Munshi, Indra. "Patrick Geddes: Sociologist, Environmentalist and Town Planner." *Economic and Political Weekly* 35, no. 6 (January 1, 2000): 485–91.

Muslim. August 30, 1979.

Mustafa, Daanish, and Amiera Sawas. "Urbanisation and Political Change in Pakistan: Exploring the Known Unknowns." *Third World Quarterly* 34, no. 7 (2013): 1293–304.

Muzaffar, Ijlal. "Boundary Games: Ecochard, Doxiadis, and the Refugee Housing Projects Under Military Rule in Pakistan, 1953–59." In *Governing by Design: Architecture, Economy, and Politics in the Twentieth Century,* edited by Aggregate, 142–78. Pittsburgh: University of Pittsburgh Press, 2012.

Naqvi, Hameeda K. *Urbanisation and Urban Centres Under the Great Mughals, 1556–1707: An Essay in Interpretation.* Vol 1. Simla: Indian Institute of Advanced Study, 1972.

Naqvi, Ijlal. "Contesting Access to Power in Urban Pakistan." *Urban Studies* 55, no. 6 (2018): 1242–56.

Nawa-i-Waqt. October 23, 1977.

———. August 23, 1979.

———. August 30, 1979.

Nenova, Tatiana. "Expanding Housing Finance to the Underserved in South Asia: Market Review and Forward Agenda." Washington, DC: World Bank, 2010.

Nilsson, Sten. *The New Capitals of India, Pakistan, and Bangladesh.* Scandinavian Institute of Asian Studies Monograph Series no. 12. Lund, Sweden: Studentlitteratur, 1973.

Nizamani, Haider K. "The Planned City That Forgot the Poor." *The News*. February 25, 1991.

O'Brien, John. *The Construction of Pakistani Christian Identity*. Lahore: Research Society of Pakistan, 2006.

"An Operation Cleanup or a Raid on Enemy's Post: CDA Demolishes Tuck Shops, Kiosks in Front of PIMS." *City News: The News*. February 23, 2013.

Pakistan Bureau of Statistics, Government of Pakistan. "Population by Sex, Religion and Rural/Urban." 2017. https://www.pbs.gov.pk/sites/default/files/population/2017/tables/pakistan/Table09n.pdf(accessed June 29, 2022).

———. "District at a Glance: Islamabad." https://www.pbs.gov.pk/sites/default/files/tables/district_at_glance/Islamabad.pdf (accessed June 29, 2022).

Pakistan Housing Authority Foundation, Ministry of Housing and Works, Government of Pakistan. 2009. http://www.pha.gov.pk/Projects.aspx?cityid=3&cityname=ISLAMABAD (accessed June 29, 2022).

Pakistan Peoples Party. *Manifesto of Pakistan Peoples Party*. 1977. http://www.ppp.org.pk/manifestos.html (accessed April 21, 2022).

Pareto, Vilfredo. *The Rise and Fall of Elites: An Application of Theoretical Sociology*. New Brunswick, NJ: Transaction, 1991.

Peattie, Lisa. *Planning and Rethinking Ciudad Guayana*. Ann Arbor: University of Michigan Press, 1987.

Peoples' Rights Movement. "Katchi Abadi Diary." *Monthly Awami Mazahamat* 4, no. 5 (July 2006).

Perlman, Janice E. *The Myth of Marginality: Urban Poverty and Politics in Rio de Janeiro*. Berkeley: University of California Press, 1976.

"Permission to Turn Squatter Settlements into Jail-house Will Not Be Given." *Nawa-i-waqt*. March 2, 2004.

Perry, Clarence. "The Neighborhood Unit." In *The City Reader*, edited by R. T. LeGates and F. Stout, 486–98. New York: Routledge, 2011.

Plan Pakistan. http://www.planpakistan.org/TORs_Awareness_Raising_on_Labor_Laws.pdf (accessed May 19, 2013).

Prakash, Vikramaditya. *Chandigarh's Le Corbusier: The Struggle for Modernity in Postcolonial India*. Seattle: University of Washington Press, 2002.

"Protest Against the Lack of Basic Facilities in Squatter Settlements." *Khabrain*. March 2, 2004.

Pyla, Panayiota. "Ekistics, Architecture and Environmental Politics, 1945–1976: A Prehistory of Sustainable Development." PhD dissertation, Massachusetts Institute of Technology, Department of Architecture, Cambridge, MA, 2002.

Qadeer, Mohammad A. "An Assessment of Pakistan's Urban Policies: 1947–1997." *Pakistan Development Review* 354 (January 1, 1996): 443–65.

Qadir, Rana G. "CDA Demolishes Bahria Dastarkhwan." *The News*. April 10, 2013. http://www.thenews.com.pk/Todays-News-13-22176-CDA-demolishes-Bahria-Dastarkhwan.

Qaiser, Aileen. "Not in My Backyard." *Dawn*. June 4, 2008. https://www.dawn.com/news/1071245.

Rabinow, Paul. "Ordonnance, Discipline, Regulation: Some Reflections on Urbanism." *Human Society* 5 (1982): 267–78.

———. *French Modern: Norms and Forms of the Social Environment*. Chicago: University of Chicago Press, 1989.

Rao, Ursula. "Tolerated Encroachment: Resettlement Policies and the Negotiation of the Licit/ Illicit Divide in an Indian Metropolis." *Cultural Anthropology* 28 (2013): 760–79.

Rauf, Muhammad A., and Olaf Weber. "Urban Infrastructure Finance and Its Relationship to Land Markets, Land Development, and Sustainability: A Case Study of the City of Islamabad, Pakistan." *Environment, Development and Sustainability* 23, no. 4 (2021): 5016–34.

"Readers' Column." *Nation*. July 5, 1992.

Realproperty.pk. September 2, 2014. http://www.realproperty.pk/property/Islamabad-G-11-865 -Sft,-PHA-,D-Type-Flat-is-for-Sale-on-First-Floor-At-G-11/4,-Islamabad-12074.html.

"Residents Threaten to Take Direct Action and Move Court." *News International*. August 30, 2012.

Reyes, Emily A. "FBI Investigating Possible Wrongdoing by Inspector on Bel-Air Mansion, City Investigator Testifies." *Los Angeles Times*. October 26, 2018. https://www.latimes.com /local/lanow/la-me-ln-bel-air-investigation-20181025-story.html.

———. "Bel-Air Mega-Mansion That Led to Charges for Mohamed Hadid Must Be Torn Down." *Los Angeles Times*. December 20, 2019. https://www.latimes.com/california/story /2019-12-20/hadid-house-bel-air-megamansion-demolition.

Riis, Jacob. A. *How the Other Half Lives: Authoritative Text, Contexts, Criticism*. New York: Charles Scribner's Sons, 1890.

Roever, Sally, and Caroline Skinner. "Street Vendors and Cities." *Environment & Urbanization* 28, no. 2 (2016): 359–74.

Routray, Sanjeev. "The Postcolonial City and Its Displaced Poor: Rethinking 'Political Society' in Delhi." *International Journal of Urban and Regional Research* 38, no. 6 (2014): 2292–308.

Roy, Ananya. "Urban Informality: Toward an Epistemology of Planning." *Journal of the American Planning Association* 71, no. 2 (2005): 147–58.

———. "Why India Cannot Plan Its Cities: Informality, Insurgence and the Idiom of Urbanization." *Planning Theory* 8 (2009): 76–87.

Roy, Ananya, and Nezar AlSayyad,. *Urban Informality: Transnational Perspectives from the Middle East, Latin America, and South Asia*. Lanham, MD: Lexington, 2004.

Sabri, Farid. "CDA Deputy Commissioner Finalises Sector C-15 Award." *Daily Times*. August 17, 2016. https://dailytimes.com.pk/63032/cda-deputy-commissioner-finalises-sector -c-15-award/.

Sampat, Preeti. "The 'Goan Impasse': Land Rights and Resistance to SEZs in Goa, India." *Journal of Peasant Studies* 42, no. 3–4 (2015): 765–90.

Sarin, Madhu. *Urban Planning in the Third World: The Chandigarh Experience*. London: Mansell, 1982.

Schindler, Seth. "Producing and Contesting the Formal/Informal Divide: Regulating Street Hawking in Delhi, India." *Urban Studies* 51, no. 12 (2014): 2596–612.

Scott, James C. *Seeing Like a State: How Certain Schemes to Improve the Human Condition Have Failed*. New Haven, CT: Yale University Press, 1998.

———. *Weapons of the Weak: Everyday Forms of Peasant Resistance*. New Haven, CT: Yale University Press, 2008.

Sennett, Richard. "The Open City." 2019. https://newformalism.aaschool.ac.uk/wp-content /uploads/2019/02/The-Open-City.pdf (accessed February 1, 2020).

———. *Together: The Rituals, Pleasures, and Politics of Cooperation*. New Haven, CT: Yale University Press, 2012.

Shatkin, Gavin. "Planning Privatopolis: Representation and Contestation in the Development of Urban Integrated Mega-Projects." In *Worlding Cities: Asian Experiments and the Art of Being Global*, edited by A. Roy and A. Ong, 77–97. Chichester, U.K.: Wiley-Blackwell, 2011.

Shehzad, Rizwan. "Land Compensation Case: Report on Pending, Disbursed Payments Due on Jan 11." *Express Tribune*. January 10, 2017. https://tribune.com.pk/story/1290633/land -compensation-case-report-pending-disbursed-payments-due-jan-11/.

Singha, Sara. "Dalit Christians and Caste Consciousness in Pakistan." PhD dissertation, Georgetown University, Graduate School of Arts and Sciences, Washington, DC, 2015.

Solomon, Benjamin. "Governance, Economic Settings and Poverty in Bangalore." *Environment and Urbanization* 12, no. 1 (April 2000): 35–56.

Srivastava, Sanjay. *Entangled Urbanism: Slum, Gated Community, and Shopping Mall in Delhi and Gurgaon*. New Delhi: Oxford University Press, 2015.

Stadiem, William. "Mohamed Hadid's Fight to Become the King of Bel Air Real Estate." *Town and Country*. February 3, 2017. https://www.townandcountrymag.com/society/money-and -power/a9120/mohamed-hadid-los-angeles-real-estate/.

Streefland, Pieter. *The Sweepers of Slaughterhouse: Conflict and Survival in a Karachi Neighbourhood*. Assen, Netherlands: Van Gorcum, 1979.

Sundaresan, Jayaraj. "Urban Planning in Vernacular Governance: Land Use Planning and Violations in Bangalore, India." *Progress in Planning* 127 (2019): 1–23.

Sutcliffe, Anthony. *Towards the Planned City: Germany, Britain, the United States, and France, 1780–1914*. New York: St. Martin's, 1981.

Takhar, Jaspreet, ed. *Celebrating Chandigarh: 50 Years of the Idea*. Chandigarh, India: Mapin, 2002.

Tarlo, Emma. "Ethnic Chic: The Transformation of Hauz Khas Village." *India International Centre Quarterly* 23, no. 2 (1996): 30–59.

———. "Paper Truths: The Emergency and Slum Clearance Through Forgotten Files." In *The Everyday State in Modern India*, edited by C. J. Fuller and B. Veronique, 68–90. London: C. Hurst, 2001.

Teepu, Imran Ali. "Businesses in Houses to Close." *Dawn*. July 27, 2013. http://www.dawn.com /news/1032247/businesses-in-houses-to-close.

Thompson, Catharine W. "Linking Landscape and Health: The Recurring Theme." *Landscape and Urban Planning* 99, no. 3–4 (2011): 187–95.

Turner, John F. C. *Housing by People: Towards Autonomy in Building Environments*. New York: Pantheon, 1977.

Turner, John F. C., and Robert Fichter, eds. *Freedom to Build: Dweller Control of the Housing Process*. New York: Macmillan, 1972.

Tyrwhitt, Jaqueline. *Patrick Geddes in India*. London: Lund Humphries, 1947.

United Nations Centre for Human Settlements (Habitats). "The Incremental-Development Scheme: A Case Study of Khuda-ki-basti in Hyderabad, Pakistan." Nairobi, 1991.

Vale, Lawrence J. *Architecture, Power, and National Identity*. New Haven, CT: Yale University Press, 1992.

Van Heur, Bas, and David Bassens. "An Urban Studies Approach to Elites: Nurturing Conceptual Rigor and Methodological Pluralism." *Urban Geography* 40, no. 5 (2019): 591–603.

Vidyarthi, Sanjeev. "'Inappropriate' Appropriations of Planning Ideas: Informalizing the Formal and Localizing the Global." PhD dissertation, University of Michigan, Ann Arbor, 2008.

Virk, Mobarik. "Violation of Law: A Prerogative of the Elite." *Muslim*. January 14, 1992.

Virk, Saqib. "PM Imran Owns Assets Worth over Rs108m: ECP." *Express Tribune*. July 2, 2019. https://tribune.com.pk/story/2004647/asset-details-pm-imran-owns-assets-worth-rs100m.

Tameer. August 30, 1979.

Thompson, Catharine, W. "Linking Landscape and Health: The Recurring Theme." *Landscape and Urban Planning* 99, no. 3–4 (2011): 187–95.

Tirmizi, Farooq. "Why (and How Much) Pakistanis Overinvest in Real Estate." *Profit: Pakistan Today*. July 11, 2020. https://profit.pakistantoday.com.pk/2020/07/11/why-and-how-much-pakistanis-overinvest-in-real-estate/.

Wigley, Mark. "Network Fever." *Grey Room* 1, no. 4 (July 1, 2001): 82–122.

Wright, Gwendolyn. "Tradition in the Service of Modernity: Architecture and Urbanism in French Colonial Policy, 1900–1930." *Journal of Modern History* 55, no. 2 (1987): 291–316.

Yakas, Orestes. *Islamabad: The Birth of a Capital*. Karachi: Oxford University Press, 2001.

Yeo, Su-Jan, Hee Limin, and Heng Chye Kiang. "Urban Informality and Everyday (Night)life: A Field Study in Singapore." *International Development Planning Review* 34, no. 4 (2012): 369–90.

Yiftachel, Oren. "Critical Theory and 'Gray Space': Mobilization of the Colonized." *City* 13 (2010): 246–63.

Zahir-ud Deen, Khwaja. *Memoirs of an Architect*. Lahore: Ferozesons, 1998.

Zameen.com. September 2, 2014. http://www.zameen.com/Flats_Apartments/Islamabad_G_11_G_11/4-3333-1.html.

Zameen blog. "Know About the Key Differences Between a Plot and a Plot File." Zameen.com. 2021. https://www.zameen.com/blog/difference-between-plot-and-plot-file.html (accessed January 15, 2022).

INDEX

ACKNOWLEDGMENTS

I was able to write this book because of the unreserved support of so many extraordinary people. I am indebted to the generosity of the residents and businesspeople of Islamabad whose stories, memories, and knowledge have been fundamental to the writing of this book but whose identities must remain anonymous. I am indebted to the insights and support of my friends, colleagues, and mentors in Islamabad, including Fawad Suhail Abbasi, Aasim Sajjad Akhtar, Faisal Arshad, Muhammad Bin Naveed, Naeem Pasha, Muhammad Saifullah Siddiqui, and Sajida Haider Vandal. I am grateful to my dear friend Mariam Hashmi and her loving family, Masood uncle, Shaheen aunty, and Zehra Hashmi, for providing fundamental insights and introductions for my research. I received critical information and documents for my work thanks to the helpful individuals at the Capital Development Authority, Islamabad Capital Territory Administration, Islamabad High Court, Lahore High Court (Rawalpindi Bench), Supreme Court of Pakistan, National Archives of Pakistan, Press Information Department, and Wafaqi Mohtasib's (Ombudsman) Secretariat. Many thanks to archivist Giota Pavlidou for her help with getting access and permission to use materials at the Doxiadis Archives in Athens. I am forever grateful to Cynthia Hammond for her infinite encouragement and guidance in my academic pursuits.

My extraordinary teachers at the University of Michigan provided me with intellectual guidance and encouragement for my dissertation work that provided the foundation for this book. From the moment I arrived in Ann Arbor, I found a rigorous yet caring PhD adviser in William Glover and a compassionate mentor in Farina Mir. I am inspired by their brilliance, integrity, and humor and am forever grateful for their unyielding commitment toward my professional success and mental well-being. I owe special thanks to Claire Zimmerman and Andrew Herscher for providing constant inspiration and encouragement as my teachers and dissertation advisers. In addition to providing critical guidance for my work, they have also deeply influenced the way I teach histories of architecture. I am intellectually indebted to Matthew Hull whose own work and insights have been transformative for my thinking on Islamabad and the writing of this book. Matt encouraged me to think about informality beyond the disenfranchised, gave me confidence in my work when I needed it the most, and provided relentless support for this book.

Friends at the University of Michigan including Sean Chauhan, Leslie Hempson, Diwas Kc, Elizabeth Keslacy, Gurveen Khurana, Mick McCulloch, Ben Smith, and Lori Smithey, provided me with camaraderie and community in Ann Arbor. Dana Kornberg's unlimited support to me and for my work at different stages of its development has sustained me over the years. I have relied on the good acumen of Hafsa Kanjwal and Tapsi Mathur in all aspects of my life. They have both been like sisters to me, even if one of them (mainly Tapsi) does not quite understand the geographical limits of Kerrytown or Delhi. Hafsa has inspired me with her kindness and resilience, and from Tapsi I have learned the meaning of unconditional support.

Beyond Michigan, I am indebted to Gyan Panday and his doctoral students at the time—Moyukh Chatterjee, Navyug Gill, Hemangini Gupta, Shatam Ray, Sydney Silverstein, Shreyas Sreenath, and Adeem Suhail—for welcoming me so warmly into their community in Atlanta. I am thankful for the strong support I received from Jaime Kucinskas, Meredith Madden, Pavitra Sundar, Lisa Trivedi, Robin Vanderwall, and Tom Wilson at Hamilton College. I am particularly grateful to Celeste Day Moore and Julie Starr for their friendship and wisdom that have helped me weather many storms. At the University of Southern California, my mentors and friends like Ken Breisch, Milton Curry, Vittoria Di Palma, Diane Ghirardo, and Ginger Nolan have provided me with a supportive and motivating work environment.

I am grateful for Jonathan Shapiro Anjaria, Vittoria Di Palma, William Glover, and Anastasia Loukaitou-Sideris for reading my book manuscript in its entirety and providing excellent advice on how to develop it further. At the University of Pennsylvania Press, I am grateful to Robert Lockhart for believing in my project and carefully guiding it to fruition. Matthew Somoroff's excellent editorial and moral support were integral to the completion of this book.

Publication of this book was aided by the Graham Foundation for Advanced Studies in the Fine Arts. The research and writing for this book would have been impossible without the generous financial support of the University of Michigan's Taubman College of Architecture and Urban Planning, Rackham

Graduate School, and Center for the Education of Women; the Social Science Research Council; American Institute of Pakistan Studies; Foundation for Urban and Regional Studies; Hamilton College; and the University of Southern California.

My family's *duas,* long internet calls, and conviction that this book would be written and published have sustained me over the many years I have spent doing research and writing. My deepest gratitude is for two people to whom I owe everything: my father, Mir Moatasim, and my mother, Farzana Moatasim. They are symbols of selfless love and integrity. But above all, they are people who have defied social and familial pressures by supporting their daughters' dreams and career goals. I am blessed with the most caring and courageous sister, Ambreen Moatasim, who provides me with comfort and reassurance when I need it the most. I am thankful to Osama Malik for giving me motivation to complete this project and for accompanying me on work-related travels to care for our young child. Last but not least, I am sustained by the love and prudence of three amazing humans in my life: my niece, Maham, and nephew, Hamza, who are the kindest and wisest souls in my family, and my son, Mekaal, who has lived with all the ups and downs that came with this work and whose positive energy and perspective keeps me going.